Solar Energy Research

Solar Energy Research

edited by Farrington Daniels

and John A. Duffie

THE UNIVERSITY OF WISCONSIN PRESS

Madison, 1955

The Contributors

C. G. *Abbot*, Smithsonian Institution

Lawrence B. Anderson, Department of Architecture, Massachusetts Institute of Technology

Werner A. Baum, Department of Meteorology, Florida State University

L. M. K. Boelter, Department of Engineering, University of California at Los Angeles

H. J. Bowlden, Department of Physics, Wayne University

F. A. Brooks, Agricultural Experiment Station, University of California, Davis

William M. Conn, Consulting Physicist, Kansas City, Missouri

Farrington Daniels, Department of Chemistry, University of Wisconsin

E. J. Drake, Australian Scientific Liaison Office, Washington, D.C.

John A. Duffie, Engineering Experiment Station, University of Wisconsin

J. Farber, Convair, a division of General Dynamics, San Diego, California

A. W. Fisher, Jr., Arthur D. Little, Inc., Cambridge, Massachusetts

Paul A. Flinn, Department of Chemistry, Wayne University

M. L. Ghai, Bush Manufacturing Company, West Hartford, Connecticut

Lawrence J. Heidt, Department of Chemistry, Massachusetts Institute of Technology

Jeremiah T. Herlihy, Department of Chemistry, University of Wisconsin

Harold Heywood, Department of Mechanical Engineering, Imperial College of Science and Technology, University of London

Hoyt C. Hottel, Department of Chemical Engineering, Massachusetts Institute of Technology

v

Everett D. Howe, Department of Engineering, Division of Mechanical Engineering, University of California at Berkeley

Henry Linschitz, Department of Chemistry, Syracuse University

George O. G. Löf, Consulting Engineer, Denver, Colorado

R. L. Meier, Program of Education and Research in Planning, University of Chicago

Ralph A. Morgen, National Science Foundation

Palmer Cosslett Putnam, Gerente General, Avicola de Cuernavaca, S.A., Mexico

Eugene Rabinowitch, Department of Botany, University of Illinois

K. S. Spiegler, Gulf Research and Development Company, P.O.D. 2038, Pittsburgh 30, Pennsylvania

Maria Telkes, Solar Energy Project, New York University

D. Trivich, Department of Chemistry, Wayne University

Felix Trombe, Mont-Louis Solar Energy Laboratory, Mont-Louis, France

Austin Whillier, Department of Mechanical Engineering, Massachusetts Institute of Technology

Oliver R. Wulf, U. S. Weather Bureau, California Institute of Technology

Preface

A comprehensive symposium on all phases of the utilization of solar energy was held in Madison, Wisconsin, on September 12–14, 1953. It was sponsored and supported in large part by the U.S. National Science Foundation and planned and carried out by the University of Wisconsin. An attempt was made to bring together all the scientists who had worked on the utilization of solar energy, to discuss the possibilities of utilization and the areas where research should be encouraged. Two early pioneers were unable to attend—Mr. Godfrey L. Cabot, who established a fund for solar energy research at the Massachusetts Institute of Technology and Harvard University, and Dr. Charles F. Kettering, who set up the Kettering Foundation for solar energy research at Yellow Springs, Ohio. There were about thirty scientists interested in the field, several of whom had experience in foreign countries. Probably never before had meteorologists, engineers, chemists, and physicists gathered together to consider the common problem of solar energy. Their language and points of view were different. Each was an expert in his own field: there were scientists with laboratory facts and laws, scientists and engineers who had vision for new approaches, and engineers who made critical evaluations and insisted on practicality. There were no formal papers. The participants reviewed past accomplishments and present progress, and gave glimpses of future possibilities. Then followed criticisms and suggestions.

This book is based rather loosely on the Wisconsin symposium. It is not a detailed account of the proceedings, nor is it a well-organized treatise or textbook on the utilization of solar energy. Rather it is a co-operative effort of most of the experts in the field to point the way to needed research. At the symposium, it was agreed that each of the participants be invited to write a brief report on the subject of his particular interest. These have coincided in part, but not entirely, with the material presented at the symposium. A few additional experts, who had been unable to attend the symposium, were invited to contribute also.

The contributions by the thirty-one different authors vary greatly. Some are mere abstracts, while others are complete and detailed reports of scientific research. Some make interesting reading for the layman, and others are highly technical. No apology is offered for this lack of uniformity. The reader may select the parts that he finds interesting. The purpose of the book is to make available to everyone the status of the utilization of solar energy as of 1954 and to provide a springboard from which other scientists, engineers, and inventors may take off in unpredictable directions to advance fundamental knowledge and hasten the time when the sun's abundant energy may be put to more general use for the benefit of mankind.

To further aid interested readers, extensive bibliographic information has been included for each section, and a list of general references on solar energy utilization will be found at the beginning of the collected references for the various sections. Inevitably some references are found in several different sections.

The editors of this book wish to express their appreciation to all the authors who have given freely of their time and their experience to make available this authoritative information on the utilization of solar energy and these suggestions for further research. They are glad to acknowledge the help of Miss Patricia Struck, who has been active in the plans for both the symposium and the book, Miss Marjorie Schroeder, Miss Ann Evans, and Miss Constance Paris, who have done much of the typing, and Mr. and Mrs. Fredrick Orcutt, who have helped with the preparation of figures and the literature and patent studies. The editorial assistance of Miss Joan Krager of the University of Wisconsin Press is very much appreciated.

The writer wishes also to express his appreciation to the John Simon Guggenheim Foundation for a generous grant to be used for solar energy research. He is particularly indebted to the U.S. National Science Foundation, which made the Wisconsin symposium possible and subsidized in part the publication of this book.

To Dr. Ralph A. Morgan, formerly of the National Science Foundation, goes much credit for helping to plan and organize the symposium. Other members of the symposium committee were W. A. Baum of Florida State University, F. G. Brickwedde of the U.S. Bureau of Standards, H. C. Hottel of the Massachusetts Institute of Technology, and E. D. Howe of the University of California at Berkeley.

Madison, Wisconsin   Farrington Daniels
October, 1954

Contents

List of figures

List of tables

Introduction

Introduction

Farrington Daniels

If he had been asked in 1938 which would come first—utilization of atomic energy or nonagricultural utilization of solar energy—the writer of this introduction would have said "solar energy." The discovery of fission in 1939 and the rapid development of atomic energy show how wrong he would have been. However, many billions of dollars have gone into the development of atomic energy and almost nothing into the study of solar energy. If a tiny fraction of the effort which has been given to atomic energy were now to be invested in research on the utilization of solar energy, significant progress would certainly be forthcoming. This book is offered in the hope that interest may be aroused and research encouraged toward the utilization of solar energy.

The energy in all our food and fuel comes originally from the sun through photosynthesis in plants. By this process the carbon dioxide of the air is combined with water in the presence of green chlorophyll to give carbohydrates and other organic material. Our foods are grown annually, but our fuels were produced millions of years ago and through geological accident preserved for us in the form of coal, oil, and gas. These are essentially irreplaceable, yet we are using them up at a rapid rate. Although exhaustion of our fossil fuels is not imminent, it is inevitable. Water power supplements our fuels to some extent. Atomic energy will soon be able to supplement them effectively, but uranium, too, is irreplaceable and will eventually become exhausted.

The sun's radiation, however, is our great source of continuing power. Solar energy will be available as long as there are people on the earth to use it. Theoretically, the sun's rays bring to the earth far more heat than is needed even for our present great energy-consuming civilization. The world's people consume food equivalent to 2,500 kilocalories per person per day while they consume fuel equivalent to 25,000 kilocalories per person per day. Thus, in the world at large, ten times as much energy is needed for our machines as for ourselves. But in the United States, where the ratio of fuel energy to food energy is 50 to 1, 150,000 kilocalories of heat per person per day is used to heat houses, run automobiles, trains, and tractors, furnish light and carry out manufacturing operations, and do most of the nation's mechanical work.

3

The average daily supply of solar energy, in much of the world, is of the order of 500 kilocalories per square foot, or about 20 million calories per acre. In the United States, the statistical land area per person is about 13.5 acres, making about 280 million kilocalories per person per day. This is nearly 2,000 times as much as the per capita requirements for fuel, but this heat is of little significance for direct utilization because it comes to the earth in so diffuse a form and at such a low temperature that it is not now being converted into useful work except through agriculture. It is very difficult to make practical use of solar energy, but it is not impossible. Moreover, easily storable fossil fuel in the form of coal, gas, and oil, suitable for operating our engines efficiently, has been so abundant and so cheap that we have had little incentive to put the sun to work.

Two new situations are now leading to an accelerated emphasis on the possible utilization of solar energy. In the first place, we know that the world's population is growing very rapidly, while its demands for electricity and mechanical power are increasing still more rapidly; and secondly, we realize that our irreplaceable fossil fuels are being rapidly depleted. If we make great inroads on the supply of fossil fuels, should we not leave to our descendants a heritage of science and technology for utilizing solar energy?

And there is a desire of the nations with more advanced technologies to assist the less industrialized areas of the world. In those areas, which have much sunshine and little coal or oil, solar energy may well be used to advantage, even if it cannot compete economically in areas where fuel is plentiful.

In the long-range development of new energy resources to supplement our fossil fuels, it is likely that atomic energy, with its concentrated energy, its complicated safety devices, and its requirement of a minimum "critical size," will be used in large, expensive central stations near urban centers. Solar energy, on the other hand, with its universal availability and simplicity and its need to cover large areas, will find its place first in isolated and rural areas.

As evidence of increasing interest in the utilization of solar energy may be cited the fact that following the symposium on the utilization of solar energy on which this book is based, and while this book was going through the press, there were three other symposia which were concerned in part with solar energy—the Mid-Century Conference on Resources in Washington, D. C., the Population Conference of the United Nations in Rome, and the symposium in India on solar and wind energy. Another symposium on the utilization of solar energy is planned to be held in Arizona.

Section I

Expected World Energy Demands

Much of our present material prosperity depends on an abundant supply of coal, gas, and oil, which provide energy to operate our machines. These fossil fuels are limited in quantity and are essentially irreplaceable. Although the world will not suffer a shortage of fuel in this generation, we cannot blithely assume that our descendants can continue indefinitely to have all the fuel that they desire. The author of this section is well qualified to look ahead with the eyes of an Energy Trustee for future generations. He has made an exhaustive study of the needs and the energy resources which will probably be available. Rapidly increasing populations and the still more rapidly increasing demands for electricity and other forms of power throughout the world leave thoughtful people with an impression of solemn responsibility for conservation and a desire to start at once an adequate research program for the direct utilization of solar energy.

Maximum Plausible Demands for Energy in the Future

Palmer Cosslett Putnam

Population and Per Capita Demands for Energy.—Many of the illiterate subsistence-farming populations of the world are in demographic transition toward literate industrial-urban-farm patterns of life. Conceivably they could make the transition without a great increase in numbers. But not plausibly. Everything we know suggests that world population will double and may treble if the balance of forces, now favoring transition and gathering momentum, should persist for a century or so. And the reverse is the Malthusian truth. Everything we know suggests that world population cannot treble unless the transition becomes general. Illiterate subsistence farmers cannot feed many nonfarmers.

The "maximum plausible" world population of 6 billion to 8 billion in A.D. 2050 is not the largest possible one on that date. A hypothetical Trustee of World Energy who plans for at least the smaller number— 6 billions, or 2.5 times the 1950 population of 2.4 billions—will hardly be criticized for imprudence.

Such a large, industrial and urban world population implies a large per capita demand for low-cost energy—a world demand whose growth, measured at the point of end use, is already averaging about 3 per cent a year, while reaching some 5 per cent in the U.S.S.R. and other underdeveloped countries.

The population of the United States is growing nearly twice as fast as world population. Even if its growth rate should decline to zero in a hundred years, our population will be nearly 375 million by A.D. 2050. And per capita demands for energy, already large, are growing at 3 or 4 per cent a year, measured at the point of end use.

Living High Off the Cream of Coal-Oil-Gas.—The United States and much of the free world have been living high off accumulated capital energy in the cream of the coal, oil, and gas reserves. Rates of extraction of these nonrenewable fossil fuels have been unbelievable and efficiencies of use have trebled. Until quite recently the average efficiency of use has increased faster than the average cost of extracting the raw fuel. We

7

cannot again treble the efficiency of use. Yet the costs of extraction continue to rise, while the average heat content in a ton of coal has begun to decline, at least in the United States. And the heavy conversion losses, when solid fuels are converted to the preferred fluid fuels and when both fuels are increasingly consumed in the generation of the more convenient but thermally less efficient electricity, are rising.

Low-Cost Reserves are Growing Scarce.—By "low cost" is meant a cost, measured in 1950 dollars, that is no higher than two times 1950 costs. Reserves of such low-cost capital energy in the fossil fuels are small—some 30 Q^*—by comparison with the maximum plausible cumulative demands—several hundred Q by A.D. 2050 (Figure 1).

If, as is supposed, low-cost energy is essential to the liveliness of an economy, then new sources of low-cost energy must begin to carry some of the load by A.D. 1975 or sooner, and much of it by A.D. 2000, if we are not to run the risk of seeing economic systems throughout the noncommunist world falter in the face of steeply rising costs of energy.

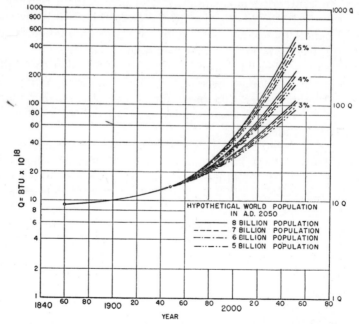

Figure 1.—Estimates of the maximum plausible world demand for the input of energy, A.D. 1947 to 2050, assuming four different maximum populations, three different maximum rates of growth in the per capita demand for the output of energy, and one minimum trend in the weighted average efficiency of the world energy system (*3*).

*1Q = 10^18 Btu.

Low-Cost Income Energy is Limited.—Known sources of income energy that are economical could make only minor contributions to the great hypothetical energy systems of the future. Fuel wood, farm wastes, water power, solar-heat collectors for comfort heating in middle latitudes, solar cookers and power collectors in arid zones, wind power in certain regions, temperature differences in certain tropical waters, tidal power at a dozen special sites, and the heat pump are sources of continuously available income energy. But, in aggregate, they could hardly carry over 15 per cent of the total load at low cost.

How can the balance of more than 85 per cent be carried at low cost?

Solar Income Energy as a General Solution Would be Prohibitively Expensive in 1953.—The direct collection of solar energy on a vast scale by myriads of tracking mirrors, thermocouples, or other devices, its overnight storage, its conversion to transportable electricity, and its delivery at low cost, from Arizona to Pittsburgh or from the Sahara to the Midlands or from the Gobi to Manchuria, appear remote in the light of what we know today. And moving industry to the deserts would be equivalent to a heavy capital charge against this source of income energy. Nor can these systems as yet economically yield those fluid fuels upon which about half of today's system directly rests.

Chlorophyll today is without promise as a means of harnessing solar income energy at low cost. So far as can be seen, the energy from Chlorella fuel, although not restricted to arid zones, would be 50 or more times as costly as from coal.

Other means of harnessing solar income energy are more attractive, in theory, than mirrors, thermocouples, or chlorophyll. But today, at least, not enough is known about the direct conversion of sunlight to electricity in photochemical reactions or its storage in crystal lattices, as examples, to suggest that these systems hold promise as sources of solar income energy able to supply the bulk of the World's needs at low cost.

Nuclear Fuels Abundant but Unsuitable Today for General Application.— Nuclear fuels are a source of abundant capital energy. They hold promise of competing with 1953 coal costs, or nearly so—principally in the generation of electricity. But they are not suitable for carrying much more than 10 or 20 per cent of a total energy system, whatever its size, so long as its pattern is like ours of today.

In 1950, 15 per cent of the energy system of the United States would have consumed the heat from a block of nuclear furnaces (reactors) producing some 170 million kilowatts. Fifty years later the same fraction of domestic requirement might plausibly amount to 750 million kilowatts, of equivalent heat. And the world requirement might be three times as much, or some 2,250 million kilowatts of nuclear furnace capacity (not generating capacity).

More Effort Required to Live Off Income than Off Capital.—Everything we know today tells us that far more effort would be required to live off solar income energy than has been required to live off the capital energy in the coal, oil, and gas reserves. If the extra effort required was very great, it would doubtless have a very great and depressing effect on living standards. The demographic transition would be denied to many. Lively economies would be checked in their growth. Before we reconciled ourselves to so bleak an outcome, we would doubtless study any alternative that appeared less undesirable.

Could We Rely More Heavily on Nuclear Capital Energy?—Perhaps it would be less costly, for example, to modify the pattern of the energy system so that nuclear fuels might bear half to three-fourths of the load.

Blanket electrification would be one way. Could we electrify most of the railroads and much of industry? Could we run overhead power lines along main toll roads and redesign trucks, buses, and cars for electric operation, relying on batteries for off-highway travel? Could we look

TABLE 1

A Hypothetical Energy System of A.D. 2050

Source of energy	% of total energy input to the system
Income energy:	
Fuel wood	2.7
Farm wastes	1.8
Water power	0.9
Solar heat collectors for comfort heating in middle latitudes	9.1
Solar cookers and solar power collectors, in arid zones	0.1
Wind power in certain regions	0.2
Temperature differences in certain tropical waters	small
Tidal power at a dozen sites	small
The heat pump	small
Total income energy	15.0
Capital energy:	
Residual fossil fuels	25.0
Nuclear fuels	60.0
Total capital energy	85.0
Total system	100.0

forward to an energy system 50 or 100 years hence, which would draw its energy from sources somewhat as suggested in Table 1?

Such a major transition to nuclear fuels clearly would be very costly. Perhaps the transition will never be made except in certain most favored countries. Perhaps it would come more easily in those countries not yet heavily committed to present patterns of energy consumption—countries like the U.S.S.R., India, Manchuria, Brazil, and China.

And in countries like the United States the costs of such a program would doubtless justify us in first digging deeper for coal, and in working harder to solve the economic problems of harnessing solar energy.

Energy in the reserves of low-cost nuclear fuels is some 20 times as abundant as in the reserves of low-cost coal-oil-gas—575 Q compared with 27 Q. Even if a great expansion of electrification should take place by A.D. 2000, the known supplies of nuclear fuels could support the bulk of the maximum plausible energy system of the United States and the Free World for a century or so thereafter.

CONCLUSIONS

The Time for Action Has Come.—Our hypothetical Trustee recognizes that the economic and social pressures directed at finding new sources of abundant low-cost energy are about to become compelling. As a prudent Trustee, he would say the time for action has come.

He would urge that the nation's talents, public and private, be released for the development of nuclear furnaces (reactors) capable of furnishing heat for the generation of electricity, for district central heating, and for industrial process heating.

He would urge that we continue to explore nuclear reactions other than the fission of uranium and thorium. There is some hope that we can domesticate the fusion reaction that makes the hydrogen bomb go. Economical fusion of the hydrogen contained in a cubic mile of sea water would be a source of capital energy equal to all conceivable needs for many hundreds of years.

He would be concerned about the vast quantities of metals, some of them already in short supply, that would be required by very large nuclear power programs. He would suggest that we search for these metals by methods yet to be developed, and in novel places, including the sea.

Finally, as our ultimate anchor to windward—an anchor that may be needed sooner than many suppose—he would urge the exploration of all ways to obtain income energy from sunlight in more useful forms and at lower costs than now appear possible.

Section II

The Nature and Availability of Solar Energy

Meteorology has much to offer the solar scientist. Further research is needed in micrometeorology so that still better advice on locations, design, and orientation can be given to those who plan to use the sun's radiation. In this section, two meteorologists who have specialized in the utilization of solar energy outline the available meteorological information and note some of the areas where more research is needed.

Meteorology and the Utilization of Solar Energy

Werner A. Baum

The role of the meteorologist in the problem before us is basically different from that of the engineer or the architect. The meteorologist is not concerned primarily with the development of devices which utilize solar energy. Rather, he is an important source of information to the designer and planner. Specifically, he is the one to answer many of the "where" and "how often" questions which must be asked in determining the feasibility or advisability of a plan to utilize solar energy.

Before we pursue the above point further, it should be noted that there do exist definite possibilities of utilization of solar energy in connection with meteorological problems. For example, solar energy could be used for weather control on a very limited scale. Agriculturally damaging frost can often be averted by supplying heat locally to the atmosphere; solar energy would seem to be an ideal source of the heat. In Florida, for instance, such frosts not infrequently are preceded by clear days of ample sunshine; therefore, the energy would not have to be stored for a long period of time.

It has been reported that the Union of Soviet Socialist Republics has increased its usable agricultural area by springtime aerial dusting of snow-covered areas with coal dust. The blackening of the surface supposedly greatly increases the absorption of solar energy, which results in acceleration of snow melt and soil thawing. It seems not unlikely that considerations of this type will assume greater importance in North America in future years as our demand for agricultural products increases.

Nevertheless, it appears that the meteorologist's primary role in the solar-energy problem in the forthcoming years should be that of a consultant to the designer and planner. The importance of the term "consultant" must be emphasized. It will become clear that we are not speaking of the ordinary weather forecaster, who may be most readily available, but of the research meteorologist or the growing group of industrial and consulting meteorologists. To illustrate, let us consider the most basic question, that of the availability of solar radiation.

If the engineer or architect is assumed to be at all reasonable, he will certainly not base decisions on the preconceived notions he undoubtedly holds about distribution of solar radiation. More likely, he will turn for

15

edification to some such source as Figure 2, from Fritz and MacDonald (*13*). The figure is a map of the average amount of solar energy received on a square centimeter of horizontal plane at the earth's surface per day in June, expressed in gram calories.

Such charts can be valuable tools for gross purposes, and their importance is not to be minimized. However, the engineer who has a particular design problem or the architect who is concerned with a solar house for a particular locality is on dangerous ground in attempting to use such a tool.

First, as Fritz and MacDonald properly indicate in presentation of

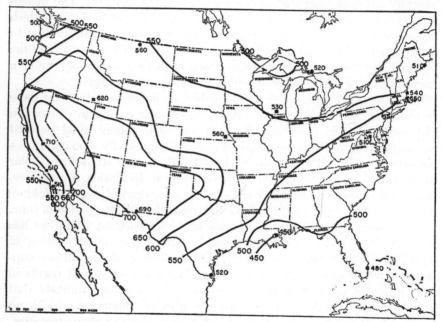

Figure 2.—Average solar energy received on a horizontal plane at the earth's surface in June, expressed as gram calories per square centimeter per day (*13*).

their material, there are important local variations in the mapped quantity. The most important factors affecting local variations are atmospheric pollution, elevation, ground reflectivity, and degree of cloudiness. Thus the reliability of the isolines varies from place to place on the map, and routine linear interpolation is risky.

Second, the chart tells us nothing about the variability of solar radiation. At any given location, how much is the variation among individual days in June, or how much is the variation among the Junes of different years? To decide whether and how much provision must be made for storage of energy, in the event a continuous supply must be available, such considerations are of fundamental importance.

Third, the chart refers to energy on a horizontal surface. Simple trigonometric considerations will not suffice to determine the corresponding energy receipt on an eastward- or westward-facing slope. Many localities have a decided diurnal variation of cloudiness with a maximum in the afternoon, so that conditions are far from symmetrical about local noon.

Further points could be made, but the above should serve to indicate the inherent inability of a general result to serve as the solution to a specific problem. We have here but one example of a basic principle in applied meteorology and climatology: no design or operational problem involving a weather factor can ever be adequately solved by falling back upon climatic generalizations; each such problem requires an individual analysis, conducted by the meteorologist in close liaison with the individual who must lay down the specifications and make the decisions.

The meteorologist's approach to a particular problem may be based entirely on observational data or entirely on theory; most frequently, both elements are needed. In the case of solar-energy problems, it appears unlikely that we shall soon have adequate observational material at our disposal. It is the meteorologist's responsibility, in connection with the apparently inevitable demand for utilization of solar energy, to develop the theoretical tools which will permit him to arrive at satisfactory answers. In the absence of detailed solar-energy observations, he must be able to make inferences on the basis of the interrelations of solar energy and other meteorological and geographical factors.

On the other hand, the meteorologist must be given an indication of what he will be expected to know. He should at least be given the opportunity to make measurements over a limited number of years. For example, perhaps we should be more concerned about insolation on vertical surfaces or on surfaces which are continually facing the sun. Or perhaps we should be concerned with special portions of the solar spectrum, rather than with the spectrum essentially in its entirety. Since it is not the meteorologist who produces the end product, he must rely on the guidance of those who do.

Because the above remarks are addressed to nonmeteorologists, primary stress has been placed on the responsibility of the engineer and the architect. It is the writer's hope that this viewpoint will not be interpreted as a lack of enthusiasm or interest on the part of meteorologists in the challenge which lies before us. Rather, it is to be hoped that the Wisconsin symposium is only one further step toward full-fledged partnership among us in the common effort.

Notes on Spectral Quality and Measurement of Solar Radiation

F. A. Brooks

SPECTRAL QUALITY OF DIRECT-BEAM IRRADIATION

A consideration of the spectral quality of direct-beam irradiation is important for photoelectric, photochemical, and thermochemical use of solar energy.

Outside the Atmosphere.—The energy distribution of solar radiation outside the atmosphere estimated in 1947 is given in Table 131 of the sixth edition of the Smithsonian Meteorological Tables (*32*). A newer energy distribution curve was given by Johnson (*25*), first presented at the joint meeting of the Royal Meteorological and American Meteorological societies, Toronto, September 9, 1953. His recommendation for the solar constant is 2.00 g-cal/cm^2 minute (= 0.1394 watts/cm^2) with a probable error of 2 per cent. This determination was based on a thorough review of all Smithsonian Reports and on spectrographic observations down to 0.24 micron wave length by rockets at altitudes up to 64 km. For wave lengths greater than 0.58 micron he recommends the determination by Moon (*34*).

Depletion by the Atmosphere.—The usual U.S. reference for spectral distributions for various air-mass paths (0 to 5) is Kimball (*29*). This figure is plotted on the wave length basis but does not show the strong water-vapor absorption lines in the near infrared which may be significant for energy transformations in the boundary layer of a surface exposed to the sun.

A recent and more specific spectral curve, plotted on a prism-angle base (labeled in wave lengths) is given by Elder and Strong (*10*). Their figure expands the scale at the short-wave end and shows the atmospheric absorption bands on both sides of a "peak" intensity at 1.2 microns. Between the solar spectrum outside the atmosphere and the envelope spectrum touching the observed transmission peaks between water-vapor absorption bands, they describe a *continuum factor F*. This nonselective absorption varies somewhat with water-vapor path but is due mostly to scattering by aerosol particles in the path. Clarifying their treatment by

19

labeling these two components separately as F_w and F_h respectively (the product $F_w \times F_h = F_p$), the water-vapor part, F_w, of the total continuum factor $F = F_p$ can be approximated according to Elder and Strong for Windows III, IV, V by the empirical formula $F_w = (0.998)^w$, where w is millimeters of precipitable moisture. Giving more credence to the distribution of observed points in their Figure 13, however, shows that 0.994 and 0.996 might well be more suitable for Windows I and II respectively. The other part, F_h, of the continuous attenuation due to scattering by haze, smoke, or droplets is reported by Gebbie and associates (*14*) as most closely related to visibility measured at 0.61 microns. Naturally haze interference is strongest in the short-wave region and tapers off at longer wave lengths. If one assumes continuous water-vapor effects as suggested in Table 2, the empirical dry-haze factor F_h for 60 per cent visibility at 0.61 microns would be 0.71 and the corresponding magnitudes for other windows would be as given in Table 2. Furthermore, judging by Elder and Strong's Fig. 14 it seems that in clearer air these factors would be improved approximately to:

$$1 - F_h = \frac{1 - \text{visibility}}{0.40}(0.235 - 0.25 \log \lambda), \qquad \lambda < 6 \text{ microns.}$$

Thus excepting the unexplained irregularity in Window III the whole continuum factor $F = F_w \cdot F_h$ for each spectrum window can be estimated reasonably well for the vertical depth of the atmosphere from a determination of precipitable moisture if the F_h factor is determined from the solar depletion at 0.61 micron wave length.

Finally, the selective transmission T' relative to the envelope can be estimated for each spectral interval (window) between strong absorption lines by the empirical formula given by Elder and Strong:

$$T' = -k \log w + t_o$$

where,

T', per cent,   = selective window transmission,
w, mm precip. H_2O, = water-vapor path length,
k, and t_o,   = empirical constants (see Table 2).

This formula is limited to the usual conditions of the atmosphere and is not meant to treat pressure effects.

Table 2 has been expanded from Elder and Strong's Table II to include the solar energy block for each window interval (Col. 3), and a haze example from Gebbie.

In any actual case the three transmission factors for direct sunshine

TABLE 2

Transmission Factors from Elder and Strong Combined with Haze Example from Gebbie, *et al.*

Window	Spectrum interval	Outside energy in interval (Smithsonian)	Charact. wave length	e^{-A} for F_w	Example F_w for 17 mm	Example F_h to suit Gebbie 2000 yd	$F = F_w F_h$	Elder and Strong selective transmission				Example 17 mm and Gebbie haze Transm.* $F \times T'$	Example Energy
								k	t_o	max. w for $T' = 100\%$	T' for 17 mm		
	microns	cal cm²min	microns							mm	%		cal cm²min
Col. [1]	[2]	[3]	[4]	[5]†	[6]	[7]	[8]	[9]	[10]	[11]	[12]	[13]	[14]
Ultraviolet	0.00– 0.30	0.0106	....	....	....	....	....	....	....	....	....	....	0.000
Visible	0.30– 0.70	0.9292	0.61	0.990	0.843	0.712	0.60	....	....	....	(100.0)	0.60	0.557
I	0.70– 0.92	0.3506	0.84	0.994	0.903	0.758	0.684	15.1	106.3	0.26	87.72	0.60	0.210
II	0.92– 1.12‡	0.2019	1.05	0.996	0.934	0.762	0.712	16.5	106.3	0.24	86.0	0.612	0.124
III	1.12– 1.4	0.1782	1.24	0.997	0.950	0.676?	0.642	17.1	96.3	0.058	75.26?	0.483	0.036
IV	1.4 – 1.9	0.1497	1.60	0.998	0.967	0.827	0.799	13.1	81.0	0.036	64.89	0.519	0.078
V	1.9 – 2.7	(0.076)	2.13	0.997	0.950	0.847	0.805	13.1	72.5	0.008	56.39	0.454	0.034
VI	2.7 – 4.3	(0.039)	3.65	(1.000)	(1.000)	(0.905)	(0.905)	12.5	72.3	0.006	56.91	0.515	0.020
VII	4.3 – 5.9	(0.009)	4.75	(0.988)	(0.814)	(0.924)	0.752	21.5	51.2	0.005	24.74	0.186	0.002
VIII	5.9 –14.	(0.005)	10.0	(0.990)	(0.843)	(0.961)	(0.81)	....	....	....	....	0.48	0.002
Total		(1.949)											1.113

*Measured by planimeter on Gebbie's Fig. 7a and 7b. †Reinterpreted from Elder and Strong's Fig. 13 instead of their constant 0.998.
‡Elder and Strong use 1.1, but Gebbie shows maximum absorption at 1.125. *Note:* Magnitudes in parentheses are estimated.

(Col. 13) applied to the energy covered in each spectral window (Col. 14) must, when totaled for all windows, match the direct-beam radiation measured by a bolometer or by the act of shading a calibrated, inclusive short-wave pyrheliometer such as the glass-covered Eppley thermopile. Absolute spectrometric observations at 1.9 and at 0.61 microns wave lengths would serve to separate the water-vapor band absorption from the poorly known continuous attenuation by fog, haze, and smoke.

Further studies are needed relating depletion of direct-beam sunshine with spectral distribution of diffuse solar radiation received at the ground from the sky hemisphere. Another study is needed to interpret spectrally the considerable world-wide data on depletion coefficients for direct sunshine for the whole short-wave region such as treated by Linke (*31*). Such a study would provide a better over-all treatment for atmospheres at various places with their characteristic haze and would serve as a starting point for interpreting the extra depletion due to smog. It seems very desirable that a translation of this excellent treatise be undertaken by the National Science Foundation.

When spectral quality is not necessary, a very useful treatment of whole-spectrum insolation on a horizontal surface for various air-mass paths based on Kimball's 1928 chart is given by Klein (*30*). This includes effects of rescattering of radiation reflected by the surface of the earth. Haurwitz (*24*) has made a careful study of insolation in relation to cloud type.

Energy Integration by Wave Length and by Wave Number.—Alternative presentations of Planckian spectral intensity distributions in wave lengths or in wave numbers give respective peak intensities which do not occur at the same position in the spectrum. This is simply because of the reciprocal relation between the two abscissae units, the intensity relation being $J_\nu = (\lambda^2/10,000) J_\lambda$. To avoid this confusion Professor Hottel (*33*) recommends discarding "peak" and instead using a common characteristic, median wave length λ, microns (or wave number ν, cm^{-1}) which divides the whole, integrated, black-body radiation Q into two equal parts. This median line occurs at

$$\lambda_{0.5Q, \text{ microns}} \times 10^{-4} \times T = T/\nu = 0.411 \text{ cm }°\text{K}$$

Another method of describing the spectral position of "most of" the black-body radiation is to delimit the central third of the whole energy. Referring to tables of integrated λT, the Smithsonian Table 129 or Dunkle's (*9*) using the revised basic constants, it is seen that the 1/3 lines are at $T/\nu = 0.327$ and 0.527 cm °K which almost includes both the peak intensity by wave length and by wave number. The wave-number basis has the advantage of expanding the short-wave end where absorption-band detail is important (Fig. 3), and of having a symmetrical pattern of absorption-line fringes.

MEASUREMENT OF SOLAR IRRADIATION RECEIVED AT THE GROUND

U. S. Weather Bureau Observations Using the Eppley Pyrheliometer.— For hourly total solar irradiation the most simple and directly useful charts for cloudless weather are those given by Hand (*17*). Tables of direct perpendicular sunshine for various altitudes of the sun are given in the A.S.H. & V.E. "Guide" (*4*). The diffuse sky radiation on vertical walls is also given for typical clear and industrial atmospheres. Hand has also compiled the distribution of average daily insolation based on U.S.A. pyrheliometer records (*18*) and has published annual curves for 35 stations (*23*). Both of the latter include typical cloudiness. Cloudiness effects by the day are treated by Kennedy (*28*).

Recommendation III 19 of the World Meteorological Organization, Commission for Instruments and Methods of Observation, adopted at the eighth meeting, Toronto, September 3, 1953(8).

NOTING—that radiation measurements within meteorological networks must contribute to the following purposes:
   (*a*) to study the transformation of energy within the system "earth and atmosphere" and its variation in time and space;
   (*b*) to analyse the atmosphere with regard to its turbidity and constituents such as dust and water vapour;
   (*c*) to study the distribution and the variations of incoming, outgoing and net radiation;
   (*d*) to satisfy the needs of biological, medical, agricultural and industrial activities with respect to radiation; and
CONSIDERING that calibrations with absolute standard pyrheliometers for direct solar radiation can, at present, be performed at the following institutes:
   (*a*) Meteorological Institute, Stockholm, Sweden;
   (*b*) Astrophysical Observatory, Smithsonian Institution, Washington, U.S.A.;
   (*c*) Institut R. Meteorologique de Belgique, Service du Rayonnement, Uccle, Belgium;
   (*d*) Physikalisch-Meteorologisches Observatorium, Davos, Switzerland;
   (*e*) Weather Bureau, Radiation Service, Pretoria, South Africa
RECOMMENDS (1) that the radiation observations in the network of each country should be controlled from a radiation centre in charge of a radiation specialist. This centre shall be responsible for the calibration and the periodic check of the instruments, for the standardization of the evaluation procedures and for the instruction of the observers;

(2) that the radiation network should include specialized radiation stations and (or) ordinary meteorological stations provided with some simple radiation instruments;
(3) that, for the specialized radiation stations, the programme should include:
   (*a*) continuous recording of the total radiation of sun and sky, and of sky, separately, on a horizontal surface;
   (*b*) regular measurements of direct solar radiation, both for total radiation and for selected spectral regions;
   (*c*) measurements of the long-wave effective outgoing radiation ("nocturnal radiation");
   (*d*) registration of the duration of sunshine;
(4) that, for ordinary meteorological stations to be provided with more simple equipment, the programme should include the registration of the duration of sunshine and, if possible, the continuous recording of the total radiation of sun and sky on a horizontal surface. . . . [For paragraphs 5 to 13 see original text (*8*).]

Measurement of Whole-Spectrum Irradiation and Separation of Long-Wave, Atmospheric Radiation.—Our common concept of irradiation on the ground as being composed of direct, beam sunshine *plus* diffuse radiation from the hemisphere of the sky is misleading because ordinarily there is net radiation *loss* to the sky which, excepting the sun itself, acts as if colder than the ground. Although atmospheric radiation is intrinsically of very low energy rate, the hemispherical sky dome has about 46,000 times the radiating area of the sun's disk and therefore radiation from the atmosphere is a considerable fraction of the total whole-spectrum irradiation such as indicated in Figure 3. The abscissa scale change at wave number 2500 (4 micron wave length) cutting off 1/2 per cent of solar energy coincides approximately with complete opacity for the Eppley glass. The opposite change in ordinate scale keeps planimeter area scale uniform for the whole figure. Outgoing black-body radiation would completely fill the long-wave Planckian distribution curve, and the net radiation loss to the cold sky occurs mainly in the 8 to 14 micron "window"; see Brooks (*7*).

To measure the radiation in each of the three modes shown in Figure 3, two calibrated hemispherical radiometers are required—uncovered and glass covered—and these must be operated shaded and unshaded from direct sunbeams, and also turned to face downward. For precise measurements the calibration needs to be known for various angles of incidence and for the inverted position. The mounting needs to provide for leveling the receiving surfaces and turning the plate blast in line with the wind, and to be high enough above ground so that the shape factor of the shadows of the apparatus will be negligible. To aid in visualizing the meaning of the positive and negative instrument responses which determine the magnitudes of the three modes of radiation, Figure 4 has been constructed with circle areas proportional to the observed intensities for May 6, 1954. This

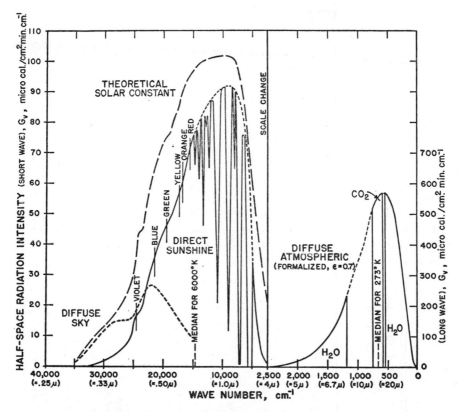

Figure 3.—Example of spectral distribution of all the radiation downward from sun, sky, and atmosphere without clouds. The diffuse sky radiation is converted from Linke and the beam radiation from Moon. The "windows" between strong absorption lines vary in transmission mainly with the water-vapor content of the atmosphere. The abscissa scale is in wave number (frequency) to suit absorption-line theory. Although the black-body "peaks" appear different from those on the wave-length scale, planimetered areas give identical energy blocks between specific spectral boundaries.

two-dimensional representation is not proper for three-dimensional diffuse radiation but conveys the idea of distribution with angle of incidence. The numbers in Figure 4 refer to lines in Table 3.

The procedure outlined in Table 3 will also yield the short-wave reflec-

TABLE 3

Observations and Calculations of Short- and Long-Wave Radiation Factors

(Left-margin section labels: lines 1–13 = FIELD OBSERVATIONS; lines 14–23 = SHORT-WAVE)

Line	Item	Calibration or calc. by line No.	Units	1428 (a)	1430 (b)	1433 (c)	1434 (a)	0735 (a)	0740 (b)	0748 (c)	0754 (a)	1203 (a)	1205 (b)	1209 (c)	1212 (a)
				6 MAY '54								8 JULY '54			
1	Date and time (P.S.T.) Davis, Calif., W.121°43', N.38°32'.	Local −7 min.+ time corr. Hrs.													
2	Exposure of radiometers	(a)=up,(b)=up,shaded,(c)=down													
3	Cloudiness			Sun clear; 0.2 Ac.				No clouds				5/6 no clouds; 0.1 thin Cs.			
4	Air temp. (aspir. I.C. couple)	mv x 35.0+32°	°F	89	—	—	—	—	72	73	—	—	89	—	89
5	Wet bulb depression (double-I.C.)	mv x 17.5	°F	20	—	—	—	—	11	14	—	—	23	13	—
6	Vapor pressure	(4),(5) table	mb.	16.3	—	—	—	—	—	—	—	—	—	—	—
7	Black globe temp. (I.C.)	mv x 35.0+32°	°F	116	—	—	—	—	94	93	88	—	101	100	103
8	Globe temp. excess (6-inch diam.)	(7)−(4)	°F	27	—	—	—	—	22	20	—	—	22	—	24
9	Soil surface temp. (I.C.)	mv x 35.0+32°	°F	—	—	—	112 av.	91	—	88	—	—	126	121	129
10	Air velocity at globe height	Pulse/min. x calib.(÷6")	Ft./min.	156	—	—	—	—	285	—	—	—	375	—	—
11	Plate radiometer temp. (I.C.)	mv x 35.0+32°	°F	98	92	93	99	73	71	73	76	99	89	91	97
12	Plate radiometer response (S.C.)	36.6 B/hr.ft².mv.	mv.	5.43	−0.24	1.54	5.50	3.02	−.40	1.10	2.92	6.23	−1.10	2.36	6.49
13	Eppley pyrheliometer response	96.3 B/hr.ft².mv.	mv	2.59	0.42	0.49	2.58	1.66	0.26	0.54	1.79	3.22	0.36	0.77	3.25
14	Altitude of sun	(1), table	deg.	—	51°04'	—	—	—	30°42'	—	—	—	74°00'	—	—
15	Air mass path of sunbeams, m.	(14), table	csc	—	1.28	—	—	—	1.96	—	—	—	1.04	—	—
16	Short-wave insola. outside atm.	(1),(15), table	B/hr.ft²	—	330	—	—	—	212	—	—	—	400	—	—
17	Short-wave dir.+diffuse (=insolation)	(13a) x 96.3	B/hr.ft²	250	—	—	249	160	—	—	172	310	—	—	313
18	Short-wave diffuse from sky	(13b) x 96.3	B/hr.ft²	—	40.4	—	—	—	25.5	—	—	—	35.1	—	—
19	Short-wave diffuse/total	(18)/(17ave.)		—	0.16	—	—	—	0.16	—	—	—	0.11	—	—
20	Direct sunbeam rad. (on horizontal)	(17)−(18)	B/hr.ft²	210	210 av.	—	209	134	137 av.	—	146	275	276 av.	—	278
21	Depleted beam	(20)/(16)		—	0.636	—	—	—	0.646	—	—	—	0.690	—	—
22	Short-wave reflected by soil surf.	(13c) x 96.3	B/hr.ft²	—	—	47	—	—	—	52.5	—	—	—	74	—
23	Short-wave reflectivity of soil surf.	(22)/(17ave.)		—	—	0.189	—	—	—	0.31	—	—	—	—	0.42

(Header span: "Observations and determinations" covers all date/time columns.)

26

TABLE 3 (Continued)

Line	Item	Calibration or calc. by line No.	Units	Observations and determinations											
WHOLE SPECTRUM															
25	Plate black emissive power	$\sigma((11)+460)^4$	B/hr.ft²	167	160	162	169	139.2	137?	139	142	168	158	159	166
26	Radia. measured rel. to plate	$(12)\times36.6$	B/hr.ft²	199	-8*	56	202	110	-14?	40	107	228	-40	86	237
27	Whole-spect. radiation toward plate	$(25)+(26)$	B/hr.ft²	366	152	218	371	250	108△	179	249	396	118	245	403
28	Direct sunbeam radia., plate(see 20)	$(27a)-(27b)$	B/hr.ft²	214	215av.	—	219	142	142av.	—	141	279	281av.	—	286
29	Net diffuse plate/beam rad.	$(26b)/(28\,\text{ave.})$		—	-0.04	—	—	—	-0.10	—	—	—	-0.14	—	—
30	Net rad. exchange at ground (input to convec., conduct. & evap.)	$(27a\,\text{ave.})-(27c)$	B/hr.ft⁴	—	—	150	—	—	—	71	—	—	—	156	—
31	Equiv. sky temp., including sun	$((27a)/\sigma)^{1/4}-460$	°F	219	—	—	221	154	—	—	157	232	—	—	235
32	Equiv. sky temp., excluding sun	$((27b)/\sigma)^{1/4}-460$	°F	—	85	—	—	—	40	—	—	—	51	—	—
33	Equiv. soil surface temp., sunlit	$((27c)/\sigma)^{1/4}-460$	°F	—	—	137	—	—	—	107	—	—	—	154	—
34	Heat convected, black globe	$(8) \times 0.169\sqrt{(10)}$	B/hr.ft²	—	57	—	—	—	63	—	—	—	75	—	—
35	Black globe emissive power**	$\varepsilon\sigma((7)+460)^4$	B/hr.ft²	—	176	—	—	—	150	—	—	—	160	—	—
36	Spherical radiation absorbed	$(34)+(35)$	B/hr.ft²	—	234	—	—	—	213	—	—	—	235	—	—
37	Mean spher. rad. temp. (M.R.T.)	$((36)/\varepsilon\sigma)^{1/4}-460$	°F	—	159	—	—	—	144	—	—	—	159	—	—
LONG-WAVE															
38	Incoming atmospheric radiation	$(27b)-(18)$	B/hr.ft²	—	112	—	—	—	82△	—	—	—	83	—	—
39	Black-body emission at soil temp.	$\sigma((9)+460)^4$	B/hr.ft²	—	—	185	—	—	—	156	—	—	—	197	—
40	Long-wave emissivity of soil surf.	$((27c)-(22)-(38))/((39)-(38))$		—	—	0.81	—	—	—	0.60?	—	—	—	0.77	—
41	Emissive power of the soil	$(39) \times (40)$	B/hr.ft²	—	150	—	—	—	?	—	—	—	152	—	—
42	Upward reflection of atm. rad.	$(38) \times (1.0-(40))$	B/hr.ft²	—	21	—	—	—	?	—	—	—	19	—	—

*Algebraic sign (−) for negative response with plate warmer than sky when shaded.   **Emissivity of Fuller's flat black taken as 0.925.   △Observed 123 but this was highly variable due to wind on soil, on radiometer, and leads to impossible incoming atm. radiation of 98.

tivity (Line 23). If the true ground-surface temperature can be measured, the approximate long-wave emissivity of the ground can be determined (Line 40) although this suffers from involving the differences of large numbers. Furthermore, comparison of the direct-beam radiation with that calculated for outside the atmosphere for the specific time and date will give the over-all shortwave depletion (Line 21) which is the total effect of the parts described in Table 2. The influence of soil reflection and emission on the effectiveness of shades in hot climates is treated by Kelly, et al. (27).

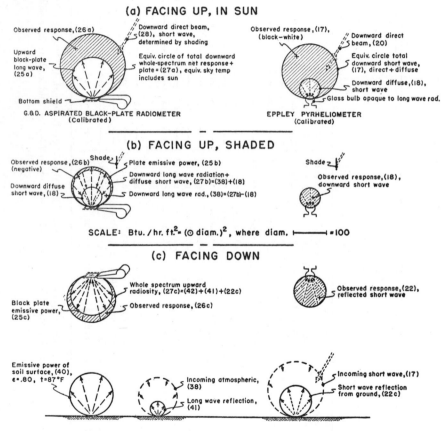

Figure 4.—Illustration of the cause of observed responses of the aspirated black-plate radiometer and the glass-enclosed Eppley pyrheliometer when exposed in three aspects: (a) facing up, unshaded, (b) facing up, shaded, and (c) facing down. The energy rates in the example of May 6, 1954, are represented arbitrarily as circle areas and the cross-hatched areas scale the measured response of each radiometer in each exposure.

It is hoped that the foregoing explanations will lead to further developments in measurement of usable solar energy and that the 0.61 and 1.9 visibility meters will be incorporated into regular observational procedures so that the haze factor can be separated from the water-vapor absorption. The apparatus and observations reported herein are primarily the work of John R. Goss (Assistant Specialist, Department of Agricultural Engineering, University of California, Davis, California, 1954), but much credit is also due the staff of Department of Agricultural Engineering at Davis.

Section III

Space Heating and Domestic
Uses of Solar Energy

Solar house-heating appears to be the simplest direct application of solar energy because a relatively slight elevation of temperature is needed. It is surprising that more attention has not been paid to research in this field, particularly in view of the fact that a thoughtful committee report (45) has predicted that by 1975 there will be 13 million houses in the United States (mostly in its southern half) which will be heated almost entirely by the sun.

The first three papers in this section were written by three of the persons or groups who have been most active in research on solar house-heating. Their research, as outlined in this section, includes three types of solar-energy collections, and both phase-transition or chemical type and specific-heat type of heat storage units. Important in this field has been the research program on heat storage and architectural design carried out by the group at the Massachusetts Institute of Technology.

Other domestic uses of solar energy are now actualities, such as hot-water heaters in California and Florida, and solar cookers in India.

The possibility of combining solar house-heating with an electrically operated heat pump is interesting, and is the subject of further research by Dr. Löf and others. Solar space-cooling and air conditioning also show some promise; and, in addition to the comments in this section, contributions in Sections IV and X also touch on these matters.

Section III. Introduction, continued

Little is said in the section about the commonly referred to "solar house," i.e., buildings with large sun-facing window areas but no collectors per se or storage facilities other than the heat capacity of the building itself; however, the bibliography includes a number of references on the subject, notably those of Hutchinson, and Parmelee *et al*.

House Heating and Cooling with Solar Energy

George O. G. Löf

Introduction.—A system for heating a dwelling with solar energy comprises essentially a solar-energy collector on the roof or south wall of the house, a container with material in which heat can be stored for one or more days, a circulating system for conducting a heated fluid from the solar collector to the house living area and the storage container, and an auxiliary heater to provide heat when solar energy is not available either from the collector or from the storage unit. If cooling is involved in the summer, an additional unit in which the household air can be cooled and dehumidified is required, along with the necessary auxiliaries for operating the apparatus with the solar-heated fluid.

A method for accomplishing the above objectives has been under investigation by the writer and associates first at the University of Colorado, later at the University of Denver, and now directly in co-operation with the American Window Glass Company of Pittsburgh, Pennsylvania. This company has supported the investigation for the past seven years; prior to that time, a two-year preliminary investigation was sponsored by the War Production Board at the University of Colorado. The experimental and development programs completed under this project have included: the design and development of the overlapped, flat-plate type of collector and the determination of its performance characteristics under a wide variety of experimental conditions; the design and testing of units employing heat storage in a gravel bin; design, installation, and testing of the complete solar-heating system in an already existing house, employing auxiliary natural-gas heat; and the design of a complete solar-heating system in a newly designed house for several climates.

General Description of System.—The distinguishing characteristics of the system on which these studies have been based are: (*a*) a unique design of solar collector which provides for the heating of air by contacting it with a series of closely spaced, overlapping, partially blackened glass plates; and (*b*) the use of a heat-storage unit consisting of a bin filled with gravel of approximately one-inch diameter, to which heat is transferred from the solar-heated air by passing the air slowly through the gravel, and from which heat is transferred to the air circulating from the living space through the bin at night.

The solar collector is thus a variation of the conventional flat-plate type, each black surface being covered by three or four air-spaced clear glass sheets. In the design found most practical, the single-strength glass panes are approximately 2 feet wide, 18 inches long (along the direction of air travel), and are coated with a dull, semifused black glass layer for a 6-inch distance along the 18-inch dimension. These plates, overlapped two-thirds their length (the clear portion) are supported 1/4 inch apart by frames between the house roof rafters, in sections 4 feet in length, which are themselves covered with a single cover glass plate (or in some tests, two plates spaced 1/4 inch apart) 2 feet by 4 feet in size. Thus, in the roof area used, a completely blackened area is provided for solar absorption, overlaid by three or four glass surfaces to reduce heat loss. Air is circulated by a blower from a supply duct to the lower ends of these 2-foot width channels, through which the air passes at low velocity (about

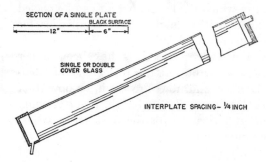

Figure 5.—Diagram of a solar collector section, consisting of an aluminum trough, 2 ft by 4 ft by 4 in. in depth, and containing a series of overlapped, partially blackened glass plates. The plates are separated by ¼–inch spacers along their two sloping edges.

1 to 2 feet per second), contacting first the warm clear portions of each glass pane and then the hot black areas. Since three or four 4-foot sections are placed in series, the air is heated stepwise to the final temperature, and is then conducted to the house rooms through conventional hot-air ducts or to the heat-storage bin. Figure 5 shows a section of a collector of the overlapped-plate type.

Temperatures of the delivered air depend primarily on solar intensity and air-circulation rate, and in a typical installation on a moderately clear but cold day would range from 90° F when the unit starts operating in the morning to nearly 200° F at noon. Air moves through the collector in relatively streamline flow, thereby minimizing convection heat loss from plate to plate and to the atmosphere. Efficiency of heat collection is dependent on numerous operating factors and weather conditions. On a clear winter day, with a solar intensity of about 1,800 Btu per square foot of collector surface and a typical 24-hour average atmospheric temperature of 35° F, approximately 800 Btu per square foot can be recovered at temperatures above 80° F by a collector having low-reflection glass and single cover plates (3 clear surfaces above the black surface) at an air circulation rate of about 1.5 cu ft per sq ft of collector per minute. Data for a clear fall day in Denver are shown on Figure 6.

Performance of four collector arrangements, indicated as heat recovered as a function of air rate, is shown in Figure 7. The use of low-reflection glass is seen to be highly advantageous, particularly at high air rates (and the corresponding lower temperatures of operation). The use of single

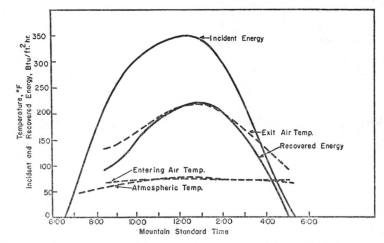

Figure 6.—Heat recovery and air temperatures during a typical clear day, for a four-section collector tilted 27°, containing surface-treated, low-reflection glass with single cover plates. Air rate through the collector was 1.48 scfm per square foot of collector area. Incident energy was 2441 Btu per ft^2, giving an efficiency of 55 per cent. Denver, October 10, 1951.

cover plates rather than double is desirable both from efficiency and economy standpoints.

Heat recovery as affected by incident energy and mean atmospheric temperature is shown in Figure 8.

The complete house-heating system involves the supply of solar-heated air directly to the living space when needed and its recirculation back to the collector from the cold-air return ducts. When heat is not needed in the rooms, a control shifts a damper and the hot air passes down through the storage bin, thence back to the collector inlet. At night, and during cloudy weather, air is drawn up through the storage bin (becoming heated) and supplied to the house rooms, from which it returns to the bottom of

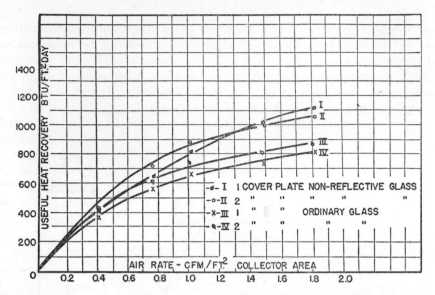

(*Above*) *Figure* 7.—Performance of four solar collector arrangements, showing heat recovery as a function of air rate, type of glass, and cover plate arrangement. Total daily incident energy was 2,200 Btu per ft² of collector surface tilted 27° to the south, and mean ambient air temperature was 40° F. (*Below*) *Figure* 8.—Performance of a solar collector under various weather conditions, showing heat recovery as a function of incident energy on sloping surface and mean (24–hour) ambient air temperature. Collector was at a slope of 27°, and contained four sections of surface-treated, low-reflection glass, with single cover plates. Air rate was 1.48 scfm/ft² collector.

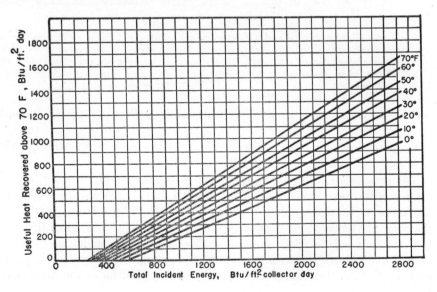

the storage bin for reheating. When there is insufficient heat either from the collector or from storage, an auxiliary duct heater, supplied with natural gas or other energy source, delivers the necessary heat into the air stream. Automatic controls make the system completely self-operating. A schematic diagram of such a system is shown in Figure 9.

Further details of the design, operation, and performance of the system

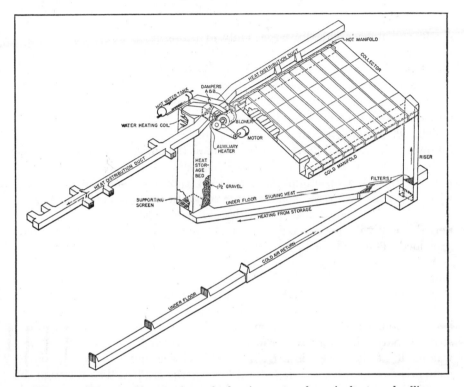

Figure 9.—Diagram of a complete solar heating system for a single-story dwelling.

have been reported in the literature and are not repeated here because of space limitations (*33, 34, 35*).

Economics of Solar Heating.—In one phase of the solar study, an economic balance of collector size, storage-bin size, and auxiliary fuel requirement was made. A 2,000–square-foot, single-story house in Denver and Dallas was used as the basis for design and cost calculations. The results show that it is entirely impractical to carry the entire heating load with solar energy. The cost of providing the necessary collector area and the resulting fixed cost on this facility considerably exceed the fixed cost on an auxiliary heater and the fuel which is required for its use. Minimum total annual fixed and operating costs are realized, in these examples, when the solar-collector area is large enough to supply about two-thirds to three-fourths of the heating load, the balance being supplied by the auxiliary heater. This generalization appears valid even in other parts of the country, with different house designs, solar-heating equipment, and fuels; that is, if central heating is definitely *required* in the dwelling, some form of auxiliary heat should be provided so that the solar-collector system need not be excessively and uneconomically large. Only in those areas where mild winter weather prevails and where house heating is not absolutely necessary could auxiliary heating be economically dispensed with.

A second result of the economic studies indicates that with the gravel type of heat storage, and in the types of climate encountered in Denver and Dallas, the economic optimum size of the storage bin is roughly that which will permit storage of one day's collected heat for use during the following night. Fixed and operating costs of the entire system were found to be rather insensitive to moderate changes in storage-bin size, and it is possible that the optimum storage-period capacity could be two days with only slightly altered conditions. Even with this storage increase, the conclusion that economical design demands relatively short heat-storage periods, equivalent to relatively small storage capacity, appears well grounded. The gains in fuel savings resulting from increasing the storage capacity an extra day are very small beyond a two-day storage period and insufficient to justify the additional cost of the heat-storage chamber, the gravel within it, and the space that the chamber occupies in the house.

The studies conducted in the solar-energy project reported here have been in connection with only one basic solar-collector design and heat-storage material. No comparison of this design and system with others was made at the outset in arriving at this choice, nor has any thorough comparison been made during the course of the studies. The criterion of superiority should be the supply of the house-heating requirements at minimum annual fixed and operating cost. Since reliable cost analyses have not been made on the various systems, it cannot be definitely stated which system may show the minimum expense. It is by no means claimed that the overlapped-plate type of system and the gravel storage used in combination with it are basically superior. It is felt, however, that the system may lend itself most readily to mass production and, for that reason, may be the cheapest to fabricate and install. The answer to this question can be reliably found only by considerably detailed cost analyses based upon construction and operation of several test installations in dwellings under various conditions. Even then, perhaps no single system will prove superior, for it may be found that certain systems lend themselves more ideally to certain climates, whereas other systems are better in other parts of the country.

Comparisons of efficiencies of various types of solar collectors are of no value in arriving at a determination of which system is "best." Only by consideration of installation and operating cost, along with efficiency, or in other words, net heat delivery per dollar of fixed and operating cost, can the performance be properly assessed as far as practicality and potentiality for house-heating application are concerned. Similarly, comparisons of various heat-storage materials in terms of heat-storage capacity per pound of material or per cubic foot of material are entirely irrelevant; the only significant figure is the heat-storage capacity of the entire storage unit per dollar of fixed and operating cost. The latter figure will, in general, be obtainable directly from heat-storage capacity per dollar of investment in the storage system. Here again, there is no clear evidence that any one of the various heat-storage systems is superior to the others.

Finally, the heat-collection and heat-storage equipment cannot be treated independently in cost analyses and comparisons of various systems, for the reason that some combinations are particularly advantageous and economical, whereas the individual components used in other combinations might be entirely impractical. Thus, if the solar collector is of the water-coil type, a water-tank storage system appears the most practical and economical; if air is being heated in the collector, storage in gravel is cheap and convenient. It would probably be impractical to combine gravel-bin storage with a water type of collector, even though the gravel-bin type were to prove more economical for application with the air-collector system. Thus, separate comparisons of costs of heat-storage materials and collector equipment fail to reflect these factors, and only by evaluation of total costs of the entire system can realistic figures be obtained.

Actual dollar costs of the overlapped plate–gravel bin combination system are still in the speculative stage, even though most of the components can be fairly accurately priced. Estimates based on factory production of equipment of this type indicate that it should be possible to install these solar collectors on an average new dwelling for about $1 per square foot of roof area occupied. In a relatively sunny, cold winter climate, such as in Denver, a 600–square-foot collector would carry two-thirds to three-fourths of the heating requirements of a 2,000–square-foot house, requiring a total investment over and above that of the conventional heating plant of about $750. Under present conditions, with a fifteen-year amortization, the resulting fixed charge of $50 per year would be roughly comparable with the fuel saving in such a house. Costs and savings will vary tremendously, depending upon the climate in the particular location, the availability and cost of fuel, and numerous other factors. It is therefore impossible to state that certain areas of the country represent "feasible" zones of solar heating and other areas "unfeasible." It may be observed that solar heating is *feasible* in all areas of the United States, whereas *economical* solar heating will be possible where there is a combination of comparatively expensive fuel, plentiful sunshine, and at least moderate heating requirement.

Objectives and Plans in Heating Development.—The principal objective in the study is the practical application of this system to the heating of dwellings at as early a date and in as wide an area as economically practical. Since the efficiencies of the several types of flat-plate collectors do not differ greatly (lying in the range of 35–55 per cent of the normal incident solar energy), the development of a low-cost, factory-made solar collector appears to be the greatest need. Studies have therefore been oriented in the direction of developing a relatively cheap system, rather than necessarily the most efficient system, for converting solar energy to heat. Because fuels are generally cheap in this country, particularly in most of the areas where solar energy is plentiful, competition of solar heating with conventional heating will be close. Wide application of solar heating can be expected only if the required investment in the solar-heating system will not be unduly great; the annual fixed cost on this added investment will therefore have to be appreciably less than the value of the fuel saved. Although some applications of solar energy are undoubtedly decades in the future, the sponsor and participants in this study are convinced that considerable use of the system will be seen well within ten years.

Plans for continuing the development of solar heating involve the construction of one or more test houses in which the system will be installed. Detailed consideration of installation and operating costs will be made, and thorough evaluation of the performance of the system, in light of its cost, will be performed. When the results of operating these heating systems have been computed and when the fuel savings have been balanced against the additional costs of the system, plans for further development can then be realistically made. Improvements in design will undoubtedly be effected as the development proceeds. Such steps as the use of glass, surface-treated to reduce reflection, have been very significant, and other improvements will no doubt be developed.

Heat Storage in Pebble Beds.—Storage of solar heat collected in a heated-air stream can be conveniently accomplished in a bed of gravel or pebbles.

In such application, the gravel serves the dual purpose of a heat exchanger and a heat-storage medium. Hot air from the solar collector at temperatures ordinarily ranging from 80° to 200° F enters the top of a vertical bed or one end of a horizontal bed, travels through the bed by passage between the pebbles, transferring its sensible heat to the pebbles and leaving the opposite end of the bin at a temperature essentially equal to that of the pebbles at the cooler end. The air is then recirculated to the collector for reheating. At night or during cloudy periods, air from the house is circulated through the pebble bed in the reverse direction, resulting in a transfer of heat from the pebbles to the air; the hot air is then circulated back to the rooms of the dwelling.

Tests with a small bin (*33*), later confirmed in a full-sized storage bed, indicate that pebbles of a size ranging from 1-1½ inch in diameter are close to ideal for this application. Use of considerably larger pebbles would result in reduced heat-transfer surface and appreciable temperature gradients within the pebbles; the use of smaller pebbles would result in a considerable increase in pressure-drop and fan-power requirements in forcing the air through the storage bed. Close sizing of the gravel is important in order that the voids between pebbles be of adequate size to permit passage of air with sufficiently low pressure drop.

Due to the very low rate of heat transfer from pebble to pebble, it is possible to obtain a high degree of heat stratification in the bed. If a vertical bin 4 feet by 4 feet in floor area and 8 feet in height is considered, the pebbles at the top of the bed are heated almost immediately to the entering air temperature, whereas the balance of the bed remains at its initial temperature; air leaving the bed is also at the initial temperature of the bottom of the bed. As heating of the bed progresses, the fairly sharp boundary between hot and cold pebbles gradually moves downward. Only when the entire storage bin is "filled with heat" will the temperature of the air leaving the bottom of the bed begin to rise.

When the house air is being heated, the reverse action takes place. Cool house air is heated by passing it up through the storage bed, a process causing the boundary between hot and cold portions to move upward and reduce the total amount of heat stored in the bed. Air leaving the top of the bed is at a temperature nearly equal to that of the gravel at that point, which in turn is nearly equal to the temperature of the hot air entering during the heating portion of the cycle. Thus, even though the storage bed may be only half filled with heat, air can be delivered from it substantially at the top temperature of operation. The low conductivity from one pebble to another, due to very small points of contact, also permits storage of the heat for considerable periods of time with only a small amount of vertical heat flow and external loss even from an uninsulated bin. Neither of these types of heat flow represent losses, however, the former simply resulting in a slight lowering of the temperature at which air can be delivered from the storage bed, and the latter merely representing a small amount of heat which is conducted directly into the house through the storage-bin walls.

In a 4 × 4 × 8 foot bin, 1½-inch gravel can be supported on a heavy screen at the bottom and can be contained in walls of cinder block or some other suitable material. The total heat-storage capacity of such a bed is about 300,000 Btu, assuming a temperature range of about 120° F between the hot and cold conditions of the bed. About six tons of gravel would be required for this storage unit. A house with about 2,000 square feet of floor area and, for example, a heat requirement of 20,000 Btu per degree day could therefore be heated overnight from storage if the bed were initially full of heat and if the outdoor night temperature averaged about 40°. If the night temperature were lower or if the bed were not completely filled with heat at the end of the sunny portion of the day, auxiliary heat would have to be employed during part of the night. A larger storage bed would provide additional nighttime heat supply, but the collector would have to be of sufficient size to supply enough heat during the daytime, under ordinary conditions, to heat the storage bed to capacity and also to supply daytime house heating needs.

Departure from ideal operation is of course observed because of variation in the temperature of the air entering the top of the bed. Thus, if a constant air-circulation rate is employed, comparatively low air temperatures are observed in the early morning and late afternoon, whereas high temperatures are obtained at noon. The heated portion of the storage bed will therefore not be at uniform temperature and there will be zones of higher and lower temperatures in the heated portion. This is not a serious drawback, however, because ordinary house-heating controls operate on an on-off principle. Hot air being delivered from the storage bed would simply be supplied for a longer period when it is not at maximum temperature; as the hottest portion of the bed is being "used"—that is, when the hottest zone is at the top of the bed—the circulating fan will be running a smaller fraction of the time. Although some of the heat-storage capacity of the bed is not being utilized when there are zones of temperature in it less than the maximum, a slight enlargement in storage-bed size can compensate for this factor.

Technical advantages which the pebble type of heat storage system has are: (1) very large heat-transfer area in the pebble bed, requiring only small temperature driving forces for substantially complete transfer of heat; (2) the combination of a heat exchanger and a heat-storage system in one unit; (3) a counter-current heat-exchange system wherein advantageous temperature stratification is realized; (4) comparatively low energy requirements for circulating air through the heat-storage bed. As a result of the technical advantages cited, and the obvious advantage in the very low cost of gravel and the container for it, use of the pebble-bed type of heat storage is considered advantageous with the solar-collector system previously described.

Air Conditioning with Solar Energy.—There are several attractive features in a system which will cool, as well as heat, a dwelling with solar energy as the primary supply. In those sections of the country where domestic air conditioning is becoming important, the fixed cost on a solar-heating system could be partially defrayed by utilizing the solar energy to operate an air-conditioning unit which would save power or fuel in the summer months also. Solar energy is much more plentiful in the summer, and, in addition, the cooling or air-conditioning load is greatest when the solar intensity is at its maximum. The several advantages of a solar-heating system also apply to a solar-cooling system, and year-around use of a considerable part of the equipment is an added economy.

During the past three years two principal systems of air conditioning with solar energy have been investigated. The first of these involved the supply of solar-heated air to a steam generator operating at atmospheric pressure, from which the steam would be supplied to a Servel home air-conditioning unit. The principle on which the Servel unit operates is similar to the absorption refrigerator in which heat is utilized to operate the refrigeration cycle. Steam supplied to the refrigerant generator, either from the solar-heat exchanger or from a small gas-fired boiler, produces the refrigerant vapor which then is condensed and effects cooling and dehumidification of the house air being circulated past coils in which the refrigerant is again vaporized. This system was discarded, however, because the solar-collector temperatures necessary for production of steam at about 200° F were too high to permit satisfactory heat-recovery efficiency. Over-all conversions of solar energy to heat of vaporization in steam were below 10 per cent, and it was felt that use of this system would not be practical at these low efficiencies. Some reduction in steam temperature could probably be effected by operating at a reduced pressure in the steam generator, but probably not enough to yield satisfactory efficiencies.

The second method of solar air conditioning involves the dehumidification of the house air by absorption of moisture in a hygroscopic solution of triethylene glycol. Household air is circulated through a chamber in which a cool, concentrated solution of triethylene glycol is being sprayed; moisture is removed from the air by the glycol solution, and the dried air is then either recirculated directly to the rooms of the house, or a portion of it is cooled by partially rehumidifying it in an evaporative cooler. The moisture received by the glycol solution is then removed from it by spraying the liquid into a second chamber through which solar-heated air is passing. Water is evaporated from the glycol solution and vented to the atmosphere in the solar-air stream. The reconcentrated glycol solution is then returned to the absorber-spray chamber. Heat exchangers are employed wherever practical, and the heat of condensation of the moisture removed from the house air is ultimately removed in cooling water. Circulating pumps and blowers are provided in the design. This system is illustrated schematically in Figure 10.

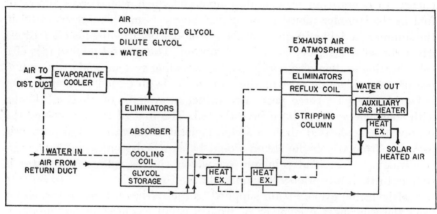

Figure 10.—Schematic drawing of triethylene glycol air-conditioning system.

Experimental tests with components of the glycol air-conditioning system were made in conjunction with an experimental solar collector, showing that the system would perform satisfactorily under normally encountered weather conditions. Numerous operating variables are involved in correlations of performance; but, under conditions which would usually be encountered, an over-all efficiency of converting solar energy to house-heat removal is about 25 per cent. Collector temperature need not be much higher than in winter use, and maximum temperatures of 200° to 250° would ordinarily be employed. The minimum temperature at which solar-heated air is effective in the operation of the conditioner is about 150° F, but temperatures of at least 175° F would usually be employed. Air is supplied to the collector directly from the atmosphere during summer operation.

Although the construction of the air-conditioner unit is considerably more complicated than the heating system, it is of approximately the same complexity as conventional types of air-conditioning equipment. Automatic operation is completely practical, and maintenance problems should not be substantially greater than with other types of air-conditioning equipment. A brief consideration of costs of this apparatus indicates that at the outset the unit will be slightly more costly than conventional equipment. It is believed, however, that after several units have been built, and factory production becomes possible, the cost should become competitive.

Finally, preliminary estimates of the cost of operating the entire solar heating and cooling system, including the associated fixed costs, are slightly greater than those of a conventional system in a typical dwelling in Dallas. It is believed that with further development of the equipment and its production on a quantity basis the total cost of solar heating and air conditioning can be brought advantageously below the corresponding costs with fuel-operated or power-operated systems. As is the case with solar heating, however, large general areas of practicality cannot be identified, and cost comparison requires a consideration of weather conditions, fuel costs, and other factors in a given location. It is felt, however, that the dehumidification system of air conditioning, in combination with a solar collector and an auxiliary heater both for winter and summer use, will prove to be a satisfactory and economical means for cooling and heating of homes in many areas of the United States, and to this objective the development is being carried forward.

Solar Heating Design Problems

Lawrence B. Anderson, Hoyt C. Hottel, Austin Whillier

Publication No. 36 of the Godfrey L. Cabot Solar Energy Conversion Research Project, Massachusetts Institute of Technology.

Four topics are covered in this contribution. The first section is a discussion of the numerous architectural problems that arise in the design of solar-heated dwellings. The next two sections summarize recent developments in the thermal design of solar collectors; the energy-balance equation for the solar collector is put into a form most suitable for general use, and a method of describing solar weather to permit rapid calculation of the performance of any kind of solar collector is presented. The final section, on energy storage, presents a brief discussion of unsolved problems in regard to phase-change storage materials, followed by a quantitative analysis for determining the optimum storage capacity for a given application. In this analysis account is taken of the day-to-day weather pattern, the performance characteristics of the solar collector, and the cost of the collector-storage system.

Architectural Problems.—To avoid confusion it is necessary to discern the various levels on which it is possible to mobilize solar energy for better comfort in buildings. To begin at the lowest, every architect should know how to design for most favorable climatic response of his enclosure so that, other factors being equal, he will minimize summer discomfort, require less fuel during temperature extremes, or extend the zones in which no mechanical equipment is required. Site selection to protect from cold winds, use of tree shade in summer on roofs, design of windows to admit sunshine in cold weather but exclude it in hot weather, control of diurnal ventilation cycles, and selection of materials with consideration for their heat-storage capacities are some of the most fruitful methods at the designer's disposal.

Greater reliance on solar energy requires specially constructed equipment, a flat-plate collector, a storage system, a means of transporting heat from collector to storage, and integration of the storage system either with the domestic hot-water supply or the house-heating system, or both. Two levels of use are discernible here. If the solar collector and storage are

47

conceived merely as supplementary to conventional energy sources, their efficiency can be relatively high because the system can always use almost immediately any collected heat; but the solar equipment has to be supplied as an addition to conventional equipment, and the only saving is in fuel costs. If the solar equipment is to become the principal energy source, the supplementary fuel-consumption device can be reduced to a stand-by heater of lesser capacity and more compact design. However, at this level of use of the sun the collector and storage requirements become important controls in the architectural design of the buildings, at least in the temperate zones where the main climatic problem is winter heating. Using reasonably attainable values for heat losses through good construction, and estimating the efficiency of collector and storage from known limits of operating conditions, it is clear that with presently available techniques it will be necessary to control dwelling profile and insulation so as to minimize the over-all heat requirement, and also to convert as much as possible of the house-envelope area seen by the sun in winter to favorably oriented flat-plate collector. Figure 11 shows a house designed, without regard for convention, to present a minimum area of exposure, maximum area of solar roof-collector, and optimum tilt of collector for a latitude of about 40°. Figure 12 represents a compromise with convention and practicality of construction.

Largely because of the variability of solar weather, the design of a solar-heated building in which comfort can always be maintained without the use of any auxiliary heat source becomes quite difficult, yet this situation must also be considered in view of the possible eventual exhaustion of convenient and economical fuels. It appears to require long-term storage with a less favorable load factor and a diminished over-all efficiency.

Analysis supported by experiment is now available for reasonably accurate design of collector and storage devices integrated with buildings, and for sound prediction of operation as related to climate. In general it seems clear from experience that the storage element cannot be combined with the collector without greatly reduced efficiency due to backward heat losses. The storage bin or tank must be kept within the building envelope, so that heat lost by leakage through its insulation may still contribute to the maintenance of interior comfort. By the same token, the collector must be considered part of the envelope of the building in order to recover its backside losses, to make 24-hour use of its insulation, and to diminish the expense of the collector to the difference between its cost and that of a comparable area of ordinary roof or wall. These considerations rule out treatment of the equipment as separate from the architectural design and require its arrangement to be involved with all the other con-

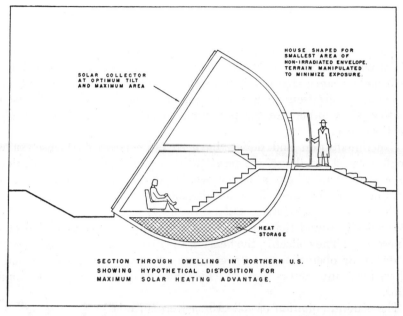

(*Above*) *Figure* 11.—A section of an idealized house having maximum collector area with optimum tilt and minimum nonirradiated area. (*Below*) *Figure* 12.—A section of a house representing a compromise with convention and practicality of construction.

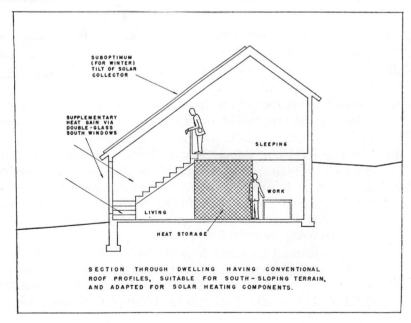

siderations of appearance, comfort, view, lighting, circulation, and general economy and amenity that are the concern of the architectural designer.

Additional developmental research is needed to simplify the construction of flat-plate collectors so that their first cost will be as low as possible and their maintenance characteristics good. It will be desirable to find means of energy utilization on a winter-summer basis, for cooling as well as heating, since otherwise the potentialities of an installation are only in fractional use.

Experimentation and design have so far concerned themselves with small isolated dwellings, yet possibilities may exist in the application to large structures where a larger scale and a radically different aspect ratio may provide more favorable installation conditions.

The Flat-Plate Collector.—Solar heating is so near the edge of being economically sound that careful attention to optimizing all design factors is necessary. The collector, the heart of the system, can be varied so greatly in design or operation as to necessitate an analysis which for generality allows for many factors some of which may be omitted in certain applications.

The general equation of collector performance is

$$Q_u/A = F_R(HR\tau\alpha - Q_L/A) \tag{1}$$

with the term in parenthesis representing performance if all heat extraction is at a uniform blackened-plate temperature t_p. The terms are:

Q_u/A The hourly-total net useful heat transferred into the transport-fluid stream per unit area of tilted collector.

H The hourly-total incidence of solar energy on unit area of a horizontal surface.

R A geometrical conversion factor, the ratio of total (direct + diffuse) incidence on the tilted surface to that on a horizontal surface.

$\tau\alpha$ The mean value of the product of effective transmittance of the glass cover plates and absorptivity of the blackened receiver. As used here, it must include allowance for angle of incidence, for multiple interior reflections, for dirt, for shading due to the finite depth of collectors; and it must be suitably weighted for direct and diffuse components of radiation.

Q_L/A The hourly total heat loss from the collector upwards from the blackened plate through glass and air to the atmosphere at temperature t_o, and downwards through the back-insulation. $Q_L/A = U(t_p - t_o)$, where t_p is the black-plate temperature.

F_R The heat-removal efficiency (*58*), the factor by which the performance drops when the collected energy is transferred into a fluid stream of finite flow-rate and entering temperature t_1, and possibly in line-contact with the blackened plate (*21*). (In evaluating Q_L/A the temperature t_1 rather than t_p is used.)

Application of this performance equation to problems of specific interest is tedious. The results are dependent both on the weather data used and on the collector design, orientation, and mode of use; and when any one of these factors is changed, complete recalculation is conventionally necessary. A method will now be presented for carrying the weather-data analysis as far as possible without commitment as to the contribution ultimately to be made by the other factors.

Solar Weather Analysis.—It is seen from Equation 1 that a certain critical or minimum value of horizontal incidence H_c, for any hour in question, is necessary to supply the sum of outward losses plus a small useful heat collection $Q_{u,\ min}/A$ which just offsets the pumping cost on the heat-transport fluid. This is given by

$$H_c R \tau \alpha = Q_L/A + (1/F_R)\, Q_{u,\ min}/A \qquad (2)$$

If the value for Q_L/A from Equation 2 is substituted in Equation 1 then

$$\frac{Q_u/A - Q_{u,\ min}/A}{F_R R \tau \alpha} = H - H_c \qquad (3)$$

The value of $Q_{u,\ min}/A$ is so small (about 3 Btu/sq ft, hour) that its evaluation may be approximate, and in some cases it may justifiably be neglected.

If now it is assumed that for a particular pair of hours of day symmetrical about solar noon, say 10–11 and 1–2, the factors affecting R, $\tau \alpha$, U, and t_o are nearly enough constant for a month to justify use of average values, the right-hand side of Equation 3 may be summed for the hour pair in question and presented as a function of the critical radiation H_c only. To use the resultant curve to estimate Q_u/A for the month, one determines H_c from Equation 2, the corresponding $\Sigma(H - H_c)$ from the weather analysis, and then Q_u/A from Equation 3.

The value $\Sigma(H - H_c)$ for various symmetrical hour pairs has been determined for each of several months, in each of several localities, using several years' solar data. The curves have been normalized by division of both co-ordinates by H_{ave}, the monthly-average value of horizontal incidence for the hour in question. From these normalized curves one evaluates the magnitude ϕ, defined by the expression

$$\phi = \frac{\Sigma_n\,(H - H_c)}{n H_{ave}}$$

(*n* is the number of items used in the numerator summation, i.e., the total number of items of hourly irradiation *H*, for the hour pair in question, that are used in the analysis.) The term ϕ will be called the "utilizability"; it is the fraction of the total month's incidence on a horizontal surface (for one particular hour from noon) which arrives with sufficient intensity to justify attempted collection.

Figure 13 presents ϕ-curves for the month of January for Blue Hill, Massachusetts, Boulder, Colorado, and El Paso, Texas. (ϕ-curves describing solar weather at seven stations in the continental United States and at three other parts of the world have been constructed, but are not reproduced here.) From curves similar to these it has been concluded that over the range of ϕ of practical interest the different hours of day, on the normalized basis, differ much less than the year-to-year variation for any one hour. This justifies use of the curves for the hour pair 10–11, 1–2 as adequately representing the other hours of the day (although the values of H_{ave} for each of the various hours of interest must of course be known). Figure 14 shows data for Blue Hill, Massachusetts, for seven different months of the year. This plot represents the complete summary of solar weather necessary for estimation of the average performance of a flat-plate collector of *any* design, when installed in the Blue Hill area. It makes due allowance for the average day-to-day departure of solar incidence, for a particular hour of day, from the mean at that hour for the month; but it cannot of course allow for the departure of the monthly-mean value in a particular year from the long-time average of the monthly mean.

For example, Blue Hill in January, 1951, was abnormally cold but sunny; its average solar incidence was 553 Btu/sq ft, day—12 per cent higher than the three-year average value 494 Btu/sq ft, day. Use of the ϕ-curves in the design of a system requiring a critical intensity H_c of 30 Btu/sq ft, hr would lead to a prediction of performance based on 1951 data which would be 16 per cent above normally expected January performance. Although the departure in this example is probably unusually large, the example does serve to underline a kind of variability in solar collector performance which is unpredictable.

The construction of ϕ-curves for a large number of representative localities over the earth is believed to be a necessary first step in the appraisal of the economics of solar-energy utilization by flat-plate collection.

The Storage of Solar Energy.—The two major problems that arise in designing the storage system are the selection of the material in which the energy is to be stored and the determination of the capacity of the system. As for selection of the storage material, Table 4 shows that of the *sensible-*

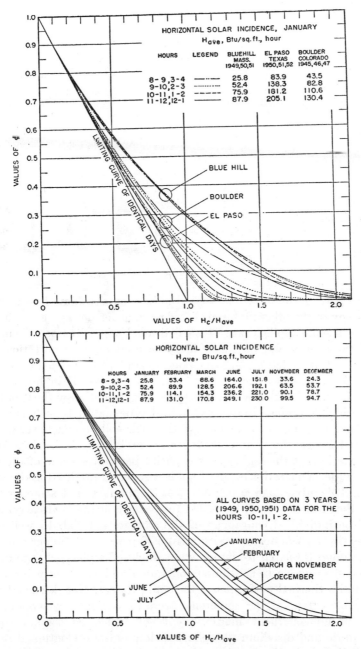

(*Upper*) *Figure* 13.—Solar weather analysis, January (three years' data), based on horizontal incidence. (*Lower*) *Figure* 14.—Solar weather analysis, Blue Hill, Massachusetts, based on three years' horizontal solar incidence data.

TABLE 4

Sensible Heat Storage Materials

| | Specific heat | Density | Unit heat capacity $\dfrac{\text{Btu}}{\text{ft}^3, \text{°F}}$ | |
	$\dfrac{\text{Btu}}{\text{lb, °F}}$	$\dfrac{\text{lb}}{\text{ft}^3}$	No voids	30% voids
Water	1.00	62	62	(62)
Scrap iron	0.112	489	55	38
Magnetite	0.165	320	53	37
Scrap aluminum	0.215	168	36	25
Concrete	0.27	140	38	26
Rock	0.205	180	37	26
Brick	0.2	140	28	20

heat type storage materials water is the best on a volume basis. Crushed rock or any of the other materials listed may, nevertheless, be economically superior in some applications. This will depend primarily upon the ultimate use of the energy and on the fluid to be used for transportation of the energy. Materials that undergo a change of state at some fixed temperature within the range of practical interest, 90° to 120° F in house-heating applications, and that have a large phase-change enthalpy (heat of fusion) are in principle preferable to sensible-heat type materials such as water or rock, since they permit operation of the solar collector at lower temperatures and hence (see Equation 1 above) at higher efficiencies. Another advantage is that the higher heat capacity per unit volume of the phase-change type of material means that less space is needed for the storage system. This advantage is partly offset by the fact that some free space within the storage system is needed for passage of the heat-carrying fluid about the individual containers of the storage material. In well packed systems these voids may constitute from 30 per cent to 50 per cent of the total volume. Research to date has not disclosed a phase-change material that is both reliable in continuous operation and sufficiently better than water in its thermal performance to justify its use. Not discussed to any appreciable extent at the conference were the serious problems of segregation in noncongruent melting-point salts such as sodium sulphate decahydrate and disodium phosphate dodecahydrate. Continued research is needed to find suitable phase-change materials and to evaluate quantitatively their thermal performance relative to that of water.

Factors of importance in determining the capacity of the storage system for a given application are the nature and magnitude of the daily demand for heat, the performance characteristics and total area of the solar collector, and the daily sequences of solar incidence for the locality in question, *all considered together*, as well as the dollar value of the collected heat based on prices of conventional fuel and the fixed charges on the storage system.

A method has been developed (*58*) for predicting for a given locality the fraction *F* of the total energy requirement in a given period that must be provided by auxiliary means, given a solar collector of area *A* and a sensible-heat type storage system of capacity *B* Btu/° F per square foot

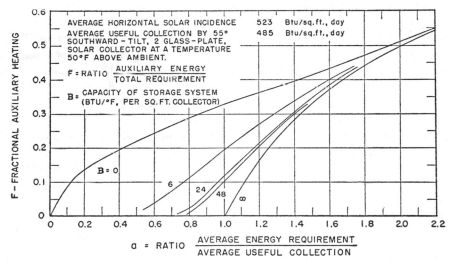

Figure 15.—Storage analysis, Blue Hill, Massachusetts, January (six years' data), (1946–51).

of collector area. (The method is also applicable to phase-change type storage systems.) A typical set of *F*(storage)–curves, for Blue Hill, Massachusetts, is presented in Figure 15. The co-ordinate "*a*" is the ratio of the energy required to heat the house for the month in question to the energy transferred from collector into transport medium. These curves indicate that the provision of even a small amount of storage results in a large decrease in the fractional auxiliary energy requirements. On the other hand, they also indicate that provision of storage capacity in excess of 20 or 30 Btu/° F per square foot of collector area (20 or 30 lb of water per square foot of collector area) causes but little further reduction in the amount of auxiliary energy required. It is apparent that complete solar heating (*F* = 0) in northern latitudes (of which Blue Hill is typical) is possible only if the collector area is so large that the average monthly collection is from 50 to 100 per cent greater than the average monthly requirement of energy ($a = 2/3$ to $1/2$), and if the storage capacity is greater than about 30 Btu/° F per square foot of collector area.

To establish quantitatively the relative merits of a given phase-change material and water, one need only construct a set of F-curves similar to the above but with the capacity B replaced by an equivalent factor to account for the heat-of-fusion storage effect. Evaluation of this equivalent factor has been discussed elsewhere (*18*).

Selection of the optimum value of storage capacity B from the above curves, based on the annual charges on the collector and on the storage system, involves minimizing the sum of the cost of the fuel corresponding to the auxiliary-energy requirement F and the total fixed charges on the solar and auxiliary heating system (after credit for replacement of a part of the roof). An analysis of this kind for year-round operation at Blue Hill, Massachusetts, showed that the optimum value of B is about 15 Btu/° F per square foot of collector. This value is in accord with the conclusions drawn from operation of the M.I.T. Solar House, where the storage capacity of 25 lb of water per square foot of collector area has been found to be too large.

In brief summary, house heating with solar energy constitutes a use of sunlight which is near enough to economic soundness to warrant an intensive study of the problem; but the study must be quantitative if the objective of minimum-cost heating is to be achieved. This paper reports some of the progress in that direction.

Solar Heat Storage

Maria Telkes

Solar house-heating requires the accumulation and storage of solar heat, when it is available on clear and partly cloudy days, to provide heating for the night and for cloudy days.

Nearly one-third of the total fuel consumed in this country is used for heating buildings. Solar house-heating therefore appears promising as a fuel saver (*4*). The Report of the President's Materials Policy Commission (*45*) predicted that by 1975 some 13 million dwelling units may be sun heated. It is obvious that large-scale research and development are needed to achieve this aim.

Solar house-heating will be economically feasible and practical only when the initial cost of this system is competitive with conventional heating systems. It may be equally important that the solar-heating system should be combined with summer cooling, in view of the recent trend and demand in this direction.

The storage of solar heat is one of the major problems to be solved, and economically acceptable solutions must use a relatively small heat-storage volume within the house, because the cost of space is at a premium. It is probable that compact, contemporary houses cannot provide more space for solar-heat storage than the volume now occupied by the "heater room." This is generally about 4 per cent of the total volume of the house. If we use as a yardstick a 10,000–cubic-foot "average house," the heat-storage bin should not occupy more than 400 cubic feet, i.e., that in a cubicle about 6 ft × 8 ft × 8 ft high.

The mythical "average modern house" is generally well insulated. With a heating load of 5,000 degree-days per heating season (New York–Washington area) its average daily winter heat loss may be around 300,000 Btu per day, with twice this loss on exceptionally cold days, which may occur on the average only six days per heating season.

Solar-heat collectors operating during the winter are limited to a moderate temperature level in the 130° to 150° F temperature region on clear days. It is probable that the temperature of the heat-storage bin should not be lower than 80° F, to deliver sufficient heat to rooms maintained at 70° F. The highest practical temperature of the heat-storage bin may not be greater than around 110° F during the winter, and a temperature increase of 30° F may represent average conditions.

Specific-Heat Type of Heat Storage.—Water and rocks have been suggested as the most practical heat-storage materials, heat being stored as their specific heat. One cubic foot of water has a heat-storage capacity of 62.5 Btu/° F, while one cubic foot of solid rock has about 36 Btu/° F. Assuming a temperature rise of 30° F, the heat-storage capacity of one cubic foot of water will be 1,880 Btu and that of rock 1,080 Btu. The above-mentioned average house with a daily heat loss (average) of 300,000 Btu will therefore require about 160 cubic feet of water (= 1,200 gallons = 5 tons) and about 280 cubic feet of solid rock (= 25 tons). It is necessary to provide additional space for the circulation of air or water to deliver solar heat to the storage and to recover the heat when needed. Thus the economically available space of some 400 cubic feet may be sufficient for the storage of the heating requirement for about 2 average days when using water and for about 1.3 days when using rocks.

Although the cost of water and rocks may appear to be negligible, the cost of tanks or containers for the water and the cost of handling rocks and the cost of the space occupied by the heat-storage bin and that of the heat-circulating equipment are the determining factors.

Heat-of-Fusion Type of Heat Storage.—The writer suggested the use of heat-storage materials which melt at a moderate temperature level and store heat as their heat of fusion, or heat of transition (*49, 55*). Low-cost salt hydrates, which are easily available—some of them being obtainable as by-products—can be used for this purpose. A typical example is sodium sulphate decahydrate, $Na_2SO_4 \cdot 10H_2O$, which almost entirely melts in its water of crystallization when heated to its transition temperature at 90° F. Its heat of fusion is 104 Btu/lb, density is 92 lb/cubic foot, and therefore one cubic foot of this material can store 9,500 Btu as its heat of fusion at the transition temperature. The specific heat of this material is comparable to that of water on an equal-volume basis. The stored heat can be recovered as the material crystallizes again. With a temperature rise of 30° F, the total heat-storage capacity of this material can be as high as 11,900 Btu per cubic foot. This is six times greater than that of water and eleven times greater than that of rocks, on an equal-volume basis. (When other temperature intervals are used, these values may be different.) With the heat-of-fusion type materials it is possible, therefore, to store more heat per cubic foot or conversely to use a smaller heat-storage volume.

The cost of these materials may be quite low, being in the range of $10 to $20 per ton, or about 50 cents to $1 per cubic foot. The heat-of-

fusion type of materials change from the solid to the liquid state and therefore these materials must be stored in suitable containers, their cost being
additional. Ultimate cost comparison of the heat-of-fusion materials with
water or rocks may be similar to the amounts in Table 5. It appears

TABLE 5

Ultimate Cost Comparison of Heat-of-Fusion Materials with Water or Rocks

| | Storage of 300,000 Btu with 30° F temperature rise using | | |
	Water	Rocks	Heat-of-fusion materials
Volume required, cu ft	160	280	25.
Weight, tons	5	25	1.1
Cost of container at $0.80/cu ft	$128	$ 0	$20
House volume at $1.20/cu ft	192	336	30
Cost of materials	0	25	20
Total cost	$320	$361	$70

probable, therefore, that the cost of the heat-of-fusion type of solar-heat
storage is economically more attractive than that of the other storage
materials.

The writer has suggested the use of several salt hydrates which are
listed in Table 6 (*50*). The transition temperature varies according to the

TABLE 6

Properties of Heat-of-Fusion Storage Materials

Compound	Transition temperature °F	Heat of fusion Btu per lb
$CaCl_2 \cdot 6H_2O$	84–102	75
$Na_2CO_3 \cdot 10H_2O$	90–97	115
$Na_2HPO_4 \cdot 12H_2O$	97	114
$Ca(NO_3)_2 \cdot 4H_2O$	104–108	90
$Na_2SO_4 \cdot 10H_2O$	90	104
$Na_2S_2O_3 \cdot 5H_2O$	120–124	90

formation of salt hydrates containing fewer water molecules, and the heat of fusion may change accordingly.

Tests have been made in the Dover house, owned by Amelia Peabody and designed by Eleanor Raymond, architect. The heating system and its operation in this house have been described (*51*, *54*). The solar-heat collector was mounted on the south-facing vertical part of the roof. The living space was situated on the first floor and additional heat was obtained through south-facing windows. The heat-storage material was located in heat-storage bins, between the rooms. Air was used as the heat-transfer medium.

Another house was designed (*52*) using the entire south wall on a one-story house as the heat collector and only one centrally located heat-storage bin, thereby decreasing the construction costs, which were estimated as being nearly the same as those of a conventionally heated house.

Several problems must be considered to obtain the most favorable results from the use of the heat-of-fusion materials. This process is theoretically reversible; that is, the entire heat delivered should be recoverable. There are several limitations which may delay the prompt recovery of the stored heat. When these materials are melted completely, in sealed containers, they may not solidify on cooling, but undercool below their melting points. Undercooling can be prevented by using crystallization catalysts, or nucleating agents. The principles of their selection have been described by the writer (*53*). The other limiting factor is the rate of crystal growth, which limits the rate of heat exchange between the solid and liquid phases. Most of the salt hydrates mentioned above have a limited crystallization velocity, of the order of 0.02 inch per hour per degree F temperature difference between solid and liquid. Thus heat cannot be withdrawn more rapidly than it can be supplied by the growth of the crystals and for practical purposes the formation of crystals does not progress more rapidly than at the rate of 0.5 inch/day. It is necessary to provide sufficiently large heat-transfer area between the heat-transfer fluid (air) and the heat-storage material, which is sealed into containers of suitable geometrical shape.

Further tests have been conducted with disodium phosphate dodeca-hydrate, in co-operation with the Edison Electric Institute and the joint A.E.I.C.-E.E.I. Heat Pump Committee, in the Laboratories of the American Gas and Electric Service Corporation, with the writer acting as consultant, (*1*, *2*). One hundred alternate heating and cooling cycles have been carried out with this material. A large number of small containers have been filled and have been used for the storage of heat, produced by heat-pump systems, for tests being conducted in five homes.

The possible combination of the heat-of-fusion heat-storage materials with the heat pump and a solar-heat collector is being investigated as a possible solution to winter-summer air conditioning.

The use of the heat-of-fusion method provides maximum heat-storage capacity in a given volume; therefore it should be useful for the storage of solar heat. It is desirable that further tests should be conducted in houses to obtain valid economical results on the use of the heat-of-fusion method.

Applications of Solar Energy for Heating, Air Conditioning, and Cooking

M. L. Ghai

Sunshine is the biggest blessing that the earth has. Coal, oil, hydroelectric power, wind power, and other sources of energy that are normally used have their origin in solar energy. Yet, if one thinks of the various parts of the world, one wonders about an amazing fact—the backward parts of the earth are generally the parts which receive this blessing in largest quantities. These parts are richer, in a way, because they receive more energy, but the fact is that man has been unable to use the biggest blessing he has.

Whereas large-scale utilization of solar energy appears uneconomical at present, it is likely that utilization of solar energy to a limited extent might be made possible within the next few decades. The present paper is devoted to some of these fields of research which, in the opinion of the author, might bring fruitful results in the immediate future.

Space Heating.—Heating of houses with solar energy has been under experimentation at several research institutions in the United States. The importance of this research can hardly be underestimated when it is considered that a large percentage of the total fuel consumption goes towards keeping the houses warm. As this topic is covered in detail by other authors, a brief mention of certain suggestions is considered adequate.

The most important problem in space heating is to develop means of collecting and storing heat which would have low initial cost, because even though there is no recurring cost of fuel there would be few people willing to buy a system much more expensive than the presently available systems of heating. To achieve this, one might give more serious thought to the simplest method of heating houses with solar energy—that is, by direct transmission through transparent windows and walls. Direct transmission of solar energy through specially developed walls and barriers having high transmissivity and low coefficient of heat transfer could make the house itself a good, efficient solar-heat collector. This might be combined with double-layered curtains in front of the transparent walls and barriers, with water as heat-storage fluid circulated through the

63

space between the two layers of the curtains. Such special curtains could be further useful in summer when air conditioning is required and it is necessary to exclude solar heating.

Air Conditioning and Refrigeration.—This aspect of utilization of solar energy has received much less attention as compared to the other fields of application, even though the excess of solar heat in summer makes so many parts of the earth almost unbearably hot. The possibility of creating air conditioning in localities receiving excessive heat is made more attractive by the fact that the air-conditioning load of a building is maximum at noontime when the available solar energy is also maximum. Furthermore, there are applications of air conditioning and refrigeration which do not require continuous operation and are therefore not handicapped by the difficulties of storage of solar heat.

In 1889, Tellier first suggested the use of solar energy for refrigeration and air conditioning. He proposed the use of a "hot-box" with ammonium hydrate to raise ammonia to a high pressure and then use it for refrigeration. It is considered doubtful whether he ever made such equipment. According to a *Science News-Letter* published in 1938, Mohr suggested the operation of an absorption refrigeration machine by burning hydrogen obtained from the electrolytic decomposition of water employing thermoelectric couples heated by solar energy. The over-all thermal efficiency of the system is of the order of 0.01 per cent, which makes its use very unlikely. More recent experiments of Dr. Löf, using a dehumidification system, are covered in detail elsewhere in this publication.

Most of the present-day refrigeration equipment is what is called "mechanical refrigeration equipment," which employs mechanical compressors in conjunction with different refrigerants to pump heat from a lower-temperature level to a higher level. The small window types of residential cooling units normally have a capacity ranging from $\frac{1}{3}$ ton to 2 tons (one ton of refrigeration is equivalent to 12,000 Btu/hr). These units normally require one horsepower per ton of refrigeration. In order to operate these units from solar energy, it would be necessary to have solar engines having an output of $\frac{1}{3}$ to 2 horsepower. Assuming that it is possible to convert solar energy into mechanical energy with an over-all thermal efficiency of 5 per cent, these units would necessitate collecting solar heat from an area normal to the rays ranging from 7 to 40 sq yd with incident solar energy at the rate of one horsepower per square yard—about 20 sq yd per ton of refrigeration. Additional surface must be allowed for energy storage if the system is required to run continuously. The over-all coefficient of performance of such a system would be about one-fourth—

that is, the refrigeration effect would be one-fourth the input of solar energy.

Absorption refrigeration machines, such as the Electrolux household refrigerator, which do not require mechanical energy but can be operated directly from thermal energy, are also available commercially although to a limited extent. The coefficient of performance of the ammonia absorption-machine is nearly 0.5, so that the area required per ton of refrigeration is reduced to about 10 sq yd. The lithium-bromide-water system of absorption refrigeration, which has come into use comparatively recently, gives a somewhat higher coefficient of performance.

In an attempt to obtain engineering data regarding the performance of an ammonia absorption-refrigeration machine with solar energy, experiments were started by the author. Figure 16 shows the installation of a cylindrical parabolic reflector with flattened metal pipe enclosed in a glass tube placed at the focal line of the reflector. The reflector is built up of aluminum sheets attached to three parabolic plates, two at the ends and one at the center. This type of arrangement is likely to be suitable for refrigeration machines of small capacities, of about ⅛ ton or less. For machines of larger capacities, hot-box types of solar-heat collectors are likely to prove more suitable.

An absorption system has another advantage which makes it attractive for use with solar energy. With a specially designed system it is possible to eliminate the storage of energy in the form of heat. By the processes of generating and condensing additional amounts of refrigerant during the daytime and continuing to operate the evaporator and absorber at night, refrigeration may be obtained at night with the solar heat collected during the day. This type of storage of energy, avoiding the difficulties of storage of heat energy, necessitates the use of larger quantities of refrigerant. It is therefore economical only to a limited extent.

Cooking of Food.—During 1950 to 1952, the author led an investigation at the National Physical Laboratory of India to develop a simple and inexpensive solar cooker. The cooker developed, shown in Figure 17, has been taken up for production on a commercial scale by a leading firm in India.

The cooking of food requires primarily the attainment of appropriate temperatures. Maximum amount of energy is required only at the start of cooking to enable quick heating of the food; once the appropriate temperature has been reached, the energy requirement is small since the cooking of food itself requires very little energy. This makes the solar-heat collector suitable for cooking, as the efficiency of solar-heat collectors is high at low temperatures and decreases as the temperature increases. Figure 18 shows the net heat output available for raising the temperature of the food and the utensil at different operating temperatures. For a typical solar cooker, the net output is maximum at the start of heating and diminishes as the utensil-temperature increases.

The temperatures required for cooking may be attained in a hot-box—a stationery, insulated, airtight box, blackened on the inside and covered with one or more glass sheets—as was done by DeSaussure, Hershel, and Langley. Alternatively, concentration of rays as done by Mouchot, Adams, and Abbot may be employed. The hot-box has the advantage of being simple and convenient to use since the equipment requires no focusing devices; but its favorable performance is limited to a few hours at noon, whereas the concentration equipment may be operated over a wider range of solar altitudes. If the hot-box is mounted on a support capable of tilting, it loses its chief advantage of simplicity. Furthermore, horizontal hot-boxes of convenient sizes give only a small amount of net heat available for cooking, as shown in Figure 19. The high heat inertia of the box results in a slow rate of cooking. Condensation of moisture given out by the food being cooked, on the glass sheets covering the box, creates further practical difficulties in a hot-box.

Cooking food with concentration equipment such as reflectors may be done by concentrating rays directly on the cooking utensil or by concentrating the rays first on a container holding a liquid and then circulating the liquid through a cooking oven. The direct cooker is inherently more efficient and simple, but it has the disadvantage of being able to operate only during the periods of sunshine. It may be mentioned that the cooking by concentration of rays directly on the food is not practical since it causes uneven heating resulting in uneven cooking.

The investigation mentioned above was restricted to direct-reflector type of cookers. Reflectors with different focal lengths, apertures, and various industrially feasible reflecting surfaces and different focusing mechanisms were tried. Paraboloidal reflectors were considered more suitable for manually controlled cookers, although concave spherical reflectors could also be considered suitable when an automatic turning mechanism was provided. Reflectors with effective face area of about 8 to 10 sq ft (specular reflectivity 75 per cent) were found most suitable. Larger sizes were inconvenient to handle and required elaborate supports, and the smaller sizes did not give sufficient output for cooking, as also indicated by Figure 19. A focal length of about 18 inches was found to be most suitable for the sizes desired. Besides convenience of handling and simplicity of supports, with this focal length the shift of the focus is such

(*Above*) *Figure* 16.—Cylindrical parabolic reflector for use with absorption-refrigeration machine. (*Below*) *Figure* 17.—Solar cooker developed by M. L. Ghai at the National Physical Laboratory of India.

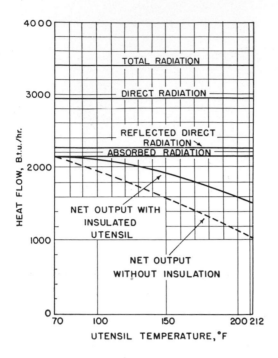

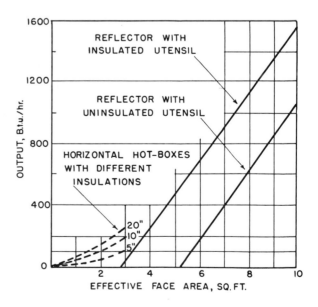

(*Above*) *Figure* 18.—Heat balance of a direct-reflector type of cooker, with reflector of effective face area of 10 sq ft, working at a solar altitude of 90°, on a normal clear day. (*Below*) *Figure* 19.—Output available for cooking versus effective face area for direct-reflector type of cookers and hot-boxes.

that it is necessary to adjust the reflector only once in about twenty minutes.

A good part of the total cost of a simple cooker, such as shown in Figure 17, is covered by the supports and the turning mechanism required for the reflector. A number of designs, both of equatorial mounting type and nonequatorial mounting type, were built and tried for convenience of operation. In nonequatorial mountings, special convenience was found in having one of the two axes of rotation as vertical axis. The support shown in Figure 17 consists of a base with a central turning pin having vertical axis of rotation, and a tilting bracket controlled by the circular knob at the upper end of the pin. The paraboloidal reflector is truncated on one side, which enables the reflector to have the entire face area fully effective for low solar altitudes in mornings and evenings.

The development of the cooker described above was restricted to a particular type of cooker suited for operation during the sunny hours. Further research might extend the utility of solar heat for cooking.

Water Heating.—Hot-water heaters working with solar energy have been in use in the southern parts of the United States and are being gradually introduced in other countries. It is, however, believed that the initial cost of the equipment is too high at present to make the solar water-heaters generally acceptable. Mention might be made of the experiments conducted by the author at the National Physical Laboratory of India in an attempt to develop a specialized form of solar water-heater suited for tropical countries and localities having latitudes less than about 30° and minimum day temperatures of higher than about 45° F in winter. Flat roofs of concrete are commonly used in several tropical countries; the roofs are flat since there are no heavy snow loads to be allowed for and the concrete is laid to keep the house cool during the daytime by making use of the time lag involved in the transmission of heat through the heavy masonry materials. A suitable hot-water heating system is needed mostly for use in winter, because for summer there could be hardly anything more simple or inexpensive than letting a tank of water be exposed to solar heat—a method which is in use at present in tropical countries. The method of heating water which is being used in the southern parts of the United States—i.e., use of a hot-box consisting of an insulated box with transparent top of one or two glass sheets and water pipes attached to a blackened metal sheet—was considered to be too expensive. The experiments were conducted with water pipes imbedded in concrete on the roof. Reasonably satisfactory temperature of hot water could be obtained and the temperature could be further raised by blackening the concrete surface and plastering it with pieces of glass sheets.

The Heat Pump

Ralph A. Morgen

The amount of energy reaching the earth from the sun, annually, is many times the present annual consumption by man. It is estimated (46) that the total amount of solar energy reaching the earth's surface is 3,200 Q* per year and of that total, 830 Q impinge on land areas. The present total energy use is only about 0.1 Q per year.

With this enormous amount of energy available and waiting for utilization, it seems incredible that man should be unduly concerned with the depletion of his stored hoard of solar energy in the form of fossil fuels. The fact that the energy is here should be a spur to unlock the secrets so that ample amounts can be made available for use.

The two greatest deterrents to the fuller use of solar energy at the present time are (*a*) the "low level" of the energy, and (*b*) its intermittent nature. Fortunately these are only temporary blocks to progress caused by lack of knowledge and the need for more research. As will be shown below, the heat pump is one tool which may be used to attack both the level of energy and the storage problem. It may do this at present by extending fossil fuels by a 3– or 4–to–1 ratio of solar energy used to fossil fuel used. Eventually the fossil fuel used could be eliminated by getting the power requirements of the heat-pump cycle from the sun, by means such as those discussed in the following section of this book.

With the limitations imposed by the laws of thermodynamics in mind, the concept of the heat pump may be considered. The heat pump is a device which through the expenditure of energy (usually in the form of work) raises low-temperature level energy to a higher temperature. The usual household refrigerator is the most common form of heat pump in operation today. While in this instance the purpose is to segregate and protect the low-level energy, the principle is the same whether the purpose is refrigeration or heating. Through the expenditure of a smaller amount of electrical, gas, or other fuel energy, a larger amount of low-level heat energy is removed from the interior of the refrigerated area and discharged through a condenser at a higher level.

*1Q = 10^{18} Btu.

Oceans, lakes, rivers, the atmosphere, and the ground itself contain large quantities of low-level energy originally solar in origin. This energy is usually at a temperature level below that at which it can be used for comfort heating. If a heat pump is employed, comfort heating is obtainable from this low-level energy. Through the expenditure of a certain amount of work energy in a compressor or other device, several times that amount of energy can be extracted from the earth, the rivers, the ocean, or even the atmosphere. This extracted energy is then raised in potential and poured into the area to be heated through a radiator.

With present knowledge, it is not unusual to have a "coefficient of performance" of 4. In other words, for the expenditure of 25 units of energy in the form of work, 100 units of energy are available for space heating. The coefficient of performance (COP) increases as the temperature differential between the heat source and the space to which heat is added decreases.

It should be noted that the removal of energy from the ground, rivers, and other places lowers the temperature and depletes the source until more solar energy arrives to replenish the energy. In concentrated areas, large numbers of heat pumps may cause temporary source dislocations, and proper precautions must be taken to insure equity to all persons involved.

Examples may be cited to illustrate this point. A Swiss city planned a major heat-pump installation for comfort heating, with river water as the best heat source. It was calculated that sufficient heat would have been removed from the rivers as to make possible freezing of the water, with the attendant threat to water supply of a downstream community. In Miami, Florida, the number of heat pumps used for comfort cooling is quite extensive; common practice is to use well water for condenser water. So much water was being used for this purpose that salt water was intruding from the ocean into the fresh-water supply. The law now requires that warmed water be returned to the underground system to protect the drinking-water supply.

In addition to legal difficulties, the technical value of the heat-pump principle has been obscured by economic questions. In the United States the economy of the heat pump has been geared to the problem of air conditioning—or more specifically, space cooling. Significantly most of the heat-pump experiments have centered around electricity as the prime-mover power source. As a result, the problem has revolved around two important economic questions. The first problem is that of maintaining a high year-round electric load in order to maintain the necessary facilities to supply power when needed (7). The second problem is due to the high unit cost of energy as electric power compared to other energy sources. In order to produce electric power (except in the case of water power), fossil fuels must be burned to convert the energy into electric power which in turn must be transported and be reconverted to mechanical power as a prime mover for the heat pump. Goethe (12) and his co-workers have shown that the economics move much in favor of the heat pump when direct-connected diesel-fuel engines instead of electric power supply the motive power for heat pumps.

As long as the success of the heat pump is tied to comfort cooling, its real value in conserving fossil fuel will be obscured. Any fuel used for comfort cooling is a net loss to the world supply of energy. It is in the field of cooling that the use of solar energy should be exploited most immediately and to the greatest advantage. Here the question of storage is least significant since the greatest cooling load is needed when the solar radiation is at its maximum. Therefore, direct use of solar energy for cooling will spotlight the value of the heat pump as a fuel saver for comfort heating.

The possibilities for combined systems of solar energy and the heat pump appear to have some promise. The problem can be approached from two standpoints: to use solar heat as an auxiliary source of energy for space heating in order to decrease the heating load on the heat pump; and to use low-temperature solar collectors to supply part or all of the energy to the heat-pump evaporator.

Chemical heat-storage methods for heat pumps have been under investigation by a joint committee of the Association of Edison Illuminating Companies and the Edison Electric Institute (2). Published data on the heat-of-fusion type of storage systems indicate the feasibility of a system in which heat from a heat pump may be accumulated during periods of low heating demand for use during periods of high heating demand. Similar considerations would apply to the specific-heat type of storage systems. Heat from a solar-energy collector could be added directly to the heated space or could be added to the storage system to augment the heat-pump output.

Collectors of solar energy used in either specific-heat type or heat-of-fusion type of storage systems or for direct space heating must operate at temperatures higher than that of the heat-storage unit or the heated space—i.e., usually 100° F or higher. Since collector efficiency varies inversely with the temperature difference between the collector and the outside air, collector efficiencies could be improved by operating in the range of 50°–60° F. This would also permit collection of radiation on hazy days and in the early morning and late afternoon, which would otherwise not be possible. Heat sources with temperatures in this range can be used effectively by heat pumps.

The design of systems combining solar energy and the heat pump has been treated by Jordan and Threlkeld (*28, 29, 56*). They discuss collectors, storage, and heat-pump requirements for a particular house design in Lincoln, Nebraska, Madison, Wisconsin, Nashville, Tennessee, and New Orleans, Louisiana. They suggest that higher coefficients of perform-ance can be realized by the use of multiple-stage vapor compression and evaporation cycles, and note that evaporator-side heat storage would have advantages over condenser-side storage if a suitable storage system could be found.

Two experimental installations of combined systems have been described by Ambrose (*20*). In these systems the solar collectors served as the evaporators of the heat pumps and were operated at a temperature of 50° F. Storage was provided on the condenser side by water tanks, from which water was circulated to the heating units. Complete data on these installations have not as yet been published.

A review of progress made in heat-pump developments during the past decade has been presented by Sporn and Ambrose (*48*); they note that as of January, 1953, over 1,000 heat-pump air-conditioning installations had been made throughout the country, but that further research on energy sources, storage systems, solar-energy collectors, and the heat pumps themselves is needed. An extensive bibliography of heat-pump literature has been published by the Edison Electric Institute (*6*).

An analysis of the total energy uses in the United States shows that between 30 and 35 per cent of the total fuel consumption (*46*) goes for comfort heating. If the heat-pump principle could be used for all comfort heating at a coefficient of performance of 4, then 75 per cent of that fuel could be conserved; this would amount to about one-fourth of the total fuel consumption.

The questions naturally arise: Why are there not more heat pumps in operation? Why with pending fuel shortages isn't this fuel saver utilized?

There is no simple answer, but a variety of explanations can be given. The first and foremost is the question of economics. Until fuel costs increase significantly, there will not be the urge to make the necessary capital expenditures. Meanwhile there is much research to be done and technical success may alter the case economically. Some of the more important research problems whose solution would be of great significance to develop-ment of wider heat-pump utilization are these: (1) a simple, self-contained, direct-operated machine which would operate a heat pump using coal, gas, or oil for fuel with high direct conversion of fuel energy to work energy; (2) a combination solar-energy heat storage and heat pump which could greatly increase the storage effectiveness; (3) storage of solar energy in a form that could be converted into work during the hours when solar energy is unavailable; (4) improved methods of extracting energy stored in the earth or other sources.

The heat pump is in reality, therefore, a device for transferring energy from a place where it is not needed to a place where it is needed. The expenditure of energy in doing the transferring job is now about 25 per cent of the energy transferred. Any improvements in the transferring mechanism, the heat pump, provides a potential for fuel conservation. If solar energy can also operate the prime mover, the fuel saving for comfort heating can be 100 per cent. For the distant future this does not seem to be either impossible or improbable.

Use of Solar Energy for Heating Water

F. A. Brooks

An excellent review of utilization of solar energy is given by Heywood (*15*). For water heating he shows that the temperature at absorber top should not exceed half the possible rise from air temperature to the equilibrium temperature of the absorber when no useful heat is being withdrawn. His experiments with a 10–square-foot absorber for maximum sunshine days near London gave an average heat gain of only 904 Btu per square foot. A 50 per cent advantage of more southerly latitudes is seen in our results (*8*) of 1,360 Btu per square foot per day in September under single glass and 7,500 Btu per day in July from a plain uncovered tank 12 inches in diameter and 5 feet long. For solar water-heating with forced circulation, see the report by Anderson *et al.* in this section or reference (*21*).

Before about 1930, widespread rural practice in California for heating water was by solid-fuel cooking range from November to March, and by solar energy which was generally dependable from April to October. Thus, there were only two rather brief transition periods when seasonal cloudiness interfered with a rather simple two-way water-heating system and many thousand solar water-heaters were in use. Most of the absorbers in the cities were installed by local plumbers. Almost all of the systems depended on closed thermosiphon circulation subject to the regular water-service pressure. Occasional failures in circulation were traced usually to too low a connection between the stove heater coil and the solar absorber relative to the storage tank (which was necessarily higher than both heater coils to prevent reversed flow at night). In the daytime, however, hot water in a considerable length of riser common to both systems might cause wasteful circulation in the unused parallel circuit. The self-limiting requirement is that the density-difference head in the common (heated) riser be overbalanced by the drawdown of warmish water from tank bottom toward the unused heater coil. This is opposed by the greater density of unheated water in the outflow riser below the junction.

In our main tests the rate of thermosiphon circulation was unsteady in the morning because the first hot water from the absorber on entering the

75

vertical riser suddenly produced excess density difference relative to water from the tank bottom.

A temperature rise of 30° F at midday in one pass through a 3/4-inch pipe required over 70 feet in the absorber. A length of 170 feet gave nearly 60° temperature rise. This is excessive. Multiple-channel flow in large absorbers is, therefore, more efficient and the practical length of a single run of 3/4-inch pipe seems to be 10 to 15 feet per foot of effective riser height. The practical size of absorber area in the interior valleys of California should be about 1 square foot per gallon of insulated storage capacity. With ordinary care, a family of five uses about 100 gallons of hot water per day with an extra 25 gallons for clothes washing.

With the general adoption of cheap, kerosene, "side-arm" heaters to provide hot water in cloudy weather, the economics of the system changed so that the only cash justification is that the investment and maintenance charges on the solar absorber be less than the actual cost of the auxiliary fuel. Furthermore, with the advent of the automatic water-heater the household demand for hot water increased, often exceeding the capacity of the previously acceptable solar absorber. So, because of cheap fuel and rising standard of living, only a few solar water-heaters can now be found in California.

There is today, however, an unsatisfied demand for solar water-heating in mountain cabins and locations remote from gas or liquid-fuel supplies. For some of these in spots without much wind the exposed 30-gallon water tanks mounted with axis sloped should be useful, providing two or three hot showers in late afternoon. The self-storage is desirable in itself and provides frost protection except during the winter. Such a tank loses practically all its heat at night. Enclosure of three such tanks under ordinary hotbed glass sash could provide 30 gallons at night at temperatures above 120° F in September and still give lots of warm water about 25° F above air temperature in the morning. The main precautions needed in such an installation are to provide strong structural support and arrangements for draining the tanks.

Solar energy is the natural heating agent for swimming pools by direct absorption. When this is insufficient, especially in windy locations, probably the simplest means of increasing water temperature is to cover the pool with a transparent plastic to minimize evaporation cooling, which usually carries away over half the incident solar energy.

Heating water by flowing it over broad areas with shallow depth is used in agriculture particularly for rice paddies. Without such precaution there is low production around cold-water inlets. Conversely, when the ditch water is disagreeably hot as drinking water for cattle (90° F near

El Centro in summer), forced evaporation using 1/2 hp either by cooling tower or by direct air blast on a 6-foot diameter tank (*13*) can cool water at least 12 inches deep to within 2° F of the wet-bulb temperature in one night.

Finally solar water-heating is an essential part of industrial production of salt from tideland pools (see Section V). Related to this is the small absorber model for 4-H club projects designed to provide farms with distilled water for storage batteries and steam irons. H. D. Lewis (associate in Agricultural Engineering, University of California, Davis) has found that a 20° slope is sufficient to collect water condensed on the bottom side of the glass, and a simple box 2 × 3 feet will regularly produce over 0.6 gallon per day in cloudless weather through most of the year. This approaches the performance of large solar evaporators.

Section IV

Solar Power

The conversion of solar radiation into mechanical power through heat engines has attracted inventors for many years. The temperatures can be increased so as to give higher engine efficiency by using multiple–glass-plate collectors or by using parabolic reflectors. Scientific studies of solar engines by leading authorities are presented here. Although the use of large power installations seems to be quite far away, in competition with fuel-powered engines, the outlook for small units in isolated areas is more hopeful. In view of the availability of sunshine in undeveloped or arid regions, a low efficiency can be tolerated provided a simple engine can be devised with sufficiently low capital investment.

Small Solar Power-Plants

M. L. Ghai

Large-scale production of power from solar energy necessitates collection of solar heat from large areas. The situation is further complicated by the intermittency of the solar radiation. As a result, large investment is involved, and the recurring cost in the form of depreciation on this investment makes production of power from solar energy more expensive than methods currently in use, even though there is no fuel cost with solar power. Unless the cost of oil and coal becomes much higher than it is today, it seems unlikely that large solar power-plants will become economical in the near future. The discussion here is limited to small power-generating plants for which more favorable conditions exist.

Wherever power is not easily available or is available at a high premium, one might consider the immediate possibility of solar power. For instance, there are several metropolitan areas in the world where power generated on a large scale exists, but the supply lags behind the increasing demand. The shortage is generally met by the use of small diesel and gasoline engines. Power generation on a small scale is, as a rule, very inefficient and the cost per unit of power is high. The solar power-plant might be used, but it is necessary that the initial cost of the plant be comparable to that of internal combustion engines of the same output, that the engine be compact, and that the maintenance and repair of the engine be not more difficult than that of an internal-combustion engine. The intermittency of power supply would be considered a serious handicap. The competition against solar power offered by the internal-combustion engines would necessitate considerable research and development in solar power-plants before they can be made practical in this field of application.

Several parts of the world—the arid zones and the rural areas—where power generation on a large scale is not available, are more likely to find it economical to avail themselves of solar power-plants. The power requirement is generally in the range of about 1/2 hp to 10 hp and is at present being met by diesel and gasoline engines. It might be mentioned that for small power requirements the internal-combustion engine has several advantages over the steam engine and it is almost universal practice to use internal-combustion engines. In fact, there are hardly any complete steam

81

plants of small capacities available on the market. The solar power-plant has therefore to offer advantages over the internal-combustion engines. A solar power-plant could never be as compact as an internal-combustion engine; but it is probable that the cost of power could be comparable. In certain areas where the cost of fuels is forbiddingly high, or the use of diesel oil and gasoline is discouraged by the country, or the maintenance and repairs of diesel engines are considered by the people too complicated and tedious, there is actually no source of energy except the animal power in use. In such cases, the availability of solar power should be welcomed, provided the initial cost of the equipment is low and the equipment does not require any skilled attention in the form of maintenance.

As to what type of solar power-plant is likely to meet these requirements, it is difficult to judge at this stage. Some of the possibilities might be briefly stated. Engines of low temperature difference employing working fluids of low boiling points have the advantage of requiring simple solar-heat collectors, and the disadvantage of having very low efficiency which necessitates large-sized solar-heat collectors. The noncondensing and condensing types of steam engines have higher efficiency, but the efficiency of their solar-heat collectors is less because of the higher temperature of heat collection. The over-all thermal efficiency is higher than that of low-temperature engines and therefore the surface area required is less. This does not necessarily indicate an advantage, since the cost per square foot of low-temperature heat collectors is less than that of high-temperature heat collectors.

If the operating temperature is further raised to say 1000° to 2000° F, which can be easily achieved with paraboloidal reflectors, the over-all efficiency is increased and the area of heat collection is decreased, thus making the engine compact. These temperatures, of course, require hot-air engines. This type of arrangement has certain advantages. A hot-air engine run by solar energy simply needs a reflector and a heat exchanger. The hot-air engine does not require any watching of pressures or control of water level as is necessary for steam engines. The disadvantage, however, is that the paraboloidal reflectors are restricted in size on account of convenience of handling. The size of the engine is therefore limited. In view of the simplicity and compactness of the arrangement using hot-air engines and considering the fact that hot-air engines had received the least attention by the previous experimenters, the author erected a setup using a hot-air engine of small power. The engine was run at first at a working temperature of 700° F. The temperature was then raised to 1100° F, which resulted in an appreciable increase of power. It was found difficult to raise the temperature further with the engine available, as the materials of the engine could not withstand the higher temperatures. As far as the reflector is concerned, the raising of the temperature could easily be done even though the method of fabrication of the reflector was such that it did not necessarily give a very accurate surface. The reflector was constructed by forming a sheet of metal in cup shape to match a plate template.

The use of thermoelectric generators is highly desirable because of the least amount of maintenance required. However, a thermoelectric generator constructed on a commercial scale with inexpensive thermocouple materials gives very low efficiency. Another arrangement which is desirable from maintenance point of view but has very low efficiency is the pumping of water for irrigation and other purposes by a steam injector. A steam-injector pump has no moving parts, can operate with low-pressure steam, and is commercially available. A hot-box type of equipment could be used to supply the low-pressure steam. The hot-box can be so designed that it could never reach very high pressures, which eliminates the necessity of pressure gauges, safety valves, or water-level indicators normally needed for steam-raising equipment. An injector is a simple and inexpensive device consisting simply of a steam-expansion nozzle, a combining tube, where steam is condensed by the water thus creating a vacuum, and a delivery tube which delivers the water and the condensed steam. The thermal efficiency of the device is only 1 to 2 per cent. It therefore needs hot-boxes of large areas. Yet another device, which is also simple but unfortunately inefficient, is the air-operated water pump of the slow-pulsating type. If it is possible to make improvements on these methods, they are likely to help in the task of putting solar energy to the service of mankind.

Whereas long-term fundamental research in several fields is highly desirable and necessary to permit utilization of solar energy on a large scale, there are several fields of application where research and development are likely to bear fruit in the near future. It is, however, necessary to pick these fields carefully after a thorough survey of needs and possibilities.

Power Generation with Solar Energy

Hoyt C. Hottel

Publication No. 37 of the Godfrey L. Cabot Solar Energy Conversion Research Project, Massachusetts Institute of Technology.

Recent advances in glass technology indicate that in the not too distant future glass plates with low internal absorption for solar radiation, which are surface treated to reduce the reflection losses at the air-glass interfaces, may be produced in quantity at prices not greatly exceeding present-day glass costs. Multiple-glass, flat-plate solar collectors may then be constructed at moderate cost, and may possibly find application in the collection of solar energy at relatively high temperatures for use in suitable heat engines to produce work. It may reasonably be assumed that high-quality glass which has been surface treated to produce a reflectivity for total sunlight of one-half the value for ordinary glass will become available. Based on this assumption, an analysis has been made and is presented in outline below, to determine the magnitude of the work obtainable from such a solar power-plant of optimum design. In the course of the analysis the optimum operating temperature of the solar collector and the optimum number of glass cover plates are established.

The following assumptions are made: (1) A heat engine is available that will operate between a source temperature of from 220° to 300° F and a sink temperature of 100° F. (2) The transport fluid enters the solar collector at a temperature equal to the source temperature; the fluid flow rate gives the optimum combination of pressure drop and heat transfer. (3) Cooling water is available at a sufficiently low temperature, say 70° F, to make reasonable the assumption of an engine sink temperature of 100° F. (4) The efficiency of conversion of heat into work by the heat engine is equal to the Carnot efficiency for the same source and sink temperatures. (5) The heat-removal efficiency, F_R (see Section 3), allowing for temperature differences in the collector necessary to transfer the energy absorbed at the blackened surface into the fluid stream, and for the finite fluid flow rate, is 0.9. (6) The collector, located at latitude 30° N., is tilted towards the equator at an angle of 30° from the horizontal. And (7) the solar weather is identical to that of El Paso, Texas.

The calculations have been based on El Paso data, not because that is considered the best area for economic development of solar power, but rather because the climate of that area is representative of localities elsewhere in the world where power is scarce but sunshine abundant.

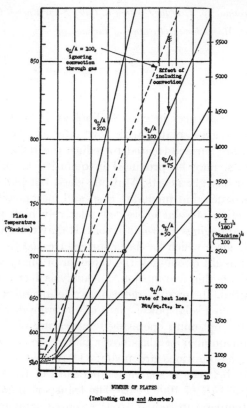

Figure 20.—Temperature distribution in a system of air-spaced thin glass plates over a blackened surface. *Conditions:* Mutual radiation exchange between adjacent plates is 92 per cent of that between black plates. Convection coefficient on outer plate is 3 Btu per sq ft, hr, °F (corresponding to a wind velocity of about 6 mph). Convection coefficient between plates is $0.166\Delta^{1/4}$, where Δ is the temperature difference between adjacent plates. Outer air temperature is 80° F. If plates are much closer together than 3/4″, allowance for additional conduction through air must be made, and all curves will be lowered.

Necessary for the calculation of the useful energy output of multiple-glass solar collectors is a knowledge of the rate of heat loss from the collector as a function of the number of glass plates and the temperature of the blackened absorber. This is shown in Figure 20, which is derived from

Equation 13 of reference (7). Lines of constant heat loss, q_L/A, are plotted as plate temperature (on a scale linear in the fourth power of temperature) versus position of the plate, counting from the outside plate. These are very nearly straight because radiation accounts for most of the total heat transfer from plate to plate. The convection, however, cannot be neglected, as is shown by the dashed line for $q_L/A \equiv 100$ Btu/sq ft hr. To illustrate the use of the curves, a 4–glass-plate collector with blackened absorbing-surface temperature 246° F (706° Rankine) will lose heat to the surroundings at a rate of 75 Btu/(sq ft)(hr), and the temperatures of the four glass plates will be 214° F, 181° F, 143° F, and 98° F, respectively. The useful heat collection at 246° F from such a system will be the excess of the incident-and-transmitted solar radiation over 75 Btu/(sq ft)(hr).

To establish the optimum number of glass cover plates and the optimum temperature of collection, calculations were made (using the ϕ-curves for El Paso, Texas, discussed earlier in Section 3) for the months of January and June, for 3–, 6–, and 9–glass-plate solar collectors. In each case the net useful energy collection at different temperatures and thence the net work output of the heat engine were determined. The results are shown in Figure 21, in which the work output is plotted against the temperature of collection. It is seen that for a given number of glass cover plates there is a maximum work output and a corresponding optimum collection temperature. The June curves are higher than those for January primarily because of the longer duration of sunshine and less cloudiness in the summer months. The maximum work output increases as the number of glass cover plates is increased, up to about 10 or 11 glass plates. Since the proportional increase in output per glass plate falls off as the number of glass plates is increased, it is necessary to determine the optimum number of cover plates from cost data. For use in this analysis the optima curves of Figure 21 have been replotted in Figure 22, as obtainable work, W, versus number of glass plates, n.

If the fixed charge on the collector and associated piping, per square foot of collector, is C, and if the work output per square foot is W, then the work output per dollar is W/C. The number of glass plates n, should be chosen so as to make this ratio a maximum. Thus

$$\frac{d(W/C)}{dn} = 0, \quad \text{or} \quad \frac{1}{C} \cdot \frac{dW}{dn} - \frac{W}{C^2} \cdot \frac{dC}{dn} = 0, \quad \text{or} \quad \left(\frac{W}{C}\right)_{\text{opt}} = \frac{dW}{dn} \Big/ \frac{dC}{dn} \ .$$

The fixed charge may be represented by a function of the form $C = a + bn$, where a is the fixed charge on the collector and associated equipment exclusive of the glass, and b is the fixed charge on a single glass plate.

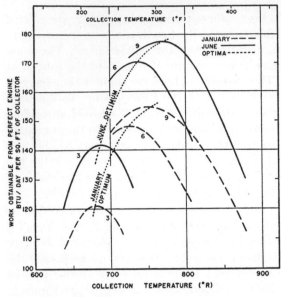

(*Left*) *Figure* 21.— Work output of a solar collector–heat engine combination.

Conditions for Figures 21 *and* 22: Solar collector located at El Paso, Texas, tilted southward at an angle equal to latitude. Good quality, surface-treated glass. Heat-removal efficiency $F_R = 0.9$. Carnot engine operating between a source temperature equal to the collection temperature, and a sink at 100° F.

(*Right*) *Figure* 22.— Work output of an n-plate solar collector–Carnot heat engine operating at the optimum collection (and hence source) temperature.

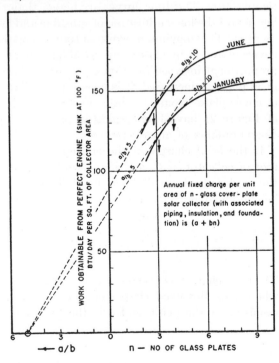

Substitution for C in the above expression gives

$$W_{opt} = \left(\frac{a}{b} + n_{opt}\right)\frac{dW}{dn}$$

(Note that the ratio a/b may be interpreted as the number of unit-area glass plates that have the same fixed charge as unit area of collector and associated equipment, exclusive of glass.) The solution of this equation may be found graphically by drawing a tangent to the curves in Figure 22 from the point $\left(-\frac{a}{b}, 0\right)$. The point of tangency with the curves gives the desired optimum number of glass plates. If $a/b = 5$, the optimum is three glass plates; if $a/b = 10$, the optimum is four.

Assuming that *four glass plates* is the optimum, then the optimum temperature of collection is 230° F in January and 240° F in June. The corresponding work output is 135 Btu/sq ft day in January and 155 Btu/sq ft day in June. (Variations in temperature of 10° F on either side of the optimum temperatures will have little effect on the work output.) On a yearly basis the average annual work output of 145 Btu/(sq ft)(day) is equivalent to $\frac{145 \times 365}{3413} = 15.5$ kilowatt hours/(sq ft)(year), or $\frac{145}{3413 \times 24} = 0.00177$ continuous kw per sq ft (565 square feet of collector per continuous kw output; 77 continuous kw per acre).

A rigorous comparison of flat-plate, solar-power systems with conventional power systems is beyond the scope of this study. However, a rough indication of the possible economic position of solar power can be readily obtained. Let it be assumed that the *fuel* cost in conventional systems is 0.5¢ per kwhr produced. (This may be realized, by use, at 25 per cent over-all efficiency, of coal at $10 per ton, oil at 5¢ per gallon, or gas at 30¢ per 1,000 cu ft.) Also it will be assumed that the annual fixed charge on the conventional installation is $15 per kw installed. With a load factor of two-thirds, this is equivalent to a charge of 0.26¢ per kwhr output. If the charge is split into 0.08¢ for the furnace and the boiler, and 0.18¢ for the turbine, generator, etc., then the solar plant must compete with the steam-from-fuel cost of $0.5 + 0.08 = 0.58$¢ per kwhr, since the 0.18¢ charge on the turbine, generator, etc., is common to both systems. A solar plant costing $1 per sq ft, with 10 per cent fixed charge, will produce steam at 10/15.5 or 0.65¢ per kwhr. A solar plant costing $2 per sq ft is more reasonable, though perhaps still optimistic, and would produce steam at 1.3¢ kwhr output.

The conclusion to be drawn is that power generation from solar energy, using high-quality, surface-treated glass in flat-plate solar collectors operating at temperatures in the low-pressure steam range, is entirely feasible. However, because the cost would probably be at least three times present-day power costs, solar power from flat-plate collectors is not generally interesting in the United States today. Applications of the idea, if they come, will first appear in localities where fuel costs are high or where intermittent power can be consumed locally in a task such as irrigation, which holds the possibility of by-passing the conventional steam-electric power plant in favor of a direct-operated, water-pumping plant. Such applications appear to justify continued study of the problem, particularly in the direction of development of cheaper ways of constructing flat-plate collectors.

Solar Power from Collecting Mirrors

C. G. Abbot

Described below are my designs of two solar boilers, with details of construction of the most easily constructed, that employing a cylindric concave parabolic mirror. As the cost of producing power by these machines has been questioned, I have also included my estimate of the cost of such power.

Two Types of Solar-Heat Collectors.—My most efficient solar boiler employs a circular concave parabolic mirror, mounted equatorially, as shown by Figure 23, a picture of the small model now on exhibition at the Smithsonian Institution. To fabricate accurate circular parabolic mirrors of sufficient dimensions would require expensive tooling. This will come only after solar power has been proved economically practicable. This type of engine is described in my Patent No. 2,460,482 of February 1, 1945.

Figure 24 shows a model, now on exhibition at the Smithsonian Institution, of a solar-heat collector with a rectangular cylindric parabolic mirror. Such mirrors are readily fabricated, and require no expensive special tools. The efficiency of this type is only about 6/10 as great as that of the type with the circular mirror. It is described by Patent No. 2.247,830 of July 1, 1941.

Obstacles to Large Solar Power-Plants.—A solar-ray collector for power purposes has to be inconveniently large. My most efficient design requires a mirror 10 feet in diameter for 2 horsepower. At that efficiency a mirror 50 feet in diameter would produce 50 hp, and one 100 feet in diameter, 200 hp. Great manufacturing plants require thousands of horsepower. It is therefore clear that many unit mirrors would be required, even if mirrors 100 feet in diameter are found practical. Again, the sun shines only half the time, even in cloudless regions, and much less in cloudy regions, where large manufacturing enterprises are now mainly carried on.

These obstacles might, it is true, be overcome if necessary. As for sunless nights, the boiler capacity may be sufficient to provide high-pressure steam, both night and day, for power purposes. Half a dozen mirrors might be grouped so as to heat one common boiler, if the heat–exchanger fluid should be circulated by a pump. Manufacturing enterprises might be carried on in desert lands. This would demand a movement of population, but there is a precedent. American cotton manufacturing used to be confined to New England and is now almost all in the southern states. Finally, power may be distributed electrically for many hundred miles from its source. By electrolyzing water, and storing the hydrogen at high pressure in steel containers, power potential may even be transported to any required distance. But large solar power is in the future.

Small Solar-Power Possibilities.—I receive nearly every week an inquiry, from some arid region of the earth, as to whether my solar-power devices are available. Thousands of ranchers, prospectors, and others, in our southwestern states, in South America, in Africa, in Australia, in India, and in Israel, are interested. Small power machines might pump water for irrigation, lift oil from deep wells, charge batteries, light lamps, cool rooms, and supply heat for cooking and for small jobs of house heating. For such uses the obstacles, which as yet hinder large solar-power projects, are not serious. There is only the question whether solar-power installations are not too expensive.

Efficiency of the Engine Employing a Rectangular Cylindric Parabolic Mirror.—I am assuming provisionally that 15 per cent of the solar energy of radiation intercepted by the mirror may be converted into mechanical work. You will wish to know how I arrive at this figure.

I propose a rectangular cylindric parabolic mirror 11 by 10 feet, rotating on an axis parallel to the earth's, and automatically kept at right angles to the incident beam. Its surface is of the specularly reflecting "Alcoa" sheets, fabricated by the Aluminum Company of America. The reflecting power of such a surface for solar rays is 82 per cent, as measured at the Smithsonian Institution on a clear day. These reflectors do not tarnish appreciably over long periods of time. Records of the intensity of solar radiation, made by the Smithsonian Astrophysical Observatory in many countries, show that 1.35 calories per square centimeter per minute is a moderate estimate for average conditions in desert lands. The surface of the mirror being 102,000 cm^2, its take of solar energy becomes 138,000 calories per minute.

The mirror focuses sunrays on a vacuum-jacketed, Pyrex-glass tube, parallel to the earth's axis, containing a dark, high-boiling liquid, "Aroch-lor," so thick in dimension as to be perfectly absorbing. The liquid and the glass have nearly equal indices of refraction; hence the reflection losses may be neglected at the surface of the liquid and regarded as from three, not four, glass surfaces. These losses are estimated at a total of 12 per cent. Hence, of the intercepted rays, there are absorbed in the dark liquid $82 \times 88 = 72$ per cent. The vacuum jacket is not as efficient to conserve this heat as the well-known thermos bottle, because the evacu-

Figure 24.—Model of solar machine described in U.S. Patent No. 2,247,830, arranged as a solar cooker, with cover removed to show inner parts.

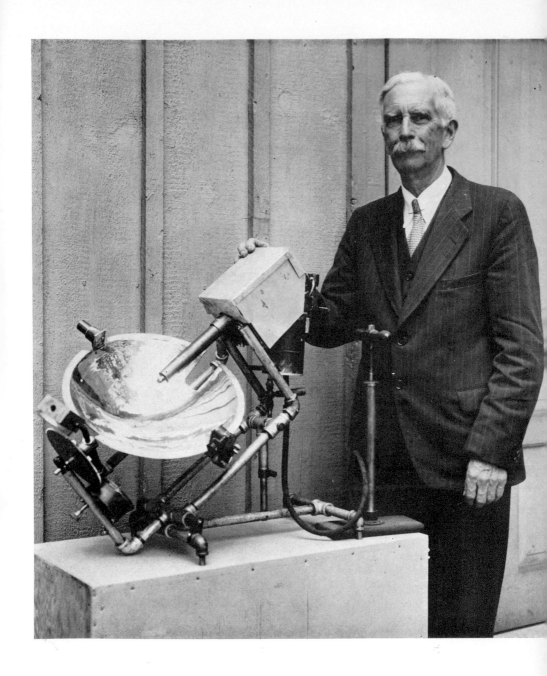

Figure 23.—Model of solar machine described in U.S. Patent No. 2,460,482, arranged for use as a flash boiler.

ated space cannot be fully enclosed by metal plating. The sun's rays must be admitted from beneath. However, it is possible by painting the uppermost 120° of the surface of the inner tube with gold paint, and flashing it, to deposit a gold plate on one third of the surface. The tube is 15 feet long so as to catch the sunrays which are reflected to the north and to the south of the 10-foot mirror, in December and June, respectively.

Estimate of Loss of Heat from the Focus Tube.—Since glass is opaque to long-wave rays, it must be regarded as a "black body," or perfect radiator, for rays emitted from the outer surface of the inner glass tube through the vacuum. The inner tube is 5 centimeters in outer diameter and 457 centimeters long. Its total area is about 7,200 square centimeters. Of this area one third is gold plated, and radiates little or nothing. There remains 4,800 square centimeters to radiate. It is intended to use the collected heat at a temperature of 500° Kelvin. At this temperature the outgoing radiation from the outer wall of the inner glass tube is 0.492 calories per cm^2 per second, or 29.5 calories per cm^2 per minute. For 4,800 cm^2 it amounts to 142,000 cal. But the outer glass tube is also hot and radiates inward. Its inner diameter being 8 centimeters, and its temperature conservatively estimated at 375° Kelvin, about that of boiling water, and with one third of the inner tube plated so that radiation from without cannot reach that part of its surface, it is found that 8,700 cm^2 of the inner wall of the outer tube will radiate inward to the inner tube 13 calories per cm^2 per minute, or 113,000 calories altogether. Thus the radiation loss from the inner tube is 142,000 − 113,000, or 29,000 calories per minute.

Of the 138,000 calories per minute intercepted by the mirror, 72 per cent, or 100,000 calories, is absorbed by the liquid. Of this amount, 29,000 calories being lost by radiation through the vacuum, there remains 71,000 calories for use. By sufficient insulation nearly all of this heat may be conserved within the water boiler.

Let the engine operate between 500° and 300° Kelvin. Then the thermodynamic efficiency is $\frac{T_1 - T_2}{T_1}$ = 0.40. Assume the engine 75 per cent efficient mechanically. Then 0.40 × 75, or 30 per cent of 71,000 calories per minute, 21,300 calories, is converted to mechanical energy. Thus the maximum of over-all efficiency of the combined machines which one may hope to realize is 21,300 ÷ 138,000 = 15.5 per cent.

The equivalent of 21,300 calories per minute is 151.6 kilogram meters per second, which is almost exactly 2 horsepower.

Modification for a Practical Estimate.—But I am aware that these figures contemplate ideal, not actual efficiency in using boiler heat. From a standard work on steam engineering I found an actual test in which

10,000 Btu in the boiler produced 1 horsepower hour of work. That amount of heat corresponds to 2,520,000 calories per hour, or 42,000 calories per minute. On that basis the 71,000 calories per minute, computed as remaining in the boiler of the solar machine, after losses, would produce 1.7, not 2.0, horsepower.

In the estimate of the costs of solar power, which I shall give later, I shall still further discount my solar machine, and regard it as able to furnish only 1.5 horsepower, or an over-all efficiency of 11.7 per cent.

Modification of the Patented Design.—You will note that I use a nearly square mirror instead of the long narrow one shown in Patent No. 2,247,830. The solar rays reflected south of the mirror in June, and north of the mirror in December, are caught on the focus tube, because it is about 5 feet longer than the mirror. As mentioned above, the inner glass tube, containing the "Arochlor," is gold plated for one third of its upper circumference. This admits the solar rays from below, but materially diminishes the long-wave radiation from the inner to the outer glass tube. As one knows, for bare glass the radiation outwards is proportional to the fourth power of the absolute temperature. The higher efficiency of the machine with circular mirror depends on the fact that the sunrays all converge upon a small circular focal spot, and the heat-conveying "Arochlor" liquid circulates from there in a vacuum-jacketed channel, in which the tubes are silvered completely within, as in a thermos bottle. The efficiency of conversion of solar energy to mechanical energy with that type is computed to be 25 per cent, as against 15 per cent for rectangular mirrors.

Details of the Solar Machine.—The rectangular parabolic mirror type of solar boiler has a cradle of parabolic cross section, framed of lightweight steel shapes, which carries a sheet of treated polished Alcoa, specularly reflecting about 82 per cent of solar radiation. A vacuum-jacketed boiler tube, of Pyrex glass, contains the nearly black liquid, Arochlor, of the Monsanto Chemical Company. This liquid circulates by gravity to a tubular heat exchanger within a strong steel boiler of water. As the liquid, Arochlor, boils at 355° C, and the machine operates at 500° Kelvin, or 227° C, the liquid is at atmospheric pressure, and the water in the boiler is superheated at some 370 lb, or 25 atmospheres pressure. Thus very hot steam may be drawn from the boiler, even at night, if the boiler has sufficient capacity.

Estimated Costs of Solar Power.—Having prepared a scale drawing of the machine designed as described, and having obtained wholesale costs of materials from several prominent manufacturers, I computed the weights and costs of the semifabricated materials for all parts of the device. I assume their use on a mass-production basis. The estimated total cost of the semifabricated materials for the solar boiler is $300. When this is multiplied by 10/6 to pass to costs of completed machines on a mass-production basis, and by 2 to give the selling cost, the total is $1,000 for the solar boiler.

In arid regions I estimate 10 hours a day of sun for 300 days per year. At 1½ horsepower output, this provides 4,500 horsepower hours of mechanical energy. I assume an interest rate of 5 per cent, which for one year amounts to $50 on the estimated cost of the solar boiler. Thus, according to my estimate, the solar plant may produce power at $50/4,500 = 1.1 cents per horsepower hour. I omit cost of engines, as they must be provided with other power sources.

I have sought to make fair, even generous, estimates in this calculation, but there are points of doubt. These can be resolved only by tests on a solar machine in a favorable region under engineering conditions. A plausible design is a good design only where it is tested in field conditions. I feel that a promising case is made for solar power from collecting mirrors. But only if some agency or organization appears able and willing to invest a few thousand dollars in an adequate field test can we know if the promise is justified.

Notes on Solar Power
and Other Uses of Solar Energy

E. J. Drake

The Heat Sink.—The generation of power or the distillation of water may be effected whenever a temperature difference can be established. In the absence of intervention by man, the energy arriving from the sun on the surface of the earth, apart from the small fraction utilized by plants, is ultimately reflected or reradiated to space; such temperature differences as are set up are transient and rarely become sufficiently great for economic exploitation.

Current thinking on means of increasing temperature differences sufficiently for economic exploitation appears to be directed almost exclusively to elevating the source temperature of the heat engine or the evaporator of the still, and it is worth considering whether in some circumstances it might be cheaper to depress the temperature of the heat sink of the heat engine or the condenser of the still. In considering the term $(T_1 - T_2)/T_1$ attention is currently directed almost exclusively to T_1; it is proposed in this discussion to compare the relative cost of, and gain from, equal increments of T_1 and decrements of T_2.

The cost of controlling the heat-sink temperature is important in any case; the condensing section of a power plant and the radiator of an automobile both represent a substantial capital cost, and the lower is the temperature range the more important is T_2. Solar engines are inherently low-temperature projects and the conditions that make them feasible—a high rate of insolation—are likely to be associated with an absence of abundant cooling water. Since the efficiency is not likely to be much above 10 per cent, if the cost of heat abstraction is comparable to the cost of collection, the capital cost of the heat sink will be of the same order as the capital cost of the collector.

If the mean temperature of the environment is 80° F, then raising T_1 by 50° will give a Carnot cycle efficiency of 8.47 per cent, while lowering T_2 by 50° will give a Carnot cycle efficiency of 10.02 per cent.

An obvious method of depressing temperature is by radiation to the night sky. If this procedure is to be used in association with solar collectors, insulated tanks must be provided for storing cold water (or brine) or hot water, or both. If continuous power is required, storage tanks must be provided in any case. The storage of energy by pumping water to elevated tanks has been proposed; yet if 1 lb of water is caused to drop through 5° F and the heat liberated is used in a heat engine of 5 per cent efficiency, it will yield work equivalent to that yielded by 1 lb of water at an elevation of 194 ft; the cost of effectively insulating a tank is probably less than the cost of elevating it to 194 ft.

The heat capacities at both T_1 and T_2 may be greatly increased by the use of a phase change associated with absorption or liberation of heat. The use by Dr. Telkes of $Na_2 SO_4 \cdot 10H_2O$ is an example. There appears to be a difference of opinion on the value of this method. Tests have been described which showed variable results; this clearly indicates a need for further research. The effect of various modes of agitation might repay study. Heat-storage studies to date have related mainly to domestic space heating, where capital charges are likely to be a limiting factor, and this must weigh against additional mechanical complications; this consideration may have less weight in the design of a solar power-plant. Where there is a tendency to form metastable solutions—as is the case with sodium sulphate—this fact, a disadvantage in an unagitated system, may in an agitated system be turned to advantage in meeting the other basic difficulty—crystallization on the heat-exchange surface. If the system is designed so that crystals of the decahydrate will always be present and these crystals are kept in suspension by agitation, then crystallization from a metastable solution is more likely to occur on the nuclei provided by existing crystals than on the heat-exchange surface.

Since the transition point from the decahydrate to anhydrous Na_2SO_4 in the solid phase is about 90° F, there would be a comparatively small temperature range available for a heat engine employing this means of storage. If a T_2 of about 30° F could be maintained by means of a night-sky radiator, then a comparatively simple collector operating at about 100° F could provide a temperature difference equivalent to a Carnot cycle efficiency of about 10 per cent. However, there are undoubtedly other systems available for obtaining higher values of T_1; Dr. Telkes' recently reported design of a solar cooker employing heat storage by means of a phase change indicates that she has investigated at least one such system.

Consider a power plant located at Phoenix, Arizona, designed to collect an average of 15,000 Btu/sq ft per month with a heat sink temperature of 90° F maintained by a slat-packed evaporative cooling tower. It is estimated that a collector with four plates of surface-treated glass will give an optimum T_1 of about 200° F, and with a T_2 of 90° F the Carnot cycle efficiency will be about 18 per cent.

If a two-plate collector were substituted, T_1 would be reduced to approximately 130° F, and to secure an equal Carnot cycle efficiency it would be necessary to reduce T_2 to approximately 30° F. Allowing for a 10° temperature difference for the condenser, a night-sky radiator would need to operate at 20° F and—assuming a surface 90 per cent "black" and an average of 12 hours per day radiating time—the heat radiated would amount to approximately 30,000 Btu/sq ft per month. (Shielding from the early morning and late afternoon sun might extend the average time of effective radiation rather beyond the 12 hours assumed.)

If the transmissivity of the atmosphere for long-range radiation is assumed to be 25 per cent, which appears to be a reasonably conservative value for the arid areas in which they would be most likely to find employment, the necessary radiator area would be about double that of the collector area, provided means can be found to prevent any substantial regain of heat by conduction or convection from the ambient air.

In the absence of high winds the influx of heat from this cause may be substantially reduced by quite simple means; if a vertical rim is provided around the periphery of the collector, a blanket of cold air may be retained on the surface and a 6-inch layer of air would—with a radiator operating at 20° F and an ambient air temperature of 50° F—reduce the influx of heat to about 1 Btu per hr per sq ft. **72660**

Recent work in microclimatology has shown that even the partial impedence of air movement resulting from the presence of grass will hold the air temperature close to the ground substantially below that a few feet higher. If high wind occurs, it is likely that in a collector of substantial area turbulance would result in the spilling of cold air over the rim. For radiators of large area it may therefore be desirable to provide baffle plates, insulated from the surface and arranged in a grid across the radiator. Radiators will, of course, require the same insulation from the earth or any structure as is provided for collectors. Clouds would reduce the performance of both the collector and the radiator but would have less effect on the radiator than on the collector. When the sky is completely overcast, there will be no substantial gain or dissipation of energy by either the collector or the radiator. Scattered cloud will have more influence on the performance of a collector than of a radiator; the passage of a small cloud between the sun and the collector will completely interrupt the collection of energy while, of the radiation reaching the earth from such a cloud, only a fraction will fall on the radiator.

The radiator would have substantially the same form as the back plate of the collector and would replace an approximately equivalent area of glass; its use would result in the replacement of the slat-packed evaporative cooling tower by an insulated storage tank for brine.

It may also be useful to study the extent to which heat can be radiated during the day from a radiator shielded from the sun, e.g., by means of vertical collectors. A cross section of a possible arrangement is shown in Figure 25.

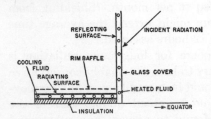

Figure 25.—Assembly of collecting and radiating surfaces.

Night Power or Distillation.—There are circumstances in which intermittent power is acceptable—for night illumination, for water pumping, or for desalting brackish water by electrodialytic processes—and in some of these cases the environment might provide a source of heat available at night. For example in arid and fuelless regions adjacent to a relatively warm sea, coils immersed in the sea could supply the heat source and a night-sky radiator the heat sink for a heat engine, or the sea might provide the evaporator and a night-sky radiator the condenser for a still. For example, suppose that a night-sky radiator having the form shown in Figure 26 is carried on piles, or, in the case of a sheltered lagoon or gulf, on pontoons, several feet above the surface of the water. It seems likely that convection currents would be set up causing a continuous flow of warm water from which evaporation would occur, with subsequent condensation on the underside of the radiator. The increase in the density of the air resulting from both the cooling and the removal of H_2O should also promote convection currents in the space between the surface of the water and the radiator.

Cooling.—Experiments have been described directed to using solar heat for the operation of an absorption-type refrigerator for air conditioning and food storage in hot climates. A simpler approach might be to use direct radiation during the night for the cooling during the day; the radiator, insulated from the walls and interior of the house, could serve as the waterproof membrane of the roof and, if fitted with two sets of coils, could act as a solar collector for a hot-water service during the day.

A radiator, forming the roof of a 1,400–square-foot, single-story house, cooling brine to 20° F would, on a clear night such as is generally experienced during the summer in many inland areas, dissipate more than a million Btu, or about the equivalent of a 4-ton refrigerator.

Working Fluids Other than Steam.—Many discussions of the comparison of the respective capital costs of a solar collector and a conventional boiler plant have assumed the engines to be comparable. However, a comparison of the first and the last rows of buckets in a steam turbine shows that this assumption is unwarranted. A glance at the Mollier

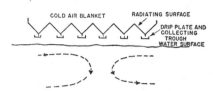

Figure 26.—Solar still utilizing nocturnal radiation to cool the condenser.

diagram will indicate that if steam enters a turbine at, say, 300 lb per sq in. and at 700° F, more than half of the available energy is converted before the specific volume reaches 32 cu ft per lb. In the solar engine operating between 200° F and 90° F the whole of the energy must be recovered from a working fluid having specific volumes in the range 32–940 cu ft per lb. Moreover the whole of the energy yield of the latter, compared with less than half of the former, must pay the toll of high windage or friction loss. Thus neither in capital cost nor in mechanical efficiency would the solar engine be comparable with an engine operating in the normal temperature range if H_2O is the working fluid.

It may be profitable therefore to investigate the use of other working fluids for the heat engine. Ammonia, for example, besides having excellent heat-exchange properties, has thermodynamic properties very suitable for the temperature range of 200° to 90° F. In this temperature range the final volume for ammonia as the working fluid would be about 0.02 cu ft per Btu enthalpy drop compared with about 5.5 cu ft if H_2O is the working fluid. If such a fluid is used, then the boiler and the condenser coils and the turbine must form a closed cycle, with a seal at the turbine shaft.

If a second working fluid is used in conjunction with a heat-storage tank for the provision of continuous power, there will be a nonreversible energy exchange at the heat-transfer surface resulting in a reduction of the availability of energy. However, a parallel nonreversible step is involved where water is the working substance and steam is generated, as is usually proposed, in a "flash" evaporator.

There is a significant difference between a collector used as an element of a power plant and one used for space heating or water heating. In the latter the heat is utilized as sensible heat and the collector operates at the mean temperature of the inlet and outlet; in the former case the collector must operate at a temperature above T_1 of the heat-engine cycle and there will be a nonreversible step in the "flash" evaporator. If the temperature drop in the evaporator is 10°, then about 100 lb of water must be pumped through it and the collector for every 1 lb of steam generated. Any attempt to reduce the unproductive temperature drop must therefore take account of an associated increase in pumping cost.

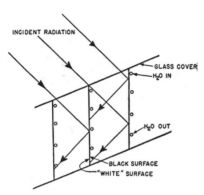

Figure 27.—Section of part of a collector having two absorbing surfaces: the first a "white" surface which is nearly "black" for long-wave radiation, and the second a black surface to absorb short-wave radiation.

Possible Alternative Collector Designs.—It has been suggested that a considerable simplification of collector design would be possible if a surface could be found which would absorb short-wave radiation and at the same time be substantially a nonemitter of long-wave radiation. There is no known surface having these properties; however there is a surface commonly used in meteorology (a white paint based on a lead sulphate pigment) which has the opposite properties, being an excellent reflector for short-wave radiation and almost "black" for long-wave radiation.

This suggests the possibility of devising a collector in which the radiation falls on the "black" collector plate only after reflection from a "white" surface such as that used by the meteorologists, so that the reradiated long-wave energy will not be reflected onto the glass cover plate but will be partly absorbed by the white surface and partly reradiated in all directions, with only a fraction falling on the glass cover plate. A possible arrangement is shown in Figure 27. The direction of water flow suggested is such that the hottest parts of the plates will be at the lower end, from which only a minor part of the reradiated energy will fall on the cover plate. This arrangement is also likely to set up rather random eddy currents in the air between the plates rather than a well defined set of convection currents carrying heat to the cover plate.

Since it would be necessary in such an arrangement to maintain the angle to the sun constant to within a few degrees, it would be necessary to construct the collector in sections fitted with jacks to allow for adjustment at about weekly intervals throughout the year.

Section V

Solar Evaporation and Distillation

The solar evaporation of sea water to give salt is one of the earliest and simplest chemical industries. The solar distillation of sea water to obtain drinking water on a small scale is described here. Discussed also is the possibility of large-scale distillation with single and multiple stills and the chance of improvement through scientific research on special plastics. Increasing population pressures provide an urge to accelerate research on the production of fresh water for seaport cities and for irrigation of farming land near the ocean.

Solar Distillation

Everett D. Howe

The State of California is faced with a continuing shortage of water for irrigation purposes and, since it is in a semiarid region, has underwritten an experimental program in the distillation of sea water. The work is being carried on by the University of California at the Engineering Field Station in Richmond and includes one project on solar distillation.

The solar-distillation units were designed by Dr. Maria Telkes and are similar in appearance to those used in Chile in the 1870's. The differences between the present design and the Chilean stills include the use of standard sizes of materials, the insulation of the pan, and the angle of the glass. The California still consists of five shallow wooden trays, 4 feet wide by 50 feet long, for holding sea water at depths of from ⅜ inch to 1¼ inches. These trays are oriented with the main axes due east and west and are covered with sloping glass panes extending from the sides of the trays to wooden ridge poles supported above the center lines of the trays. The trays slope gently from west to east so that water will flow along the trays as well as along the wooden distillate-collection troughs at the bases of the glass sides. The insides of the wooden trays are painted a dull black for maximum absorption of solar radiation.

The operation of the still involves the trapping of solar energy within the glass hood, the evaporation of water as humidity of the air inside the hood, and the condensation of part of the humidity by contact with the inside of the glass hood, which is in turn cooled by the convection of air over the outside.

The California still has been in continuous operation somewhat longer than a year and has produced a maximum of about 100 gallons per day, or at the rate of a gallon per day per 10 square feet. This production has been low because of several adverse circumstances, including excessive dust due to nearby grading of land, leakage of air into the stills, and low transmissivity of the glass (0.785). It has been observed that the first distilled water produced by the stills comes out at from three to five hours after sunrise. The probable causes of this delay include the large heat capacity of the units and the problem of grazing angle on the flat glass early in the day.

A second design of still constructed was one with an unsymmetrical glass hood. This unit has a tray 4 feet by 8 feet and the glass hood has a vertical mirror north face with sloping glass south face, on which the glass panes are 5 feet long. The general idea of this unit is that the sunlight at low angles would not pass through both faces of the hood and so be lost from the still, but would be reflected by the mirror into the water tray. Results on this unit showed about the same production per square foot as the simpler symmetrical design previously described, and it was therefore concluded that the added complication and cost of the unsymmetrical design was not warranted.

The third design tried out is a tubular type unit. In this case a tube $4\frac{1}{2}$ inches in diameter and 5 feet long is fitted with a shallow metal tray adjusted within the tube with its top edge horizontal and lying in the diametral plane of the tube. The tray is slightly narrower than the tube so that it does not touch the tube and will allow water to slide down the inside of the tube wall. The point of this design lies in the virtual elimination of air and dust leakage and the elimination of insulation. It should be noted that heat loss by radiation from the bottom of the water tray is reduced by the shielding effect of the lower half of the glass tube. Results with this unit have been encouraging, with the distillate output per square foot slightly higher than that of either of the other designs. Another unit of similar design but cheaper construction is being fabricated.

Measurements of pertinent weather data and of critical performance data on the stills are being continuously recorded so that a reasonably complete analysis of performance can be achieved. Weather data include air temperature, pressure and humidity, wind speed and direction, rainfall, solar radiation (Pyrheliometer), total radiation. Data on the stills include distillate output, temperatures of water at various points, heat-flow rates through the bottom of the water tray, glass temperatures, and air temperatures inside of the glass hood.

Results to date indicate that 4 acre-feet of distilled water per acre of ground per year is about the greatest net output which can be expected. The present cost of construction is likely to be more than the $4 per gallon per day typical of conventional water-development schemes. The operating costs would probably be less than the 20 cents per thousand gallons previously estimated. Widespread use of this equipment could come only if many small installations were feasible and if the construction and operating costs can be reduced. Costs of water in California range from approximately 12 cents per thousand gallons maximum for irrigation water to approximately 30 cents per thousand gallons maximum for domestic water supplies. Capital expenditures for water-production systems range from 50 cents per gallon per day to $4 per gallon per day. It is to be anticipated that the first prototype installations will be made in places where water supply is either very expensive or completely lacking.

Distillation with Solar Energy

Maria Telkes

In tropical, arid regions the supply of fresh water is often a serious problem. Many islands are devoid of natural fresh water, because wells produce only saline water. The present practice is to collect and store rain water, but this is relatively costly and often unsanitary, because the dry season may last for many months. The development of large areas of the globe is restricted, due to lack of rainfall and lack of water for irrigating the land.

Since 1952 the problem of demineralizing saline waters has been the subject of an extensive program within the U.S. Department of the Interior, known as the Saline Water Program. The aims of this program have been summarized in a pamphlet (*26*), which includes a list of potential water-purifying methods and a bibliography.

Review of Previous Attempts.—The history of the development of solar-distillation methods has been recently presented by the writer (*22*). The actual experimental developments are summarized briefly as follows:

Distillers using Lenses or Reflectors.—Parabolic reflectors, or lenses, were used centuries ago to concentrate solar energy to a boiler. The vapor thus produced was condensed by conventional means. Pasteur (*21*) in France and Abbot (*1*) built devices of this type and reported 50 per cent, or even higher, efficiencies. The construction costs of devices of this type are rather high and they require considerable attention during operation.

Solar-energy concentration requires a reliable moving mechanism to "follow the sun" which must be sufficiently accurate to keep the boiler in the focus. Only the direct solar beam can be concentrated and the diffuse solar energy represents a loss, which may amount to at least 10 per cent of the total incident solar energy on clear days and may be considerably higher during cloudy days. In addition the problem of producing highly reflecting *durable* parabolic reflectors at a low cost remains to be solved. Back-silvered glass reflectors or polished and anodized aluminum reflectors may concentrate 80 to 90 per cent of the direct part of the incident solar radiation, but there are no experimental records on their durability.

Inclined-Plate Type of Solar Stills.—One of the earliest and thus far the largest solar still of this type was built around 1872 (*17*) at Las Salinas

111

in Chile (lat. 24° S). This still covered slightly more than an acre and its largest daily fresh-water yield was reported at 6,000 gallons, corresponding to an efficiency of about 35 per cent. This installation was actually operating in 1908, attesting to the remarkable durability (36 years at least) of glass-covered enclosures. The solar still consisted of a black evaporator pan, resting on the ground, built of wood and waterproofed by asphalt. Inclined glass panes formed a tightly fitting roof over the pan. Solar radiation was transmitted by the glass roof and was absorbed by the black pan, heating a shallow layer of salt water contained in the pan. Water vapor was produced and it condensed on the inner surface of the glass roof, trickling down the inclined surface to a water-collecting channel at the inner periphery of the roof. The channel drained the distillate to a storage cistern. This device was relatively inexpensive; the initial invest-

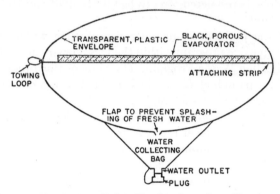

Figure 28.—Inflatable, floating solar still.

ment was about $4 per daily gallon fresh water yield, which included the local development and the rather high transportation costs.

The Salinas solar still was completely forgotten by 1926, when the French Government offered a prize for a solar still, to supply fresh water to Colonial troops in Africa. The inclined-plate principle was rediscovered at that time and several small experimental stills were built, operating at a rather low efficiency of about 25 per cent (*8, 9*).

In Italy calculations have been published by Dornig (*15*) concerning various solar still possibilities, which also had a rather low calculated efficiency. None of the above devices was used for practical applications.

Developments during World War II.—Flyers forced down at sea were equipped with inflatable rubber life rafts, but these could carry only a small supply of drinking water. Survival became a critical problem. Most flying was over tropical regions, where solar distillation could solve the problem of turning sea water into fresh water. Experimental work started at the Massachusetts Institute of Technology and was partly supported by O.S.R.D. (Office of Scientific Research and Development). Experiments were carried out by the writer to solve the basic principles of the inclined-plate type of solar still as well as those of other types (*22, 23, 24*). An inflatable solar still was built, to float next to life rafts, made of Vinylite

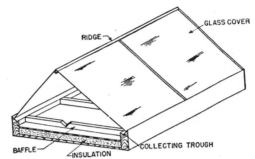

Figure 29.—Inclined-plate type of solar still.

or similar plastic materials. Figure 28 shows the schematic structure of this still. The inflated, transparent plastic envelope supported a black porous pad which was saturated with sea water. The rays of the sun heated the sea water absorbed in the porous pad and vaporized it. The vapor condensed on the colder surfaces and trickled down to a fresh-water holder at the bottom part of the solar still. The salt remained in the pad and could be flushed away at the end of the day. This device operated with a 50 to 60 per cent efficiency. The temperature of the evaporator pad reached a maximum of about 150° F during the middle of the day, on clear days. Inflatable, floating stills of this type have been developed commercially and they are currently used as standard equipment on life rafts (*25*).

Recent Developments.—The inclined-plate type of solar still shown in Figure 29, designed by the writer, was built at the seashore near Boston at Cohasset, Massachusetts. It was sponsored by the Pacific Science Board of the National Research Council. It was 4 ft wide, 50 ft long, with a total base area of 200 sq ft. Operated during the summer of 1951, it produced a maximum of 44 gallons of fresh water daily. Its estimated cost was about $4 per daily gallon of fresh-water yield and the average efficiency was 63 per cent.

Similar solar stills were built by E. D. Howe at the University of California (*20*) during the spring of 1952 and have been operating since that time.

Basic Principles, Design, and Experimental Results.—The inclined-plate types of solar stills shown in Figures 28 and 29 are single-effect stills. Their basic features combine the essential elements of atmospheric stills. The "boiler" evaporator consists of a shallow pan, or a suspended evaporator pad, saturated or filled with sea water, which also serves as an absorber of solar radiation. The "condenser" is the inclined, or curved, transparent surface, which forms an airtight envelope. It also serves as transmitter for solar radiation and it dissipates the heat of condensation, being cooled by the ambient air or wind.

The heat required to evaporate one pound of water depends upon its initial temperature and the temperature of evaporation. Starting with sea water at 80° F and evaporating at 150° F (the average noonday temperature of the water in solar stills of this type), the heat needed to raise the temperature of the feed water is 70 Btu/lb, the heat of vaporization is 1,007 Btu/lb, and the total heat is 1,077 Btu/lb. Values for other temperature levels can be obtained from steam tables. In tropical regions the average daily solar energy received on a horizontal surface can be as high as 2,500 to 3,000 Btu/sq ft. If this amount of solar energy could be used completely for the evaporation of water (meaning an efficiency of 100 per cent), the daily water yield per sq ft of evaporator surface could be about 2.3 to 2.8 lb. The actual amount of water obtained will generally be less and the ratio of actual water production to the theoretical yield is the efficiency mentioned above. To obtain the highest efficiency, all heat losses must be kept at the minimum.

Calculations of the heat losses and the equations of the performance of such stills have been published by the writer (*22, 23, 24*) and their results are summarized.

Transmission of Solar Energy.—For this purpose glass and certain plastic materials can be used, which transmit nearly 90 per cent of the incident solar energy provided that the angle of incidence is not greater than 60°. Most of this energy loss is due to surface reflection and is an unavoidable loss, unless "low-reflection" coatings can be used. Coatings of this type have been developed and, if they could be made available at a low cost, they could minimize the reflection losses to about 5 per cent. Glass and other materials which absorb appreciable amounts of solar radiation are heated, and therefore they cannot serve as a suitable solar-energy transmitter. Glass with a greenish color, or plastics which yellow on prolonged exposure, should be avoided. It is essential that the condensing water vapor should form a thin film, which is invariably formed on clean, water-wettable surfaces such as glass. Most plastics are not water wettable and the water vapor condenses on them in small droplets (drop-type condensation or "fogging") which act like small reflectors.

The appearance of such a surface is silvery white and the reflection losses may be as high as 40 per cent of the total incident solar radiation. Such surfaces should be coated with a water-wettable coating, which should not be washed off by the continuously flowing fresh water.

Heat Losses due to Incomplete Solar Absorption.—The black evaporator pan, or pad, should absorb all solar wave lengths. Most "black" surfaces are not completely black, and even the best velvety blacks are incomplete absorbers, although solar energy loss due to this effect may be kept as low as 4 per cent. Exposure to sunlight should not change the blackness of such surfaces by "bleaching." The formation of salt crusts or other mineral deposits must be avoided, because they change the black color of the absorbing surface.

Heat Loss through the Base of the Evaporator Pan.—This can be the most serious heat loss, with heat leaking off into the ground and serving no useful purpose. The early solar stills, including the large Las Salinas model, used wooden pans, which rested directly on the ground. Considerable amounts of heat can be lost through the wet ground, and this should be avoided. This can be accomplished by using a waterproof layer of heat insulation under the evaporator pan; or even better, the evaporator pan may be constructed of heat-insulating materials of low-heat capacity. When suitable materials are used, the heat loss through the base of the evaporator can be limited to 10 per cent, or even less, as proved by experiments.

Heat Loss from Evaporator Pad Suspended in Air.—The heat loss from an evaporator pad saturated with sea water (as shown in Figure 28) depends upon its surface-evaporation characteristics. If the pad is porous and evaporation occurs from both surfaces, heat is lost only due to the circulation of air saturated with water vapor and due to reradiation from the black surface. If the water evaporates from the top surface alone, heat will be lost from the bottom surface by reradiation, convection, and conduction.

Heat Loss due to Air Circulation within the Still.—The air, saturated with water vapor, circulates around within the still. In the roof-type models, the air rises in the center to the ridge of the roof and passes down the sloping transparent surfaces, as part of the vapor condenses. The heat losses due to the movement of air are not excessive and amount to about 4 per cent under average conditions.

Heat Loss due to Reradiation from the Black Pan or Pad.—The temperature of the black pan or pad is higher than that of the glass or plastic condensing surfaces and therefore continuous heat exchange will occur, which under average operating conditions is about 10 per cent of the total incident solar energy. This is an unavoidable heat loss which is inherent in the operation of the solar still.

Other Losses.—Serious losses may be caused by the leakage of water from the collecting channels, which must be avoided through proper construction. Cracks or holes in the mounting of the transparent surfaces will permit escape of water vapor, and leakage of water from the pan will likewise be unfavorable, but these may be avoided by proper construction. In the construction redwood may be used as a building material, as it resists sea water or fresh water almost indefinitely without deterioration. Plastic materials may be used for water-collecting channels and feed-water conduits.

TABLE 7

Heat Loss, Percentage of Incident Solar Energy, for Two Types of Stills

	Central evaporator pad Figure 28	Roof-type Figure 29
Transparent surface	8	8
Imperfect blackening	4	4
Reradiation	20	10
Air circulation	8	4
Base loss	0	6
Total losses	40	32
Efficiency	60	68

A summary of these losses provides the balance given in Table 7. The efficiency obtained during experimental results and found by calculations were in reasonably good agreement. The stills built according to Figure 28 gave an efficiency of 60 per cent, provided the plastic surfaces were clear and "fogging" was avoided. Solar stills built like Figure 29 attained slightly higher efficiencies, in accordance with the calculations.

Other Designs.—Inclined-plate type of solar stills have been designed using external cooling or vacuum operation. Experimental data are not available. It is probable that the efficiency of single-effect solar stills cannot be increased to much above 70 per cent and complicated designs only increase the initial cost of construction.

Multiple-Effect Solar Stills.—Such stills have been designed and built by Ginnings (*16*) for life-raft use (described in a private communication). The heat of condensation of the first stage was used to evaporate the feed water of the second stage. According to Ginnings, four-effect atmospheric stills might produce three times more fresh water than single-effect solar stills of equal area for solar-energy intercepting, but their cost of construction would be considerably more than three times that of the single-effect solar stills.

Future Improvements.—In the tropics one acre of ground, covered by single-effect solar stills, could produce about 10,000 gallons of fresh water daily, enough for the daily needs of about 1,000 families living in arid, underdeveloped regions where one acre of desert land has no value. In industrialized regions the daily water requirement may be as high as 100 gallons per person. A city of one million inhabitants may require single-effect, "solar-distiller waterworks" covering about 15 square miles. This is obviously too large for practical consideration. Future uses of solar stills depend, therefore, on the development of single-effect solar stills of relatively simple and inexpensive design and high durability for underdeveloped countries. For highly industrialized regions there is need for solar stills which can produce considerably more water per unit area than the single-effect stills.

Economics of Solar Distillation.—The initial construction cost of single-effect solar stills has been tentatively estimated at less than $4 per daily gallon of water yield. How does this compare with other processes now being used for producing fresh water from sea water? At the present time two large, fuel-operated stills which produce large quantities of fresh water from sea water exist. One of these is the $28-million plant at Kuwait, Arabia, in the Persian Gulf (*2*). At present it produces 1 million gallons of fresh water daily, but eventually it should produce 5 million gallons. The initial construction cost is therefore $5.60 per daily gallon of fresh-water yield. Operational costs are not available.

The other installation is at Curacao, Netherland West Indies, where 1,900,000 gallons of fresh water are distilled daily by multiple-effect, fuel-operated stills. The initial cost of construction was $6.30 per daily gallon of fresh-water yield and the operational costs are $3.80 per 1,000 gallons of water (private communication).

It appears, therefore, that the tentative cost estimate of the solar still, even in its present state of incipient development, is already lower than the cost of these large installations, which were able to use results and experience gained during many years of development.

The single-effect solar still may also be compared favorably with compression distillation. The initial cost of this equipment varies with capacity, being around $2.50 to $4.00 per daily gallon of water yield. The operational costs are around $1.25 per 1,000 gallons of water, under optimum conditions of operation.

Comparison with installations at natural water sources is rather difficult, due to variations in estimating "useful life" and in accounting practices of amortization and interest charges on the capital investment. The large waterworks of California, according to Howe (*20*), cost $0.96 (in 1904) and $1.56 (in 1925). If built today, these costs would be considerably higher, possibly around $3 to $4 per daily gallon of fresh water yield— that is, the cost level of single-effect solar stills. The operational costs of municipal water supplies average $0.16 per 1,000 gallons of water, but in some regions, where water shortages may be encountered, the cost is higher. Cost figures are given in Table 8.

TABLE 8

Costs of Water Supplies

Type of installation	Initial cost per daily gallon water yield	Operational costs per 1000 gallons
Multiple-effect, fuel burning:		
Kuwait	$5.60	not known
Curacao	6.30	$3.80
Compression distillation	$2.50– 4.00	1.25
California water works estimated present costs	3.00– 4.00	$0.16– 0.50
Single effect solar still, estimated on the basis of incipient development	4.00	not known

Conclusions.—Considering the limited effort and time spent thus far on the development of solar stills, the results appear encouraging. The estimated construction costs of solar stills are already lower than the costs of fuel-operated tropical installations. Comparison with compression distillation and certain developments at natural water sources indicates that solar stills are equally favorable, and this should stimulate further research and development work with solar stills.

Solar Evaporation of Salt Brines in Open Pans

K. S. Spiegler

Solar evaporation for the recovery of salt from sea water and other brines is one of the oldest unit processes of chemical engineering. There are records of its use in China several thousands of years ago, and it provided the ancient Egyptians, Phoenicians, Greeks, and Romans with common salt, one of their most important articles of trade. It was practiced on the Atlantic Coast in Massachusetts about twenty-one years after the Pilgrims landed in 1621.

While the proportion of salt manufactured by solar evaporation has been decreasing ever since because it is more economical to mine solid salt deposits, large quantities of salt are still being manufactured by solar evaporation. Thus, about 1,500,000 tons of salt are produced annually in India and Aden by this process, and the annual production of "solar salt" in the United States is about 1,000,000 tons. Moreover, interest in solar evaporation for the production of other chemicals has been revived in recent years. Thus the potash industry at the Dead Sea in Israel uses solar energy extensively for the production of the chlorides of potassium, sodium, and magnesium.

In spite of its long history, the process has not undergone fundamental changes since the days of antiquity and relatively few basic improvements have been made in the procedure during the last two thousand years. Systematic studies of solar-evaporation yields in the chemical-engineering sense have been initiated only in the recent past.

The necessary factors for successful operation of solar evaporation are a suitable climate—namely, much solar radiation and low rainfall—suitable contour of the ground for large pans, an almost impermeable soil or an economical method to make it impermeable, and the absence of dilution from fresh-water sources.

The sea water or other solutions to be evaporated flow into large open pans where the water evaporates under the influence of solar radiation. The solution, which gradually concentrates, is moved forward from one pan to the next. Eventually salts crystallize at the bottom of the pan. The nature of the salts and their relative proportions depend on the kind of solution used. By controlling the flow rate of the solutions, one can achieve the crystallization of different salts or salt mixtures in different pans. When the salt layer has reached sufficient thickness, the salts can be harvested mechanically or by hand and the pan can be used for the evaporation of additional quantities of brine. In the case of sea-water evaporation, calcium sulfate is the first salt to crystallize. When the brine reaches saturation with respect to sodium chloride, the latter crystallizes together with some calcium sulfate, and the concentration of the salts of magnesium, calcium, and potassium in the brine increases until at a specific gravity of about 1.28 the magnesium salts are ready to crystallize. At this point the brine, now known as "bittern," is drawn off and either used for the recovery of potassium and bromine or else returned to the ocean (*3*).

The rate of solar evaporation depends in the first place on the amount of solar energy absorbed by the brine, but also on the other meteorological factors, such as air temperature and humidity, wind velocity, and on the nature of the brine. Suppose the radiation on a horizontal plane in a given location amounts to 2,000 Btu per sq ft per day, which is a characteristic average value for the summer months in the tropics. If this energy could be utilized to its full extent for the evaporation of pure water, the daily evaporation would amount to about 2 lb per sq ft, or a layer of 0.4 inches of water would evaporate daily. (This figure is obtained by using a value of about 1,000 Btu per lb for the latent heat of evaporation of water at 110° F.) However, due to unavoidable losses, evaporation rarely exceeds 0.3 inches per day.

Setting up the energy balance of the unit area of a pan, for unit time, one obtains

$$LE = I - B - S - K - C \tag{1}$$

where E is the evaporation in terms of mass of water evaporated; L, its latent heat of evaporation; I, the incident radiation; B, the long–wavelength back radiation; S, the amount of heat stored in the brine as sensible heat; K, the convection loss to the air; and C, the loss to the walls and the bottom. The estimation of the rate of evaporation, E, from this equation has been discussed comprehensively by Cummings (*11–14*) in a series of papers. While S can be estimated accurately, B can be estimated with a reasonable degree of accuracy, and C can often be neglected, the estimation of the convection loss, K, seems at first sight to present difficulties. However, K is not an independent variable. Heat transfer to the air by convection and evaporation are indeed intimately related, both transfers being determined by the degree of turbulence of the air, except that the driving force for the heat transfer is the temperature difference, while for the water transfer it is the water-vapor pressure difference. Accordingly, it was shown (*10, 12*) that the ratio, R, of heat transfer to moisture transfer between the atmosphere and a water surface equals

$$R = \frac{K}{LE} = J \frac{T_w - T_A}{P_w - P_A} \frac{P}{760} \qquad (2)$$

where T_w and T_A are the temperatures, P_w and P_A are the partial pressures of water vapor in the saturated layer in immediate contact with the water and in the air respectively, and P is the barometric pressure. J is a function of the wind velocity and turbulence of the air, but Bowen (*10*) showed that it varies only within narrow limits and derived a mean value of 0.46 for it (if the pressures are expressed as mm mercury and the temperatures in degrees centigrade).

By means of Equation 2 one can thus eliminate factor K from Equation 1 and estimate the evaporation from data which can be measured more conveniently.

In shallow pans the daily average of S is usually negligible, as the brine temperature returns almost to its initial value in a 24-hour period. For free surfaces of water, B is usually only within 10–20 per cent of I and can be estimated with reasonable accuracy from Stefan-Boltzman's law.

One reason for the success of this method (*14*) is the fact that for water surfaces the convective heat transfer to the air is generally small compared to evaporation (expressed as transfer of latent heat) and its sum over a 24-hour period often almost vanishes, for during the day the water is usually warmer than the air and loses heat, while at night the opposite is the case. Thus, even if J in Equation 2 is not quite constant, the error in the estimation of the evaporation is small.

This is not the case for brine evaporation. For a given temperature the vapor pressure of the brine is lower than that of water (25 per cent lower in the case of a saturated solution of common salt), and in order to release the absorbed energy the brine surface has to reach higher temperatures. In fact, at the Dead Sea Potash Works the brine temperature is almost always higher than the air temperature and hence the daily average value of K in Equation 1 does not vanish. Possible variations in the value of J in Equation 2 are therefore more liable to cause errors than in the case of water surfaces, and the study of brine evaporation thus seems to offer a better check of this equation than the study of evaporation from water surfaces.

If one wants to express the daily variation of the brine temperature, T_B, one can set up Equation 1 for a pan in a differential form in terms of T_B and the meteorological variables (*4*). This leads to a quite complicated equation, as the different terms of Equation 1 do not depend on T_B in a very simple fashion. However, since the diurnal variation of T_B is small, one may use a linear relationship over a short temperature interval. Proceeding in such manner and assuming the brine temperature in a pan to be uniform, one obtains terms proportional to T_B, terms independent of T_B, and terms proportional to dT_B/dt (the latter being contributed by S), yielding the linear differential equation:

$$k \frac{dT_B}{dt} + l(t)T_B + m(t) = 0 \qquad (3)$$

where k is independent of time, $l(t)$ is a function of the wind velocity (which is a function of the time t) and $m(t)$ is a function of time containing such terms as solar radiation and air temperature and humidity.

This latter function being almost periodic with a period of 24 hours, $m(t)$ can be be conveniently expressed in terms of a Fourier series of this period. If $l(t)$ varies little with time (which corresponds to either constant or very low wind velocity), the solution of Equation 3 is a very simple expression, and it can easily be shown from it that the daily variation of the brine temperature depends in the following manner on the depth of the pan: (*a*) The amplitude of the daily temperature variation decreases with increasing depth. (*b*) The phase lag between solar radiation and brine-temperature variation increases with increasing depth. (*c*) For the case of constant wind velocity, and provided absorption of solar energy is the same for all depths, diurnal evaporation should be independent of the depth of the layer.

A study of solar evaporation of brines from hexagonal pans, 4 feet in diameter, which were lined with mirrors, in the Dead Sea area verified these conclusions in a qualitative manner even though the wind velocity was not constant (*4*).

Since the main factor determining the rate of evaporation in the pans is the rate of absorption of solar energy, and since in general the absorption of solar radiation by saturated brines is incomplete, an increase in the rate of evaporation may be achieved by the addition of dyes to the brine (*5–7*). The addition of 2-naphthol green to Dead Sea brines is being carried out on a large scale by the Israel Potash Company (*7*) and has caused increased absorption of solar energy and considerably higher yields per acre. The following description of the process is given in order to illustrate the optimum conditions for the addition of dyes to brines undergoing solar evaporation.

Dead Sea brine is pumped from a depth of about 150 feet into a series of large solar-evaporation pans. This brine contains the following amounts of salts in grams per 100 grams of water: magnesium chloride, 17.6; sodium chloride, 10.6; calcium chloride, 5.2; and potassium chloride, 1.6. It is almost saturated with respect to common salt, which crystallizes in the first pans. When a large proportion of the common salt has crystallized, a stage is reached when carnallite ($KCl \cdot MgCl_2 \cdot 6H_2O$) starts precipitating. This carnallite, contaminated with common salt, is harvested and potassium chloride recovered from it by treatment with different brines thus effecting complete removal of magnesium. A further wash with cold water dissolves the sodium chloride leaving pure potassium chloride. From the mother liquor remaining after the crystallization of carnallite, bromine is recovered.

The largest proportion of the pan area is covered by the "salt pans," i.e., the pans where common salt precipitates. The salt crystallizing at the bottom of the pans is white. Dead Sea brine happens to be almost completely transparent to visible light and the white salt layers reflect solar radiation like fresh snow. This reflection represents a considerable loss of energy, for almost all the visible light, which accounts for over one-third of the energy of the solar radiation entering the pans, is reflected into the atmosphere. If the solar energy spectrum at sea level is compared to the absorption spectrum of a 1-foot layer of pure water, it is seen that just in the range where solar energy reaches its maximum, the transparency of water is highest. While the infrared and ultraviolet sections of the solar energy spectrum are readily absorbed in relatively thin layers of water, a considerable fraction of the visible light passes even through tens of meters of water. An estimation of the energy loss due to the diffuse reflection of solar radiation at the bottom of the pans showed that in the case of a smooth layer of brine, 1 foot deep, about one-third of the solar radiation entering the brine surface is lost by reflection at the salt layer (*4*).

However, it would be impractical to design deep evaporation pans owing to higher construction costs per unit area and to the increase in seepage. The use of the dye causes almost complete absorption of solar energy even in shallow layers of brine. Almost complete absorption of solar energy is possible in 8-inch layers, if as little as 3.5 grains of dye are added per cubic foot of brine. In addition, the proportion of brine lost by seepage is thus reduced, owing to the increase in the rate of evaporation.

The choice of a suitable dye depends on the nature of the brine. It must not contaminate the precipitated crystals and must be sufficiently light-proof and unaffected by the high salt concentration of the brine. Salt brines sometimes contain natural contaminants causing absorption of radiation. However, when salt starts to crystallize, these contaminants often precipitate with it, leaving a clear brine. The dye is most effective in these later stages of evaporation, owing to the reflection of light from the salt layer at the bottom (4).

In spite of the ready availability of solar energy, solar evaporation in open pans as practiced today has only a low efficiency from the thermodynamic point of view since the amount of energy consumed for the evaporation of the water is usually many times higher than the minimum energy necessary to separate salt and water in a reversible process. However, one can hardly think of less expensive installations for the direct use of solar energy than evaporation pans and, wherever climatic conditions permit it, the chemical industry might again avail itself of this inexhaustible source of energy.

Solar Distillation of Sea Water in Plastic Tubes

Jeremiah T. Herlihy, Farrington Daniels

The distillation of fresh water from sea water would be attractive in many coastal areas if the installation costs could be low enough. Large areas are required and glass coverings by the acre are expensive as are satisfactory mountings for holding and condensing the water. One square foot of land receives about 500 kilocalories of solar energy per day in many parts of the world and this is theoretically sufficient to evaporate about a liter of water or roughly a quarter of a gallon of water. If some of the heat of condensation is used to raise the temperature of incoming water, the fresh water distilled per 500 kilocalories can be considerably increased, but the apparatus is more complicated and more expensive.

The object of the investigation summarized here (*18*) was to explore the possibility of using thin plastic tubing to reduce the capital cost for containing material and installation.

A long horizontal tube of plastic 9.7 cm in diameter was nearly filled with salt water and placed inside of a larger plastic tube 16.2 cm in diameter and the latter was kept in position by inflation with a slight air pressure. A diagram of the assembly is shown in Figure 30. Thin Trithene

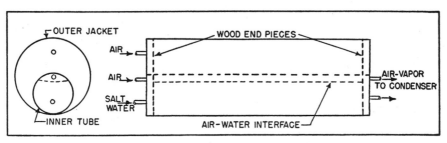

Figure 30.—Plastic solar still assembly.

tubing or Kel-F was used. It is a fluorinated vinyl plastic which has good resistance to weathering, cracking, and chemical reactions. Moreover, it has excellent transparency. It held up very well over several months during the period of the tests. The inner and the outer tubes were provided with circular wooden ends and were laid flat on a wooden table. This type of distillation tube and condenser is light in weight for easy transportation and easy to install by simply laying on flat ground.

The inner tube was nearly filled with water containing 32.1 grams of sodium chloride and 0.06 gram of a commercial black dye, "Rit," per liter. The area of water exposed was 4,000 square cm and on sunny days the temperature of the water reached 57° C. Both the black dye and the outer insulating tube were necessary. Without them the water could be heated only to a considerably lower temperature.

Air was blown along the top of the water in the inner tube and it picked up water vapor at 57° and gave it up in the condenser cooled to 25° by the incoming water.

The condensed water was collected and measured while the incident radiation was measured with a pyroheliometer.

The amount of the water collected was about 25 per cent of the theoretical maximum which would have been produced if all the solar energy had been utilized in evaporating water, without other heat losses, and if all the water vapor had been condensed and recovered. Under the conditions of these experiments the air was blown through too rapidly and it was only partially saturated with water vapor.

It seems likely that with slower passage of air an efficiency of 50 per cent in evaporation and condensation can be achieved. The simplicity and low cost of construction indicate that further experiments should be carried out to obtain cost data and length of life of the exposed plastic tubing.

Section VI

Atmospheric Phenomena, and Conversion of Solar to Electrical Energy

Solar heat can be converted directly into electricity through thermopiles of dissimilar metals, but the capital cost of large areas of metals is high. Solar heat can be converted readily into mechanical power through the use of air currents. Windmills have long provided a simple and practical means of using the solar energy indirectly. Long-range possibilities of utilizing solar energy through other atmospheric phenomena are discussed also.

Perhaps the greatest hope of utilizing solar energy is through the use of photovoltaic cells and newly developed types of transistors in which the sun's radiation is converted directly into electrical energy in solids without being transformed into heat.

Utilization of Solar Energy in Some Geophysical Processes

Oliver R. Wulf

Of the total solar radiation falling on the earth, approximately 35 per cent is reflected or scattered back into space (*8*), while the rest is absorbed, appearing principally as heat. This latter portion, too, is ultimately returned to space as radiation, since in the average over the years the earth is practically in a steady state with respect to outer space, losing the same amount of energy as it gains. But in the interval between the absorption of this solar energy and its re-emission to space as longer wave-length radiation, some of this energy appears in forms that can be utilized by man. One well-known instance is the chemical energy stored in photosynthesis. Another is the gravitational energy of water that has been lifted to the areas of high land by the atmosphere, deposited there as rain or snow, and utilized by man in turning water turbines. There are also some forms in which this solar energy appears that seem remote from utilization, but that conceivably might be utilized, and that therefore bear passing attention at least in any general considerations on the utilization of solar energy. Certain instances are described here in which solar energy is transformed and stored in atmospheric processes.

One way in which the earth utilizes solar energy is in the moving of the great mass of the atmosphere over its surface, that is, in the production of winds. On the large scale there are the trade winds of the low latitudes, the westerly winds of the middle latitudes, and the easterly winds of the polar regions. The kinetic energy of the atmosphere is very large. It has been estimated by Brunt (*2*) and found to be of the order of 10^{20} joules. In the course of the atmospheric circulation, warm air moves from low to high latitudes and cold air from high to low latitudes. The winds are thus part of a great temperature-regulating mechanism in which the higher latitudes are warmed and the lower latitudes cooled.

The moving of this air is accomplished by a heat engine comprising the surface of the earth and the atmosphere. The air is the working substance of the engine. It picks up heat at relatively high temperature and gives it up at relatively low temperature, thus insuring that a portion of the heat taken up may be converted into work if the engine is capable of doing so. The atmospheric circulation is evidence that it is indeed capable of doing so.

This kinetic energy generated by the engine is constantly being converted into heat, that is, the energy of the winds is being dissipated by turbulence and viscosity. Brunt has also estimated the rate of this dissipation (*2*), and for the entire earth this proves to be of the order of 10^{15} watts. In the average this must be equal to the rate at which kinetic energy is being produced by the engine, since over the years the energy of the atmospheric circulation is undoubtedly about constant, that is, there exists essentially a steady state condition.

The earth is constantly gaining entropy through heat realized from the absorption of radiation over a range of temperatures and losing entropy through the same amount of heat emitted as radiation over another range of temperatures. In the average the temperature at which the earth is losing this heat is lower (as mentioned above) than the temperature at which it is gaining it—that is, the earth is losing entropy at a greater rate than it is gaining it—and since this system is essentially in a steady state, entropy must be being produced at a rate equal to the difference between the rate of entropy loss and the rate of entropy gain. A portion of this entropy production occurs in the dissipation of the kinetic energy of the atmospheric circulation.

It should be possible to make an estimate of the entropy budget of the earth. Wulf and Davis (*24*) have made a rough illustrative attempt of this kind and, from the ratio of the rate of entropy production in the dissipation of the kinetic energy of the atmosphere to the total rate of entropy production, have estimated the efficiency of this atmospheric engine in producing the kinetic energy of the winds from the heat that is transported in the engine from the "boiler" to the "condenser." This proved to be of the order of one half—that is, one half of that thermodynamically possible from this heat transport—and it is perhaps a little surprising that this engine seems to operate at such a relatively high efficiency.

In the course of the atmospheric circulation, weather and the disturbances that we speak of as storms occur. It appears that one particular class of these storms is instrumental in storing energy in the atmosphere in another interesting way, namely as electrostatic energy.

In fair weather a vertical electric field (*7, 9, 18*) exists in the atmosphere which in the average is of the order of 100 volts per meter near the surface of the earth, and in the sense that the earth is negative and the sky positive. This amounts to approximately 400,000 volts between the upper atmosphere and the ground.

The air, though a very poor electrical conductor, does possess a certain conductivity because of ions produced in it, principally by cosmic radiation. Moreover, this conductivity increases with height, the vertical electric field decreasing accordingly. At some 15 or 20 kilometers altitude the potential difference of roughly 400,000 volts between sky and earth has been almost completely attained.

Thus effectively a concentric spherical condenser exists, comprising the sky and the earth, with the poorly conducting lower air serving as the dielectric. This represents storage of energy of course—that is, storage as electrical energy in this great condenser, the charge in which appears to be of the order of several hundred thousand coulombs. Due, however, to the conducting properties of the air, even though it is a poor conductor, a leakage current or discharge current is steadily flowing from sky to earth, of between one and two thousand amperes over the entire earth. Though this is a very small current per square centimeter—that is, the current density is very low—it is sufficient to discharge such a condenser in a short time, of the order of a number of minutes.

Such a discharging of the condenser does not occur, however, and it follows that its charge is in some way being steadily maintained. This brings us back to the matter of storms. It appears now very probable that the charge of the great condenser is maintained by thunderstorms, the thunderstorm being a form of static electrical machine suspended between sky and earth sending negative electricity down to the earth and positive electricity to the sky above.

There is another way in which solar energy appears to be utilized in producing electrical energy in the atmosphere. The very high atmosphere in the region known as the ionosphere is electrically conducting by virtue of ionization produced there by ultraviolet solar radiation. This maintenance of photoionization in the ionosphere by the sun has some points of similarity with the maintenance of the photochemical ozone steady state somewhat farther down in the atmosphere, and both of these represent, of course, a certain storage of solar energy. But in the electrically conducting region, i.e., the ionosphere, motion of the air may give rise to a feature not found where the air is a very poor conductor, namely, the flow of appreciable electric current under the influence of electromotive forces that arise when the electrically conducting air moves across the lines of force of the earth's permanent magnetic field. It is clear that such electric currents may be said to be generated by "dynamo" action.

The earth's magnetic field shows a characteristic daily variation (*4, 5, 7, 22, 23*). The widely accepted explanation of this attributes it to the magnetic field of diurnal electric currents flowing in the ionosphere, these currents being generated by solar-produced diurnal ionospheric winds through the dynamo action just described. This explanation is known, indeed, as the dynamo theory of the daily variation of the earth's magnetic field. It is the widely accepted explanation of the daily variation on days that are free of geomagnetic disturbance. Corpuscular radiation from the sun is believed by most workers in the field to be the cause of more violent effects and of much larger electric currents in the ionosphere that appear to flow on what are known as magnetically disturbed days.

The electric currents generated by dynamo action appear themselves to be quite large, of the order of 50,000 to 100,000 amperes. But they are spread over very large geographical areas and the current density is small.

Geomagnetic disturbance, which is attributed by the generally accepted theory to corpuscular radiation from the sun, represents at times very large amounts of energy, as in a magnetic storm. Chapman and Bartels (*5*) have estimated the energy of an active magnetic storm to be of the order of 10^{15} joules, and for the greatest storms it is even larger. Such magnetic storms usually last for a time of the order of a day.

Varying electric currents in the ionosphere appear to induce electric currents in the earth, as might be expected knowing that the material of which the earth is made has appreciable electrical conductivity. These latter are known as earth currents, and some study has been made of them.

In the geophysical instances described above, solar energy is utilized and stored in atmospheric processes. Whether man can make economical use of such energy is a question that may deserve at least some notice in the general consideration of the utilization of solar energy.

Maximum Plausible Energy
Contributions from Wind Power

Palmer Cosslett Putnam

The atmospheric envelope over the earth is a rotating, regenerative, thermal engine, fueled by radiant energy from the sun. The total kinetic energy of the rotating atmosphere has been estimated by Brunt at 3×10^{17} kw. But not all of this power is available to windmills—only that portion in the lowest stratum. Willet (personal communication) estimates the total power available to windmills at roughly 10^{10} kw, compared with total potential water power of some 10^9 kw.

The most powerful wind regimes are generally to be found between North and South latitudes 40° and 55°. Northern Scotland, northern Ireland, northern Wales, Denmark, South Island of New Zealand, northern Japan, and southern Chile are areas where there is a demand for energy and where the wind blows at 25 miles an hour or more 100 feet above the ground the year round.

Trade winds blow fairly steadily at 15 to 20 miles per hour over many power-hungry lands in the lower latitudes, where local markets for wind energy would perhaps justify small isolated installations.

The power in the wind varies as the cube of the velocity. A rule of thumb is that

$$kw = 4 \cdot D^2 \cdot V^3 \cdot 10^{-6}$$

where D is the diameter of the windmill in feet and V is the wind velocity in miles per hour.

A mean annual wind velocity of at least 25 miles an hour at hub height is required if a wind-power installation is to compete economically with modern integrated utility systems.

Wind power, like solar power, is not firm power. The proprietor of a large wind-power installation cannot offer to sell contracts for power which will be continuously available like that from a steam plant. He can only sell what is known as secondary or dump power. The worth of dump power is essentially the value of the fuel which it displaces. This credit cannot always be fully earned, however, unless the availability of wind

133

power can be definitely predicted and scheduled, thus enabling the utility despatcher to decrease the steam capacity that he has floating on the line, ready to take up load instantly, and the steam capacity that he has on immediate stand-by with banked fires. Other things being equal, the worth of dump power varies from region to region with variations in the delivered cost of coal, and with variations in the regional steam-station efficiency. In the United States, in 1953, the worth of dump power varied from about 1.5 mills per kilowatt hour to 5 mills per kilowatt hour in certain special cases.

After a review of all proposed designs, the S. Morgan Smith Company, in collaboration with the General Electric Company, built an experimental 1,250–kilowatt Smith-Putnam wind turbine on Grandpa's Knob in Vermont in 1940. The stainless steel blades swept an area 187 feet in diameter. The unit generated alternating current and fed into the lines of the Central Vermont Public Service Corporation.

In the course of five years of experiments the engineers in charge concluded that the major mechanical problems had been solved, and that a unit could be designed to remain safely on line in any wind (*15*).

Several hundred cost studies were made. It was concluded that the economically optimum wind turbine would stand about 165 feet high, with a diameter of about 225 feet and a rating of about 2,000 kilowatts— virtually regardless of the wind regime. Shifting cost patterns would alter these values somewhat.

The British now have an experimental 100–kilowatt unit under test in Scotland, where the average annual velocity may be not far from 30 miles an hour.

The Soviets had a three-bladed, 100–kilowatt unit on a hill near Yalta before the war, feeding into the 20,000–kilowatt peatburning steam station at Sebastopol.

Attractive major wind-power sites are rather rare. For example, what is needed in New England, where the prevailing wind flow is from the west, is a ridge trending north-south, with favorable and regular aerodynamic characteristics to increase the average annual velocity of the "free-air" flow, and long enough to support a battery of at least ten 2,500–kilowatt units—that is, several miles long. There are not many such ridges in New England.

In Great Britain three years of survey have disclosed several hundred wind-power sites with an aggregate potential capacity of several million kilowatts, capable, if developed, of saving 2 million to 4 million tons of coal a year. Each site would mount a 2,000–kilowatt wind turbine, which would operate at full capacity up to 4,000 hours a year.

The demand for wind-power units rated from 5 to 100 kilowatts is world-wide and lively. The Negeb of Israel is an example. Fuels are prohibitively costly in this thinly populated desert. Rural electrification is not yet justified. Wind velocities are not impressive. But water is needed. If water could be pumped, even at costs equivalent to 5 or 10 cents a kilowatt-hour, the expense would perhaps be justified during the 15 or 20 years required to transform parts of the Negeb into a latter-day land of milk and honey. By that time, local demand would perhaps justify rural electrification.

Soviet reliance on windmills is reputedly heavy in many parts of the U.S.S.R. They have announced plans to build 600,000 units of a modern design, rated at about 25 kw. These units are coupled to inertia storage batteries and are designed to provide light and power in thinly settled regions, ahead of rural electrification.

The ultimate installed capacity of "large" wind turbines in places like Great Britain, Denmark, South Island of New Zealand, southern Chile, northern Japan, and other windy regions close to growing demands for energy may amount to 100 million kilowatts. Medium-sized units may amount to as much again. Small units of less than two kilowatts are numerous, but their aggregate contribution is negligible.

Plausibly the cumulative contribution from wind power in the next 100 years may amount to 0.1 Q.*

*1.0 Q = 10^{18} Btu, equivalent to the heat in 38 billion tons of bituminous coal.

Solar Thermoelectric Generators

Maria Telkes

On clear days solar energy is received at the rate of about 100 watts per square foot, or about 0.1 watt per cm^2 at normal incidence. The direct conversion of solar-radiant energy into electrical energy may be attempted by photoelectric cells of the photovoltaic type, or by thermoelectric means. Solar thermoelectric generators, operating as heat engines, convert radiant energy into thermal energy.

The thermoelectric process has definite advantages when compared to conventional heat engines. There are no moving parts and, barring accidents or thermal deterioration, thermoelectric generators should last indefinitely. Their practical application depends upon their efficiency and construction costs. High efficiency is needed to obtain maximum power output per unit area of intercepted solar radiation. Low cost is equally essential, because thermoelectric generators will be used only if their construction cost, per kwhr capacity, is not greater than the comparable cost of conventional, fuel-operated electric-power generators.

The development of thermoelectric generators in the past was empirical and until recently the highest efficiency obtained was only around 0.5 per cent. Solar thermoelectric generators, or solar thermopiles, have been constructed by Coblentz (6), but the efficiency attained has been only 0.008 per cent.

Efficiency of Thermoelectric Generators.—The writer summarized theoretical calculations and the results of experiments with various thermoelectric materials (19) and also presented experimental results with solar thermoelectric generators in a recent article (20). These results are summarized in the following pages.

The efficiency of thermocouples is a function of the temperature difference maintained between the hot and cold junctions of the thermocouples. It is also a function of the physical properties of the positive and negative thermoelectric materials, including the following:

e = thermoelectric power, in volt/°C.
ρ', ρ'' = resistivity of thermoelectric materials as an average in the operating temperature range, in ohm-cm.

k', k'' = specific heat conductivity of the materials as an average in the operating temperature range, in Watt· cm^{-1}·deg^{-1}.

T_h = hot junction temperature, in °K.

T_c = cold junction temperature, in °K.

The following equation was derived theoretically and has been confirmed by experiments (*19, 20*):

$$\text{Thermoelectric efficiency} = \frac{1}{\dfrac{2T_h}{T_h - T_c} + \dfrac{4[(k'\rho')^{1/2} + (k''\rho'')^{1/2}]^2}{e^2(T_h - T_c)}}$$

In this equation the first part of the denominator represents the Carnot efficiency factor, while the second part gives the correlation of the physical characteristics of thermocouple materials. Their dimensions (length L; cross sections s', s''; and form factors d', d'', $d = s/L$) for optimum operation are given by:

$$\frac{d''}{d'} = \left(\frac{k'\rho''}{k''\rho'}\right)^{1/2}$$

The theoretical correlation between ρ, k, and T is given by the Wiedemann-Franz-Lorenz relation $k\rho = 2.45 \ 10^{-8}T$, which is applicable to most metals and alloys. Some alloys and semiconductors of higher thermoelectric power values may deviate considerably from the "normal" Wiedemann-Franz-Lorenz relation and this leads to a considerable decrease in their efficiency.

The thermoelectric power of most ductile alloys is rather low, even the best couple of this type, Chromel-P–constantan, having a thermoelectric power of only 65 microvolts per degree C. Certain alloys and semiconductors have e values in the 100 to 1,000 microvolt/°C range. The specific-heat conductivity of such materials, if it is not known, may be assumed as being around $k = 0.01$, the lowest value for solid insulators. The normal value of the Wiedemann-Franz-Lorenz relation at moderate temperatures is around $k\rho = 10^{-5}$ and therefore $\rho = 0.001$; that is, the resistivity of such materials should not be appreciably greater than 0.001 ohm-cm. Most semiconductors of high thermoelectric power, however, have rather high resistivities and therefore their efficiency cannot be expected to be sufficiently high. Future developments in semiconductors may lead eventually to possible improvements in efficiency.

Thermoelectric Materials.—The physical characteristics of some of the representative materials are given in Table 9 for various temperature ranges. The ductile alloys, Chromel-P and constantan, are commercially available in wire or strip form and can be welded or soldered to form

TABLE 9

Resistivity ρ (Ohm-cm), Specific Heat Conductivity k (Watt·cm^{-1}·deg^{-1}), and ρk
of Thermoelectric Materials

Material	Temperature range $T_h - T_c$, °C	$\rho \times 10^6$	k	$k\rho \times 10^6$
Chromel-P	100 to 20	71.5	0.169	12.1
"	200 to 20	73.8	0.179	13.2
"	420 to 20	76.9	0.206	16.6
constantan	100 to 20	49.	0.250	11.8
"	200 to 20	49.	0.262	12.8
"	420 to 20	49.	0.312	15.5
91Bi—9Sb	100 to 20	200.	0.041	8.2
"	200 to 20	220.	0.044	9.7
ZnSb (Sn, Ag, Bi)	100 to 20	1900.–2700.	0.0205–0.0165	34.–39.
"	200 to 20	2200.–3100.	0.0180–0.0152	40.–47.
"	420 to 20	2400.–3600.	0.0165–0.0142	40.–51.
Normal	100 to 20	. . . .		8.2
"	200 to 20	. . . .		9.4
"	420 to 20	. . . .		12.1

junctions. The negative alloy of 91 per cent bismuth plus 9 per cent antimony can be cast and formed easily, melting at 270° F. It must be soldered with special methods. The positive alloy is based on the inter-metallic compound ZnSb, with small amounts of addition agents (Sn, Bi, Ag, etc.). It melts around 560° C and requires special casting and annealing techniques. These alloys are nearly ten times more efficient than the ductile alloys.

The thermoelectric power, open-circuit emf, and efficiency of several thermocouple combinations are given in Table 10. The experimentally obtained efficiencies are shown in Figure 31 and are compared with theo-retical values for normal Wiedemann-Franz-Lorenz relation. The letters on the curves correspond to the thermocouple combinations of Table 10.

The efficiency results shown in Table 10 have been obtained with elec-trically heated thermocouples and represent the efficiency of the thermo-couples. This efficiency is influenced by the efficiency of the process for collecting solar energy and the resultant over-all efficiency will be smaller.

Flat-Plate Solar Thermoelectric Generators.—The flat-plate solar-energy collector consists of a black-coated metal plate, which is shielded by air-spaced transparent panes to diminish heat losses from it. The hot junctions of the thermocouples are attached to the black plate, which

TABLE 10

Thermoelectric Power, Open-Circuit emf, and Efficiency of Thermocouple Combinations

Positive	Negative	Temperature range $T_h - T_c$, °C		
		100 to 20	200 to 20	420 to 20
Thermoelectric power, microvolts per °C				
a) Chromel-P,	constantan	63	67	73
b) ZnSb (Sn, Ag, Bi),	constantan	210–250	225–270	240–290
c) ZnSb (Sn, Ag, Bi),	91Bi—9Sb	240–280	255–305	....
Open-circuit emf, millivolts				
a) Chromel-P,	constantan	5.0	12.1	29.1
b) ZnSb (Sn, Ag, Bi),	constantan	16.8–20.0	40.5–48.6	96.–116.
c) ZnSb (Sn, Ag, Bi),	91Bi—9Sb	19.2–22.4	48.9–55.0	....
Thermocouple efficiency, per cent				
a) Chromel-P, constantan				
Calculated		0.16	0.37	0.83
Observed		0.15	0.35	0.76
b) ZnSb (Sn, Ag, Bi), constantan				
Calculated		1.25	2.75	5.7
Observed		1.20	2.65	5.6
c) ZnSb (Sn, Ag, Bi), 91Bi—9Sb				
Calculated		1.55	3.65	....
Observed		1.5	3.4	....

may be subdivided into separate sections, to permit series connection. Figure 32 shows one thermocouple, with the attached black plate forming the hot-junction connection and with the cold junctions of the alloy bars soldered to cooling fins. Figure 33 is a front view of 25 series-connected thermocouples, mounted in a suitable insulating frame, and shows the checker-board arrangement of the couples behind air-spaced glass panes. The back view, Figure 34, shows the cooling fins which also serve as connectors. The thermoelectric generator is oriented to face south and suitable legs are provided to tilt it at an optimum angle.

Several thermoelectric generators were built, using combinations of the materials shown in Tables 9 and 10. The dimensions of the black plate, the length and cross section of the alloys were varied, and the

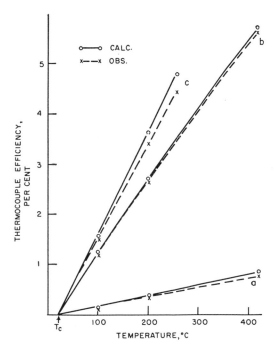

Figure 31.—The efficiency of thermocouples.

Figure 32.—One solar radiation thermocouple, with receiver, alloy bars, and two cooling fins which serve as connections.

(*Above*) *Figure* 33.—Front view of a solar radiation thermopile with 25 junctions.
(*Below*) *Figure* 34.—Back view of a solar radiation thermopile.

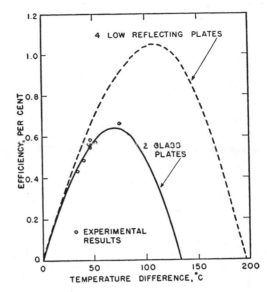

Figure 35.—Efficiency of flat-plate type of solar thermoelectric generators.

experimental results are shown in Figure 35. The theoretically calculated over-all efficiency is shown by the curves, while the experimental results are indicated by dots, showing good agreement. In these tests two air-spaced glass panes were used. Four "low reflection" coated glass panes would theoretically increase the efficiency, because greater temperature differences could be attained.

Typical results obtained with 25-junction thermocouple assemblies using combinations *a* and *c* are shown in Table 11. Nearly ten times

TABLE 11

Typical Experimental Results, 25-Couple Assemblies

	Chromel-P, constantan (*a*)	ZnSb (Sn, Ag, Bi), 91Bi—9Sb (*c*)
Area of collectors, cm²	360.	340.
Internal resistance, ohm	0.088	0.137
Open-circuit emf, volts	0.086	0.30
Load emf, volts	0.043	0.15
$T_h - T_c$, °C	54.5	47.
Current, amp	0.49	1.10
Power output, watts	0.021	0.165
Incident solar energy, watts	31.	28.
Over-all efficiency, per cent	0.068	0.59

greater efficiency was obtained with thermocouple *c*, using a negative alloy of 91 per cent bismuth and 9 per cent antimony in combination with a positive alloy of ZnSb (with small amounts of additional agents Sn, Ag, Bi). With four "low reflection" coated glass panes, it is indicated that the efficiency may be increased to slightly more than 1.0 per cent for this combination.

Solar Energy Concentration.—Higher temperatures can be obtained only by concentrating solar energy to the hot junctions. Glass lenses were used for this purpose, focusing solar energy to small collectors, forming the hot-junction connections. The best alloy combination was used. The cold junctions were cooled by larger fins, or water cooling could be used, with the possibility of producing hot water as a by-product to the electric power supplied. The highest attainable hot-junction temperature was limited by the melting point of the negative alloy. The experimental data per single couple were the following: open circuit emf, 56 millivolt; load emf, 28 millivolt; temperature difference, 247° C, current, 5.6 ampere; power output, 0.156 watt; incident solar energy, 4.7 watt; over-all efficiency, 3.35 per cent. The results indicate that at higher temperature differences the over-all efficiency increased considerably, as this may be expected on the basis of theoretical calculation and experimental results shown in Figure 31 and Tables 9 and 10.

Conclusions.—The efficiency of solar thermoelectric generators can be predicted from the physical properties of the materials and the efficiency of solar-energy collection.

Ductile alloys of Chromel-P–constantan are not suitable for the attainment of higher efficiencies. Flat-plate solar thermoelectric generators, using special alloys, attained an efficiency of 0.59 per cent with a collector shielded against heat losses by two glass panes. With four "low reflection" coated panes the efficiency may be increased to about 1 per cent.

Concentrating solar energy with lenses or other devices permits the attainment of higher temperature differences, and it was possible to obtain an efficiency of 3.35 per cent.

It is probable that solar thermoelectric generators of the flat-plate type can be used only for special purposes, where the cost of electric power is high and where tropical solar energy is available most of the time. If the problem of producing inexpensive systems of high durability for concentrating solar energy could be solved, solar thermoelectric generators of this type may offer possibilities of applications in tropical regions. Further development work is needed to produce better thermoelectric materials.

Maximum Efficiency of Solar Energy Conversion by Quantum Processes

D. Trivich, Paul A. Flinn

The ideas expressed in this communication were developed in connection with research in photochemistry sponsored by the Charles F. Kettering Foundation and research on photovoltaic cells sponsored by the United States Air Force under Contract No. AF 18(600)–481, monitored by the Office of Scientific Research. The authors are indebted to Dr. Henry J. Bowlden of the Physics Department of Wayne University for helpful discussions.

Solar energy converters, such as photovoltaic cells, photochemical reactions, and similar devices, operate by what we shall call here "quantum processes." They differ from heat-engine converters in that they have a minimum threshold frequency and therefore cannot usefully absorb quanta at wave lengths longer than the threshold value, while heat engines can usefully absorb all wave lengths of solar radiation. Heat engines are severely limited in conversion efficiency by the second law of thermodynamics. In order to be able to compare the relative utility of quantum converters with heat-engine converters, it is necessary to consider means of calculating the theoretical and practical maximum conversion efficiencies of each type.

The method of the calculation for heat engines seems fairly obvious. The net energy received by the collector by radiation processes depends on the difference between the fourth power of the absolute temperatures of the sun and the collector. The temperature of the collector builds up to a value, T_2, where the net energy received is equal to energy removed from the system by conduction and other losses and by the heat engine. Then the limiting efficiency in the heat engine, given by the second law, is $(T_2 - T_1)/T_2$. The over-all efficiency of the process can be calculated by considering the various steps involved, the most difficult being the estimation of heat losses. In a perfectly insulated system with no heat losses other than radiation, the efficiency will be of the order of $\dfrac{T_3^4 - T_2^4}{T_3^4} \cdot \dfrac{T_2 - T_1}{T_2}$ where T_3 is the black-body temperature of the sun, T_2 of the collector, and T_1 of the engine surroundings. The first term will normally be larger than the second. The present difficulty of maintaining high collector temperatures without large heat losses indicates that heat engines will usually have low efficiencies although not necessarily unusably low values.

The calculation for quantum processes is less obvious and, since it does not appear to have been considered in detail before, we shall set forth here what seems to us to be a plausible method.

The energy of the sun falling on the earth per unit area per unit time is distributed over a range of frequencies or wave lengths in a manner which can be measured, and which can be expressed by a plot of the energy at a given frequency, $E(\nu)$, against the frequency, ν. Another expression would be to plot the number of quanta at a given frequency, $n(\nu)$, against the frequency. The relation between the two terms is $E(\nu) = h\nu \cdot n(\nu)$, or the energy per unit area per unit time is equal to the number of quanta per unit area per unit time multiplied by the energy per quantum, $h\nu$. The total energy received over all frequencies is given by $E_{tot} = \int_0^\infty E(\nu)\, d\nu$ and can be found by determining the area under the curve of the plot of $E(\nu)$ vs. ν, or by direct measurement with a total-energy receiver.

As pointed out previously, devices operating by quantum processes can absorb usefully only energy above a threshold frequency, ν_0. Assuming complete absorption above the threshold, the maximum number of quanta usefully absorbed is given by

$$n_u = \int_{\nu_0}^\infty n(\nu)\, d\nu$$

or by

$$n_u = \int_0^\infty n(\nu)\, d\nu - \int_0^{\nu_0} n(\nu)\, d\nu$$

$$= n_{tot} - n_{non-u}$$

Consideration of the character of most quantum processes indicates that energy of a quantum in excess of that at the threshold is not used so that the useful energy in each quantum is $h\nu_0$. Hence, the total useful energy is

$$E_u = n_u h\nu_0$$

$$= h\nu_0 \int_{\nu_0}^\infty n(\nu)\, d\nu$$

The maximum efficiency for any given value of ν_0 then becomes

$$\xi = \frac{E_u}{E_{tot}} = \frac{h\nu_0 \int_{\nu_0}^\infty n(\nu)\, d\nu}{\int_0^\infty n(\nu) h\nu\, d\nu}$$

and this can be evaluated from experimentally determinable curves for $n(\nu)$ vs. ν, by using various values for the threshold.

Under the assumptions made, it can be seen that an optimum threshold value should exist since a decrease in the threshold value means that more of the total quanta are being used but a smaller fraction of the energy of each quantum. The optimum value can be found by finding the maximum value for $h\nu_0 \cdot \int_{\nu_0}^{\infty} n(\nu) \, d\nu$, or if an analytical expression for ξ in terms of ν_0 can be found, by setting the derivative of ξ with respect to ν_0 equal to zero and solving for ν_0, i.e.

$$\nu_{\mathrm{opt}} = \nu_0, \qquad \text{for } \frac{d\xi}{d\nu_0} = 0$$

The optimum value will vary according to the spectral distribution of solar energy as received at the earth and this in turn varies according to time of day, season, and atmospheric conditions.

The energy distribution emitted by the sun is often considered to be approximately that of a black body at 6,000° K, but the distribution as received at the earth's surface is substantially different due to absorption by water vapor, by oxygen, by ozone, and other scattering effects. A rough calculation, however, can be made (as shown below) by assuming the black-body distribution to hold at the earth's surface and neglecting the other effects. If one considers the solar radiation received at the earth's surface to be that from a black body at 6,000° K, one arrives at an optimum threshold wave length of 11,100 Å, and the efficiency for this choice of threshold is 44 per cent. An even greater efficiency can be expected when it is recalled that the chief departures of the solar spectrum at the earth from the black-body curve are due to absorption by the atmosphere in the infrared.

Several words of caution must be mentioned since the preceding discussion is so highly simplified. First, it must not be inferred that the second law of thermodynamics does not apply to this radiation reception process even though the application is not obvious. (It is to be noted that the solution below for x_0 does not contain the temperature explicitly and would predict the same efficiency for black-body radiation from the room, an obvious absurdity.) For the case of radiation received by a 300° K body from a 6,000° K body, the limitation due to the second law need not be introduced explicitly.

Another ramification is that absorption is not necessarily complete at all frequencies above the threshold. This suggests the possibility of a further increase in efficiency by passing the light through a succession of absorbing and converting systems, each with a different threshold and only a limited range of absorption above the threshold. Alternatively, light-dispersing devices can be used in front of an array of converters of various thresholds.

Another aspect to be considered is the minimization of the degradation of the energy by back drift. This is discussed elsewhere in this series for the particular case of photovoltaic cells. For photochemical reactions, the reverse reaction should be slow and not affected by light; e.g. for

$$A \underset{k_2}{\overset{k_1 + k_3 I}{\rightleftharpoons}} B,$$

the displacement of the equilibrium is increased as $k_3 I$ is made large compared to k_2. The continuous removal of products from the reaction system seems particularly useful, such as the generation of hydrogen and oxygen in the reactions studied by L. J. Heidt (Section IX).

Rough Calculation of Optimum Threshold Wave Length.—According to Planck's radiation law, the energy per cm² per second emitted at a frequency, ν, by a black body at temperature, T, is

$$E'(\nu) = \frac{2\pi\nu^2}{c^2} \cdot \frac{h\nu}{e^{h\nu/kT} - 1}$$

Under the assumptions made, the energy distribution at the earth will be proportional to this because of the geometry of the system.

$$E(\nu) = AE'(\nu)$$

This constant, A, can be evaluated since

$$E_{tot} = \int_0^\infty E(\nu)\, d\nu = \int_0^\infty A \cdot E'(\nu)\, d\nu = A\sigma T^4$$

where σ is the Stefan constant, 5.735×10^{-5} erg cm⁻² sec⁻¹ deg⁻⁴.

From the previous discussion, it follows that

$$n(\nu) = A\,\frac{2\pi\nu^2}{c^2} \cdot \frac{1}{e^{h\nu/kT} - 1}$$

It is useful to change the variable to $x = \dfrac{h\nu}{kT}$ so that

$$\xi = \frac{E_u}{E_{tot}} = \frac{x_0 \displaystyle\int_{x_0}^\infty x^2 (e^x - 1)^{-1}\, dx}{\displaystyle\int_0^\infty x^3 (e^x - 1)^{-1}\, dx}$$

The evaluation of the denominator is given by Richtmyer and Kennard (*Introduction to Modern Physics*, 3rd ed., p. 181) as $\pi^4/15$. Hence,

$$\xi = \frac{15}{\pi^4} x_0 \int_{x_0}^{\infty} x^2 (e^x - 1)^{-1} \, dx$$

The condition for finding the optimum threshold lies in maximizing the efficiency so that $d\xi/dx_0 = 0$. Hence,

$$\int_{x_0}^{\infty} x^2 (e^x - 1)^{-1} \, dx - x_0^3 (e^{x_0} - 1)^{-1} = 0$$

The evaluation of the integral which is the first term proceeds by using

$$(e^x - 1)^{-1} = \sum_{n=1}^{\infty} e^{-nx}$$

$$\int_{x_0}^{\infty} x^2 (e^x - 1)^{-1} \, dx = \sum_{n=1}^{\infty} e^{-nx_0} \left(\frac{x_0^2}{n} + \frac{2x_0}{n^2} + \frac{2}{n^3} \right)$$

The optimum value of x_0 can be found by successive approximations to be 2.17. The efficiency for this value of x_0 is 44 per cent. For a black body at $6{,}000°$ K, the optimum threshold wave length is 11,100 Å.

Photovoltaic Cells in Solar Energy Conversion

D. Trivich, Paul A. Flinn, H. J. Bowlden

Research on photovoltaic cells at Wayne University is sponsored by the United States Air Force under Contract No. AF 18(600)–481 monitored by the Office of Scientific Research.

Photovoltaic cells convert light energy directly into electrical energy; and since they do not require the consumption or cycling of any material, they offer a particularly attractive possibility for solar-energy conversion. Further possible advantages will be mentioned in the later discussion.

A previous paper by one of us (*21*) reviewed the physical constitution and properties of photovoltaic cells and the background material on semiconductors necessary for an understanding of the mechanism of the photovoltaic effect. It will, therefore, not be necessary to discuss these matters in any detail here. We shall try to focus attention on those aspects of the problem which seem to us to be most important for a consideration of the use of photovoltaic cells for conversion of solar energy.

A photovoltaic cell in its most common form consists of a thin film of a semiconductor in contact with another appropriate material, usually a metal. Recently it has been shown that photovoltaic junctions can be constructed by placing two semiconductors in contact, one semiconductor being of the excess or *n*-type, and the other being of the deficit or *p*-type. The most common examples of photovoltaic cells are the cuprous oxide cell and the selenium cell, both of which have been used extensively in photoelectric devices such as photographic exposure meters. The more recent *n-p* type of photovoltaic junction has been developed as an outgrowth of transistor research, particularly with germanium and silicon.

The mechanism of the photovoltaic effect is illustrated in Figure 36, for the case of the *n-p* junction. The intrinsic semiconductor has a lower completely filled band and an upper completely empty band separated by a forbidden energy region or gap of width ϵ. No conduction is possible unless there are current carriers (electrons) and easily available empty levels for them to move into. Thermal excitation of some electrons from the filled band to the empty band gives rise to conduction, both by the

149

electrons in the upper, the "conduction" band, and also by the "positive holes" in the lower band. In the n-type of semiconductor (Figure 36A), donor impurities, which in the case of germanium may be Group V elements such as antimony, have filled electron levels near the conduction band of the semiconductor and these electrons are easily excited thermally to the conduction band. In the p-type (Figure 36B) acceptor impurities, which in the case of germanium may be Group III elements such as gallium or aluminum, receive electrons thermally from the completely filled band, and thus create holes in this band which make conduction possible.

When the two types of semiconductors are placed in contact, the topmost electrons in the n-type are momentarily at higher energy states than the topmost electrons in the p-type. A transfer of electrons occurs

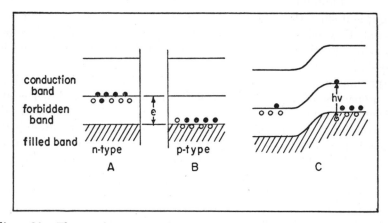

Figure 36.—The mechanism of the photovoltaic effect. Solid circles represent electrons or filled impurity levels; open circles represent holes or empty impurity levels.

from the n-type to the p-type semiconductor, charging the p side of the junction negatively with respect to the n side. This progressively raises the energy levels in the p side relative to the n side until equilibrium is attained as shown in Figure 36C (when the Fermi levels of the two are equal). This creates an energy barrier at the junction.

When such an assembly is illuminated by light of frequency greater than ϵ/h, electrons are lifted from the lower band to the upper band. These electrons may return by various degradation processes; or in the vicinity of the junction, an appreciable number may be driven by the charging potential across the junction from the p side to the n side. These latter electrons may be passed around through an external circuit, and therefore constitute a photoelectric current. In the absence of an external circuit, the flow of electrons will act to upset the normal thermal equilibrium at the junction, diminishing the magnitude of the negative charge of the p side relative to the n side. This diminution is observable externally under null-current measurements as an "open circuit potential."

Such photovoltaic cells will show response beginning at the threshold frequency and extending to higher frequencies, the actual photoelectric current depending upon the amount of light absorbed, the efficiency of production of photoelectrons, and the efficiency of delivery of the electrons to the external circuit. Under short-circuit conditions, the external current is directly proportional to light intensity. Under open-circuit conditions, the potential gradually approaches a limiting value with increasing light intensity. Under limited load conditions, the external current falls short of the linear relation by an increasingly wide margin with increasing intensity because of a variable internal shunting resistance due to a back drift of electrons across the junction. An optimum external load resistance equal to the internal resistance exists for any given set of conditions. The current output is proportional also to the area of the cell, so that another advantage of photovoltaic cells as solar-energy convertors is that they do not require bulky and expensive light concentrators such as lenses and mirrors.

The properties of photovoltaic cells needed for calculations of energy efficiency have been studied by a number of investigators. The most pertinent studies were done by Billig and Plessner (1), and we shall quote most extensively from these authors to illustrate our points. Their measurements were made on commercial selenium cells of 1.5 cm² area. Table 12

TABLE 12
Photoelectric Efficiencies of Selenium Cells

Light	Incident intensity $\mu w/cm^2$	I_{sc} μa	V_o mV	Max. power μw	Quantum yield %	Voltage eff'cy %	Power eff'cy %
Hg, 4358 Å	52.5	12.1	130.	0.61	44	4.6	0.78
5461 Å	144.	36.2	200.	2.65	38	8.8	1.22
5770, 5790 Å	177.	43.5	200.	3.18	35	9.3	1.20
5461 Å (filter)	730.	164.	307.	15.4	34	13.5	1.41
Daylight (overcast sky)	1,350.	166.	310.	19.2	..	....	0.95
Direct sunlight (Jan. 26, noon)	54,700.	935.	526.	150.	..	....	0.183
100 w incandescent lamp at 30 cm	5,380.	55.5	220.	4.78	..	....	0.059

gives measured values of short-circuit current, I_{sc}, and open-circuit potential, V_o, for various qualities and intensities of light. The maximum power output was calculated by assuming the average current under optimum load conditions to be 0.6 of the short-circuit current and the voltage under load to be 0.6 of the open-circuit potential, giving a load factor of 0.36. The power efficiency is also given.

Further, as proposed by Billig and Plessner, one can break down the power efficiency into a product of a quantum yield and voltage efficiency multiplied by the 0.36 load factor. The quantum yield is the number of short-circuit photoelectrons per incident photon, and the voltage efficiency is the open-circuit voltage divided by the voltage equivalent of the photon

$$V = \frac{hc}{e\lambda} = \frac{12,400}{\lambda_{\text{Å}}} .$$

Examination of these figures shows that the power efficiency for solar energy conversion is quite low, 0.2 per cent. Part of the reason for the low efficiency is the unfavorable spectral sensitivity of the selenium type cell, which falls off sharply at wave lengths above 6,000 Å, thus losing a considerable portion of the solar spectrum. At more favorable wave lengths, the power efficiency for the selenium cell is of the order of 1 per cent, and this figure can probably be taken as a fair representation of present attainability with cells of good spectral sensitivity match.

Various calculations could be made regarding the probable economics of solar energy conversion by photovoltaic cells, but these would be too nebulous until a detailed design is specified. On the average in the North, 1 square yard receives about 1,400 kwhr of solar energy per year, and at present the individual small consumer pays 2 cents per kwhr, or $28 for this much energy. At conversion efficiency of 1 per cent and a yearly upkeep and amortization cost equal to one-tenth of the capital cost, one could presently tolerate an investment cost of $2.80 per square yard of photocell area and associated equipment. An increase in the competitive cost of electricity or an increase in efficiency or time of amortization would lead to a higher tolerance for investment cost. It appears at present that the most logical approach lies in further research to improve the power efficiency.

If one examines the data in Table 12, it becomes evident that the quantum yield—i.e., the number of electrons per photon—is fairly high, about 35 per cent in the data quoted. Other investigators have cited even higher values; for example, Kingsbury and Ohl (*13*) found that silicon cells had a peak efficiency exceeding 70 per cent (after correcting for reflectance loss) and efficiencies exceeding 50 per cent from 5,000 Å to 8,500 Å.

A discussion of voltage efficiency cannot be divorced from a consideration of the threshold limit. As shown by us elsewhere in these pages, there should exist an optimum threshold frequency for solar-energy conversion by a single quantum process, as pictured here for photovoltaic cells. A rough calculation indicates this to be about 12,000 Å. In the photovoltaic cell, as shown in Figure 36, this indicates that a good semiconductor material should have an energy gap ϵ, of about 1.0 volts. Silicon with an energy gap of 1.2 volts should offer a promising start.

However, as shown in Table 12, only a small portion of the voltage equivalent of a photon is realized to drive electrons through an external circuit, e.g., the most favorable value for which a definite calculation could be made is 13.5 per cent. It should be noted that these measurements were made at moderate light intensities and that increasing light intensity increases the voltage efficiency and decreases the quantum yield. As shown in Table 12, direct sunlight on a selenium cell gives an open-circuit potential of 526 millivolts. Taking the threshold of selenium to be 8,000 Å or 1.5 volts, the voltage efficiency is about 30 per cent. However, the short-circuit current under full sunlight has risen much less than proportionately.

The explanation for the losses discussed apparently lies mostly in the internal shunting of photovoltaic cells, i.e., the back-diffusion of electrons across the barrier. Under short-circuit conditions and low light intensities, the back-diffusion process does not interfere seriously so that relatively high current efficiencies can be observed. At high light intensities, the current efficiency is greatly lowered because of the reverse flow. Under open-circuit conditions, illumination causes a displacement of the normal thermal distribution of electrons at the junction, resulting in a photo-potential at which the reverse flow equals the flow of photoelectrons across the barrier. Low light intensities lead to only a small displacement of equilibrium and thus low photopotentials. High intensities increase both but at a decreasing rate since the back-diffusion process is still further enhanced.

It appears that some improvement in power efficiency can be made by reducing the back-diffusion process. Presumably this can be brought about by reducing the conductivity of the photovoltaic cell in the low resistance direction, which is the direction for back diffusion. The conductivity of semiconductors, apart from some of the photoconductivity, can be decreased by reducing the impurity content. However, caution must be exercised in this direction since the existence of the necessary junction is due to the character conferred on the semiconductors by the impurities. Also the reduction of the impurity content will lead to an increase in series resistance so that thinner films may be necessary. This in turn may require a stacking of cells or some other method of improving the light-absorption process. It should be pointed out that the mobility of current carriers depends on impurity content but only at higher impurity contents than those of interest here.

The reduction of the back-diffusion process is only part of the total problem. For example, the spectral sensitivity must be improved so that current efficiency is uniformly high at all wave lengths below the threshold. Reflection losses must be reduced or multiple-reflection assemblies used. Probably any realization of practical solar-energy conversion by photovoltaic cells will come about from some improvements in several respects. It should also be mentioned that research in new and improved methods of energy storage will be required.

It is easy to envision practical use of photovoltaic cells if power efficiencies of 5–10 per cent could be consistently attained with not too expensive assemblies. At present, silicon appears to be a promising material for investigation. However, the field of semiconductors, particularly of alloys and compounds, has scarcely been touched and a wide field for further investigation remains.

Section VII

Solar Furnaces

Although the chief difficulty in producing power from the sun's energy is the limitation of low temperatures, it is true also that solar energy is used for achieving the highest possible temperatures for laboratory research. A large parabolic mirror focusing radiation on a small area can give temperatures of over 3,000° C. Pioneers in this aspect of solar-energy uses describe in this section their specialized equipment and their results. The editors are particularly pleased to include a contribution from a laboratory in France which has done important work in this field. This paper was not presented at the symposium.

Utilization of Solar Energy for the Attainment of High Temperatures

J. Farber

Introduction.—The attainment of high temperatures is a necessity for an industrial society. Metallurgy, chemical synthesis, fabrication, heating, lighting, etc., are dependent on the ability to attain high temperatures. In addition, much of present-day research is in the field of high temperatures.

The common methods used to achieve the required temperatures are flames, electrical resistance heating, induction heating, and electric arc. Short-time heating at high temperatures can be obtained by "exploding" wires, detonations, and shock waves. Finally, occasional use is made of electron bombardment.

In each case there exist some drawbacks as to possible applications. One is limited by the shortness of time, the products produced, electric and magnetic fields, the necessity of special materials that can contaminate, and limitations of furnace materials as to temperatures attainable.

Since we live in an age "confined" by the second law of thermodynamics, the attainment of high temperature comes with difficulty. Yet, "hanging" in the sky is a body radiating energy to the earth at a "surface" temperature in the neighborhood of 6,000° K (the assignment of a more definite value is dependent upon the method of estimating the surface temperature). It has run across the minds of many that it should be possible, in some manner, to approach this extremely high temperature on earth. It is towards this end that the concentration of the sun's radiation has been achieved by means of parabolic mirrors and lenses. It has been possible by these means to achieve relatively high temperatures in a short period of time and for durations up to eight hours, depending on the weather conditions, time of year, and location. It is possible, by a suitable enclosure of the samples to be heated, to obtain any desired transparent atmosphere free of electric and magnetic fields, contamination, and reaction with sample holders or furnace elements.

Historical.—The earliest use of solar radiation to attain elevated temperatures is generally attributed to Archimedes. In the year 215 B.C.

Archimedes is supposed to have used a large hexagonal mirror to burn the Roman fleet which besieged Syracuse. A similar feat is attributed to Procus, who in 614 A.D. used brass mirrors to burn the fleet besieging Constantinople. Perhaps the results of Buffon (*1*) can give an air of validity to these claims attributed to the "ancients." Buffon, using a large number of small flat mirrors and superimposing the images formed, was able to melt some metal and kindle wood at a distance of 65 meters.

Another early record reports the use of concentrated radiation by the Athenians to light the sacred fires of Vesta by means of a polished concave gold surface.

The first evidence of the attainment of high temperatures by means of solar radiation is the use by Averani and Targioni in 1695, at Florence, of a large burning glass to make a diamond, previously considered unalterable, disappear. During this same period a large number of lenses and concave mirrors were made and innumerable fusions and combustions were studied. The better concave mirrors were made of copper, tin, and arsenic. The surface curvature was obtained by careful polishing. These radiation collectors varied in size and some were reported to be as large as 3 meters in diameter.

Much research was done with these early solar furnaces. Tschirnhaus, around 1700, using a 0.97 meter diameter lens, was able to melt slate, china, talc, and tile. He observed that black materials were easier to heat than white. Lavoisier is well noted for his use of solar energy to demonstrate that diamond was another form of carbon. He was one of the first to use an adjustable mounting and envelope around his specimen. This was accomplished back in 1770!

Since that time, lenses and reflectors have been used intermittently for various purposes, but without any appreciable contribution to the development of these instruments.

Present.—The present era may be considered to begin with the building of a small two-lens, adjustable mounting, enclosed sample solar furnace by Stock and Heyneman (*9*). Because of the development for military purposes of large searchlight mirrors, which meet the needs of solar furnaces perfectly, a large number of these mirrors have been recently used for this purpose. By using these searchlight mirrors of a high aperture parabolic shape as collectors of solar radiation, one can readily attain high temperatures. For reflectors, the parabola is as near an ideal shape as can be obtained because any light parallel to its optical axis will be reflected at its surface so that the light will pass through its focal point. The higher the relative aperture (diameter/focal length of mirror), the greater will be the concentration of light at the focal area. The diameter of the image obtained is the product of the distance of the mirror from the focal point and the angle subtended by the source (for the sun the angle is 32′ or .00931 radians, on the average). In the case of small aperture mirrors as used in the telescopes, use of the product of the focal length and angle subtended by the image is precise enough for determining the diameter of the focal area. For large-aperture mirrors, the diameter of the image varies as one goes from the optical axis to the outer edge of the mirror. This property of parabolas, i.e., the increase of distance from the mirror to the focal point with increasing aperture, causes a doubling of the image diameter at 90° aperture (as measured at the focus from the optical axis to the edge of the mirror). The collecting area increases as the aperture increases; but this, to some extent, is negated by distribution of the collected radiation over a larger area. To obtain very high temperatures, it is necessary to concentrate the energy in as small an area as possible.

To attain high temperatures one needs a target for the intense radiation. This target introduces additional problems with large-aperture reflectors. At large angles, a flat target will reflect most of the light coming to it and, at 90° aperture, all the light, according to Lambert's Law. These large angles also spread the image over a large area of the focal plane. Thus, the largest area of a mirror of 90° aperture is completely ineffective. An analysis shows, taking into account reflection at the target and mirror and change of image size with angle, that the maximum input to a flat collector is at 35° and that beyond 70° no appreciable contribution is obtained to the total flux density. The situation is somewhat altered for the case of a hemispherical target, in which case the radiation is received even at 90°. However, since the area of the hemisphere is twice that of the flat target, it is found that the flux per unit area is slightly lower than for the flat target. The maximum effective area on a mirror for the hemispherical target is found to be at 40° aperture.

The other method used to concentrate light is by means of lenses. The only known large installation of this type in use is the one used by Professor Duwez at the California Institute of Technology. Here the light is refracted by lenses onto mirrors which reflect it through an almost hemispherical nest of smaller lenses, which further concentrates the light. The distances traveled by the light are almost constant. However, the problems of spherical and chromatic aberration become important. In addition, there is still the reflection problem at high angles at the target.

A question often asked is, what is the highest temperature possible with a solar furnace? Trombe (*13*) calculates the maximum temperature obtainable by taking all the energy hitting the surface of the solar furnace per unit time and assuming it all goes into the area calculated by use of the focal length and angle subtended by sun. For a perfect target and mirror above the atmosphere of the earth, such a calculation yields a temperature of 8,200° K, obviously a violation of the second law of thermodynamics. However, Trombe, by assuming losses due to atmospheric absorption and scattering and reflection losses of mirror, has calculated temperatures only to 5,300° K.

If the possible temperature attainable is calculated by taking into account the change of image size and the reflectivity of the target by use of Lambert's Law, it is found that the maximum attainable temperature would be 5,100° K above the atmosphere of the earth for a mirror of 100 per cent reflectivity and a flat black-body target. The temperature is a calculated one based on the assumption that radiation to a "surface" is equal to the radiation emitted. Under good conditions at the earth's surface, it is probable that a temperature of 4,000° K can be obtained.

Large Solar Furnaces in Use at the Present Time.—Reports of the utilization of searchlight reflectors of large aperture as solar furnaces are being made continually by various institutions. The furnaces of large diameter (over 1 meter) are few in number. Since these furnaces are the ones that give an image which is easily worked with, a brief description of some of them will be given. Conn gives further data in the following paper.

Since 1921, a series of large mirrors has been constructed. Straubel (*10*) used silvered-glass searchlight mirrors made for him at the Zeiss Works in Jena. The mirrors were 2 meters in diameter and had a focal length of 86 cm. In the first furnace Straubel had the light reflected from the parabolic mirror to a plane mirror and from there reflected to a lens which focused the light on the samples which could be enclosed in an envelope. He found that the smaller reflective mirror overheated and that it would crack in a short time. To avoid this difficulty, Straubel used a stationary parabolic mirror and used a flat mirror to follow the apparent motion of the sun, thus obtaining a fixed focal point and ease of instrumentation.

After the last war, the French government obtained a number of German searchlight mirrors. There are two principal groups in France which have used these mirrors. One of them is the group under Angot and the other at Mont-Louis under Professor F. Trombe. The mirrors obtained were 2 meters in diameter, 83 cm focal length, and had a silvered-glass surface. In addition, the Mont-Louis group set up a huge semi-industrial type of high-temperature furnace 10.5 meters in diameter, 6 meters focal length, composed of 3,500 mirrors of silvered glass. It is described in detail in Professor Trombe's contribution to this book (Section VII).

Conn (*4*) spun an aluminum mirror 3 meters in diameter and 0.86

meters focal length, having an image diameter of 0.8 cm. In addition, Conn used smaller 1.5–meter rhodium on copper mirrors inside the large mirror. Couchet (*6*) in Algiers has used a 1.5–meter solar furnace to fuse alumino silicates.

Instrumentation of Furnaces.—The apparent movement of the sun through the sky and its change of declination daily necessitates a mounting of the solar furnaces, or the auxiliary flat mirrors, that will allow for easy movement. The equatorial mounting seems to be most popular. The declination is set each day and the motion through the sky is followed by photocells, bimetallic strips, astronomical clocks (synchronous motors or falling arm with governor), or by manual operation.

The intensity at the target has been varied by means of a diaphragm over the entire mirror, by a reflecting cylinder near the target, and by defocusing.

Temperature measurements are made on the targets by optical pyrometers by the use of rotating sectors which eliminate the incident radiation. Recently, attempts have been made to measure the energy flux at the image and this has been accomplished by use of a water-cooled "blackbody" cavity, air blown through a porous plug, and by short-time heating of a cone cavity (*7*).

Future.—Very recently Trombe (*23, 28, 30*) has been investigating the possibilities of using solar furnaces as industrial tools. His major efforts have been in the field of nitrogen fixation and the melting of iron. It is Trombe's belief that it is a waste of high-temperature energy to vaporize steam when the same amount of energy can melt iron.

The past uses of the solar furnace have been primarily confined to the study of ceramic materials and their products. This instrument easily provides a high temperature, controllable atmosphere heat source. In the way of research the solar furnace is also adaptable to the study of the thermodynamic properties of refractory materials. Since it is a source of high energy density, it can be used to evaluate thermal shock resistivity.

The quantitative evaluation of the solar furnace has only begun and it is to be expected that when it is completed an optimum type of furnace may be designed and constructed and that its use as a modern research tool may be greatly enhanced.

Trombe has only, optimistically speaking, begun to scratch the surface as to the potential industrial applications of solar furnaces. The problem of low total energy flux, obtainable even with the largest of the furnaces, would tend to preclude practical applications; yet the very peculiar special conditions obtainable with solar furnaces may be just what some particular industry needs.

Solar Furnaces for Attaining High Temperatures

William M. Conn

Introduction.—Solar furnaces for attaining high temperatures may be divided into two groups: (1) experimental furnaces for pure research work, and (2) semi-industrial furnaces. The first group includes furnaces for attaining high temperatures by concentrating solar energy in a small area into which the sample to be heated is brought. Paraboloidal mirrors are used, as a rule, similar in design and definition to searchlight mirrors. The greater the focal length, the greater will be the diameter of the image of the sun; and the larger the aperture, the greater will be the amount of solar energy collected. Experimental solar furnaces may be operated with fixed values of aperture and focal length, or with variable effective aperture, or with variable focal length.

The second group of solar furnaces includes semi-industrial units. They have been used for the melting of alloy steels, the fixation of nitrogen, etc.

Principal advantages and disadvantages of a solar furnace in comparison to other means of obtaining very high temperatures may be summarized as follows: Heating samples by solar energy presents a means of carrying out experiments under very pure conditions in an atmosphere which remains oxidizing up to the highest temperatures. No interference occurs from electric or magnetic fields, from products of combustion, or from heated furnace walls made from materials different from the sample being tested. Specimens may be heated or heat-treated in predetermined cycles. Physical changes occurring in a sample may be directly observed up to the highest temperatures while the material is heating or cooling. Furnaces heated by gas, oil, coal, or electric energy can be heated for twenty-four hours, while solar furnaces can only be used during daylight hours. Solar furnaces depend on favorable atmospheric conditions. The area of heating is limited in size depending on the focal length of the main mirror and the definition of the sun's image.

Solar Furnaces Used for Experimental Work: (1) *Constant Aperture and Constant Focal Length.*—The best-known units of this type are described by Straubel (*10*) and Trombe (*13*). The incident energy from the sun is collected by means of a paraboloidal mirror in a small area. In some cases, the parabolic mirror remains stationary and a plane mirror is used as a heliostat which follows the apparent movement of the sun. In other cases, a plane or convex mirror is inserted between the main mirror and the sample in order to shift the image of the sun to a desired location or to change its size.

The sample to be tested is brought into the image of the sun where it quickly melts if sufficient energy is available. The products of melting are collected in a crucible made from or lined with the same material that is being studied. Melting can be carried out in oxidizing atmosphere or the sample and its holder can be enclosed in a transparent container for heating in vacuum or at elevated pressure, with or without protecting atmosphere.

(2) *Variable Apparent Aperture.*—A shutter in the form of a cylinder which moves along the axis of the paraboloidal mirror was introduced by Conn (*4*). It serves for control of the amount of incident radiation by varying the effective aperture of the mirror. Since the position of the control cylinder can be closely adjusted, an accurate control of the temperature of the sample is possible, the temperature equilibrium attained being a function of the amount of incident and absorbed radiation, emitted radiation, and losses by convection and conduction.

The temperature of a sample heated below its melting point can be observed on the side opposite to the incident radiation if the sample is small enough to attain uniform temperature. In most other cases, however, a small sample will melt quickly. It becomes necessary to measure the temperature of the sample or target from the same side from which it receives radiant energy. The result is that the incident radiation from the sun (reflected by the concave mirror) and the temperature radiation of the sample are superimposed. They are separated by means of two sectors which intermittently block out the incident radiation from the sample while temperature readings are taken. The sectors rotate at 2,500 rpm (*3*).

(3) *Variable Focal Length.*—The mirror made from glass or metal was replaced by a surface of liquid mercury by Wood (*11*), the mercury rotating with and in a container at constant angular velocity. The surface of the liquid forms a paraboloid of revolution, the shape of which depends upon the characteristics of the liquid and its angular velocity. A change in the rate of revolution causes a change of focal length. At the same time, the diameter of the sun's image changes, and also the amount of energy received per unit area of the sample, causing an increase or decrease of the temperature of the target. Since the rate of revolution of the liquid can be easily adjusted, close control of the temperature of the sample is attained.

Solar Furnaces for Semi-Industrial Installations.—The first units were built many years ago. A modern type was developed by Trombe (*30, 31*). The one-piece paraboloidal mirror of solar furnaces serving for experimental work is replaced by a composite mirror in which 3,500 small glass mirrors are used to obtain a large image of the sun. This permits pilot-plant development. For example, a considerable output of fixed nitrogen was obtained in this installation. This furnace is described by Trombe in the following paper.

Tabulation of Data for Solar Furnaces.—Table 13 presents a summary of dimensions of experimental and semi-industrial solar furnaces which have been in use recently (*5*). The sequence of the table is based on the apertures of the main mirror. For example, with the furnace noted in Table 13 as Kansas City IV (now at San Diego) it should be possible, according to computations by Dr. Farber of Consolidated-Vultee, to obtain a maximum temperature of 4,000° K for a flat target, and 4,200° K for a hemispherical one.

Fields of Use for Solar Furnaces.—Some of the fields of study for which solar furnaces are suggested are: the high-temperature chemistry and physics of silicates, high-melting oxides, borides, carbides, silicides, and nitrides; the thermal properties of materials in solid or gaseous form at high temperatures; the determination of liquidus curves (*2*); the production of glasses with high refractive indices; the growing of single crystals; and the development of heat-resistant alloys. Other fields of high-temperature research are: the determination of the heat flux at the focus of the concave mirror up to the highest temperatures attainable; the rate of transfer of heat for various mirror combinations; and high-temperature spectrographic work.

TABLE 13
Data for Solar Furnaces

	Kansas City I	Kansas City II	Jena I	Jena II	Jena III	Meudon	Mont-Louis I	Kansas City III	Kansas City IV††	Mont-Louis II
One piece or composite mirror	1 piece	1 piece	1 piece	1 piece	1 piece	1 piece	1 piece	3 zones	1 piece	3500 plates
Material of main mirror	Cu	Cu	glass	glass	glass	glass	glass	Al	Al	glass
Reflecting material	Rh	Rh	Ag	Ag	Ag	Ag	Ag	Al	Al	Ag
Reflecting surface	1st	1st	2d	2d	2d	2d	2d	1st	1st	2d
Aperture of main mirror	60.0"	60.0"	69.0"	78.7"	78.7"	78.7"	78.7"	120.0"	120.0"	35.0'
Focal length of main mirror	25.75"	26.0"	35.4"	33.9"	33.9"	33.5"	33.5"	34.0"	34.0"	19.7'
Focal ratio of main mirror, f/	0.43	0.43	0.51	0.43	0.43	0.43	0.43	0.28	0.28	0.56
Diameter of sun's image (computed)	0.24"	0.24"	0.33"	0.32"	0.32"	0.31"	0.31"	3"×0.32"	0.32"	2.20"
Diameter of central opening in main mirror	......	8.3"	......	12.0"	7.9"	......	......	22."	22."	66."
Auxiliary mirror	None	None	Newtonian	Cassegrainian	Heliostat*	Newtonian†	Newtonian†	None	None	Heliostat‡

166

TABLE 13 (Continued)

	Kansas City I	Kansas City II	Jena I	Jena II	Jena III	Meudon	Mont-Louis I	Kansas City III	Kansas City IV††	Mont-Louis II
Mounting	Altazimuth	Equatorial	Equatorial	Equatorial	Stationary	Altazimuth	Altazimuth	Equatorial	Equatorial	Stationary
Guiding	Manual	Astronom. controller	bimetal resistor	bimetal resistor	bimetal resistor	manual	manual	manual	astronom. controller	phototubes
Vacuum attachment	....	yes	....	yes	yes	....	....	....	yes	....
Temperature control	yes§	yes**	....	yes§	yes§	....	....	....	yes**	....

*98.4″ diameter with 33.1′ distance from main mirror. †17.7″ diameter with 3.9″ distance from focus. ‡Size 43′ × 34′ with 80′ distance from main mirror. §Shades or diaphragm. **Al cylinder and rotating sectors. ††Now in San Diego, California.

167

Development of Large-Scale Solar Furnaces

Felix Trombe

Modern solar furnaces receive their energy from convergent reflecting surfaces which are paraboloids or sections of paraboloids. The use of a reflecting surface makes possible optical apertures which are very much larger than those which are obtainable through a system of lenses. Experiments in both America and France have shown, in fact, that the concentration of solar energy in the focal point of a parabolic mirror makes it easily possible to attain a temperature of more than 3,000° C.

Until just recently, convergent assemblies made up of single-glass surfaces or of aluminum surfaces were expensive, and their net cost per square meter did not encourage their use other than for basic research. However, it can be said that the solar furnace has already rendered great service for such research and will certainly render much more. It is an exceptional tool to obtain high temperatures in conditioned environments, particularly in oxidizing atmospheres.

In order to increase the dimensions of convergent reflecting apparatus, it was necessary to adopt a completely different approach from the one which had been used to construct small mirrors. The more the dimensions of the assembly are enlarged, the less the curvature of the reflecting surface becomes, and the more difficult it becomes to make this reflecting surface effective.

Ground-glass surfaces are clearly prohibitive from the point of view of cost, and aluminum surfaces seem to be prohibitive as well; for even without taking into account the cost of stamping out of the reflectors, one must take into consideration the elasticity of the piece which has been shaped, and which is deformed after stamping. For slight curvatures, this distorting effect is important. This being the case, one is forced to adopt relatively large thicknesses of metal to avoid distortion.

Setting aside the preceding solutions, we have proposed another approach. Archimedes' arrangement of apparatus, or at least that attributed to him and used again by Buffon, is familiar. It consists of superimposing, on a single zone, the rays of the sun reflected by a number of flat mirrors. When these mirrors are very small and when their number is very large, in order to obtain the maximum energy, they are made tangent to an imaginary paraboloid fixed by the previously selected focal distance.

The preceding is true when the energy accumulates on the classic focal volume of the paraboloid, but it is perhaps slightly inexact when the energy is received on a plane perpendicular to the axis of the system. We will not examine this point in detail here.

The improvement which we have made on the apparatus of Buffon-Archimedes consists of placing flat mirrors under permanent mechanical deformations. In this way, by the proper choice of points of forward and backward loading on each of the mirrors, the mirrors can be given a curvature close to that of the paraboloid. This curvature has as its axis of revolution the axis of the paraboloid, and it is apparent that for a mirror situated very far from that axis the curvature would be dissymmetrical. Considering for example the apparatus developed at Mont-Louis, which is made up of 3,500 curved mirrors, this method made it possible to produce an energy concentration at the focal point of the apparatus equal to that which would result from the superposition of the reflections of approximately 20,000 flat mirrors.

Moreover, it is possible to do better, for the apparatus at Mont-Louis is made up of silvered window glass, adopted because of the necessity of having relatively thin mirrors, approximately 1.5 mm thick, in order to concentrate the rays 6 meters from the vertex of the paraboloid. In larger units, the window glass would be replaced by real mirror glass, approximately 4 mm thick, and the quality of the images would be very much superior. In an apparatus of 500 to 1,000 kw, for example, such mirrors could be used.

The furnace at Mont-Louis, with the concentration which has been used, produces a temperature of approximately 3,000° C. Larger units would certainly produce energy concentrations twice as large, which is to say that, under the best conditions, temperatures of 3,600° to 3,700° C will be obtained.

The Mont-Louis paraboloid was produced by adjustment, in the laboratory, in the following manner: The elementary mirrors are mounted on a support plate on which are located the guideways, the back-loading pieces, and the forward-bend crosses of the mirror, as shown in Figure 38. In a single ring of the paraboloid are placed side by side support plates which are identical in their profile, as are the bent mirrors which they support. The complete apparatus has five rings, each made up of support plates of a different model.

The adjustment is done very simply, in the laboratory, by placing the support plates along a semiparabola having the characteristics of the one

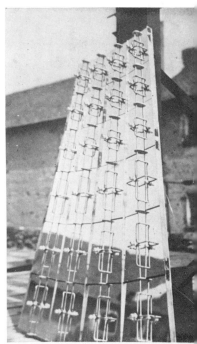

(*Above*) *Figure* 37.—Parabolic mirror with an area of 90 square meters and focal length of 6 meters. (*Right*) *Figure* 38.—Support plate and elementary mirrors of the large parabolic reflector.

Figure 39.—Heliostat having an area of 135 square meters, used with large parabolic mirror.

after which the paraboloid will be modeled. It is sufficient to arrange a radiation source to represent that of the sun and to fix the geometric position of the focal point of the system. Each support plate of the same ring will have its assigned place, tangent to the parabola, and the adjustment of each of the basic mirrors of a plate will be accomplished, the others being masked, by observing the image which it casts on a plan of the focal area of the assembly. One can thus minimize the defects of each mirror and obtain optimum curvature for the one in question. It was in this fashion that, one after another, the 3,500 mirrors of the Mont-Louis apparatus were shaped and oriented while their focusing was observed. This important work is relatively simple when one compares it to other methods of constructing the paraboloids.

Such an apparatus is relatively inexpensive and extremely strong. Moreover, it does not go out of adjustment. The Mont-Louis apparatus has successfully resisted violent winds, which in some cases have damaged the heavy slate roofs of some of the old houses in the region of Cerdagnes in which Mont-Louis is located. No disturbance of the adjustment resulted and no mirrors were broken. Indeed, glass is an extremely strong material under certain conditions. It has a good resistance to mechanical deformations and its surface remains unchanged. The silvering applied to glass is relatively fragile, but it becomes very strong when it is protected by electrolytic copper plating. Apparatus at Mont-Louis which have had more than five years of outside exposure to all the intemperate forms of a mountain climate have resisted perfectly and are in excellent condition.

The orientation on the mirror of the sun's radiation, which has been achieved at Mont-Louis with an automatic heliostat, has not been discussed. However, this orientation offers no problem.

In conclusion, it may be said that solar furnaces can become apparatus of large sizes, collecting and concentrating considerable energy in a quite inexpensive manner. It appears that we are on the road to the construction of solar furnaces at costs quite close to the cost of wrought iron. We may hope in the future to reduce the price of costly parts to that of the framework. There now remains to be drawn up an economic balance sheet of solar power compared to hydroelectric power or power from coal.

We know now that we can approach in a profitable manner the manufacture of refined products, i.e., products which are necessarily expensive. We hope that little by little the solar furnace will come into use in production of some present-day products.

Section VIII

Photosynthetic Utilization of Solar Energy

Although the symposium did not cover agricultural processes which constitute the all-important utilization of solar energy through photosynthesis, one session was devoted to certain aspects of the mass culture of algae. Pilot-plant experiments have been carried out with sufficient data to consider fuel costs, and ideas for long-range possibilities are proposed.

The maximum efficiency of photosynthesis is high. It is discussed here as a challenge to future scientists to show that in spite of physical chemical difficulties solar energy *can* be stored effectively through photochemistry.

Efficiency of Photosynthesis

Farrington Daniels

The Wisconsin symposium on the utilization of solar energy excluded discussions of agriculture, although the growth of plants constitutes the oldest and almost the sole method yet available for the storage of solar energy. Enormous effort has gone into agricultural research and it has led to remarkable improvements in crop yields; but comparatively very little research has been devoted to understanding photosynthesis, which is the primary process underlying all agriculture. It is necessary to bring photosynthesis into these discussions, briefly, because it constitutes striking proof that solar energy can actually be stored and utilized through photochemical reactions. Nature has provided us with a pace-setter for the encouragement of future photochemists who will try to duplicate and improve on photosynthesis.

In photosynthesis, solar energy is stored by using it with the help of green chlorophyll in the living plant to combine water and carbon dioxide of the air with the formation of carbohydrate or organic material. The chemical reaction is

$$CO_2 + H_2O + Chlorophyll + light = (H_2CO) + O_2 + Chlorophyll$$

The formula (H_2CO) is taken to be one unit of a sugar or other carbohydrate. When it is burned with oxygen, the reverse process takes place and carbon dioxide and water are produced. This reaction evolves 112 kilocalories of heat per gram atom of carbon. This energy as food maintains life and provides animal and human work, and as fuel it produces heat at high temperatures which operates engines.

In order that carbon dioxide and water may combine to give carbohydrate and oxygen, it is necessary to supply at least the 112 kilocalories given back on reversing the process. In red light there are only 40 kilocalories per gram atom and so at least three units of light, three photons per molecule, are required to supply the 112 kilocalories.

Actually, considerably more than three photons per molecule would be expected because other energy-consuming reactions are likely to accompany the main reaction. Measurements in many laboratories by different methods show that under optimum conditions in the laboratory growing

175

algae require about 8 to 10 photons of light per molecule of carbon dioxide converted into carbohydrate. This corresponds with red light to an efficiency of about 30 per cent (i.e., $112/[9 \times 40]$). That is, about 30 per cent of the light actually absorbed can be stored and recovered later by burning organic material produced by the photosynthesis (*4, 7, 12, 14*). In these measurements the energy absorption is measured with thermopiles and the extent of the photosynthesis is followed by pressure measurements of carbon dioxide and oxygen, electrical determination of dissolved oxygen, infrared absorption measurements of carbon dioxide, or magnetic moment measurements of oxygen. It has been followed also by calorimetric measurements and by other means. There has been a controversy concerning this maximum laboratory efficiency, Warburg and Burk and their associates reporting 4 photons per molecule of carbon dioxide or a storage of about 70 per cent of the energy absorbed (*13*). Most of these measurements of 70 per cent and more efficiency have been made with manometers which measure the total pressure of gas under conditions where there is an argument concerning the interpretation of the data (*10, 15*).

The efficiency of solar-energy storage in agricultural crops is of course much less than is indicated by photosynthesis in laboratory algae carried out under optimum conditions. In the laboratory only the light absorbed by chlorophyll is measured, the carbon dioxide concentration is 3 per cent or more, the light intensity is low, and there is an ample supply of water and fertilizers. However, half of the sun's energy is in the infrared, which is not absorbed by chlorophyll and can take no part in photosynthesis. The growing season in the temperate zones is confined to a third of the year. The carbon dioxide present in the air is only 0.03 per cent and the sunlight is much too intense for high efficiency in photosynthesis. It is not surprising then to find that the utilization of solar energy in agriculture is comparatively low. An average corn crop produces about a ton of dry organic material per acre per year and if this is burned the heat produced is about 0.1 per cent of the total amount of solar radiation falling on the acre during the whole year. Many other crops and certain forests and algae production in lakes store 0.1 or 0.2 per cent or less of the annual solar energy.

Attempts have been made to use photosynthesis on a large scale under conditions more nearly like those obtainable in the laboratory. The mass culture of algae on a large scale in plastic bags with high carbon dioxide concentration is a step in this direction (*3*). There are serious technical difficulties caused by biological contamination and by overheating, but some investigators believe that a twentyfold increase over average agriculture may well be possible. The capital investment for the containing material, the pumps and engineering equipment, and extra carbon dioxide will of course cost much more than the price of the equivalent amount of agricultural land; but, on the other hand, the photosynthesis can be carried out on cheap land unsuitable for standard agriculture.

We are just beginning to understand the mechanism of photosynthesis. It is a remarkable process. It is not possible for several photons of light and a molecule of carbon dioxide and a molecule of water to collide simultaneously. A stepwise mechanism is involved. One photon activates one molecule of chlorophyll which in turn breaks up a water molecule to give a hydrogen atom which then reduces the carbon dioxide. A second photon liberates a second hydrogen atom, continuing the reduction, and thus the process continues until the carbohydrate is formed. There are side reactions and steps in the complicated mechanism which evolve heat, and so it is necessary to supply more than the theoretical minimum of three photons per molecule.

Research is going on in several laboratories with enzyme studies, radioactive tracers, spectrographic measurements, and chromatrographic separators which will throw more light on the mechanism of photosynthesis. Then eventually it may be possible to find other photochemical systems which can store solar energy in a similar way, possibly with greater efficiency or without the requirement of good soil.

Biological Cycles in the Transformation of Solar Energy into Useful Fuels

R. L. Meier

Over the past decade probably a larger quantity of vegetation has been used for fuel than at any previous date. At the same time the proportion of all the energy employed has been less than for any earlier period. This means that the increases in utilization of vegetation have been at a lower rate than the increases in utilization of energy as a whole. The fossil fuels have become general-purpose energy sources, leaving only lower-grade, somewhat specialized applications open to wood, bagasse, straw, etc. Withdrawals from the ongoing production of plants are limited to cooking fuel, steam-raising, space heating for dwelling in isolated areas, and similar purposes. Such applications as the generation of electricity, steelmaking, internal combustion engines, and chemical technology have been found to be relatively inefficient when mainly dependent upon the direct products of vegetation.

The most important difficulties encountered are: (1) the effort required for collecting and assembling vegetation; (2) bulkiness of the products, a low caloric value per unit volume; (3) the normally high water content of plant substances. The first is responsible for the high cost of important quantities of energy when delivered to a single point on the map; while the others make it exceedingly expensive to achieve high temperatures.

The capacity of the forests can be deduced from Glesinger's survey (*6*). To this must be added some agricultural waste. The total foreseeable output is roughly 2×10^{16} cal per year, which is quite insufficient for preserving even the present production of goods. The critical needs are for charcoal (coking coal substitute) and liquid fuels, because these cannot be met if the world depends upon photosynthesis in higher plants. We will therefore be limited by the inefficiencies of soils and the vagaries of weather.

Laboratory work on photosynthesis has demonstrated that much higher efficiencies for the conversion of solar energy into cell substance are possible when microscopic plants are grown dispersed in optimal media (*3*). The yields increase from 1–10 tons per acre average for higher plants to 20–35 tons, or even more, for microscopic plants. However, cell substance

179

grown under optimum conditions becomes predominantly protein. Therefore the principal prospective use is for food; but we shall consider here only the possibilities for conversion into the familiar kinds of fuel.

In outlining a possible sequence of conversions (Figure 40), one encounters immediately a gap in the scientific and technical literature. No work has been done, utilizing modern concepts, upon the products to be expected from the pyrolysis of hydrated proteins. By the use of chemical theory one is able to deduce from the composition of algae the kinds of products that should be obtained from pyrolysis, but not much about the over-all yields of useful products.

The process blocked out in Figure 40 is probably the most efficient means for the direct conversion of cell substance. It would yield a charcoal, a combustible gas, and several fractions of combustible liquids and tars. It has several important limitations however. Not the least of these is the

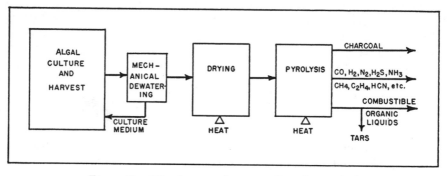

Figure 40.—Direct process for converting algae to fuel.

penetrating stench of pyrolysing proteins, but perhaps more significant is the energy required to separate the water of hydration from the organic material. Indeed, much engineering development would be necessary to reduce the energy required for processing to a level less than the caloric value of the products. Preliminary analysis of the possibilities for direct conversion of algae to useful fuels indicates that these processes are not very promising. It suggests that indirect methods, using two or more biological cycles, ought to be investigated.

Ideally one should try to find a biological process which uses algae as a feedstuff and converts it to a mixture of simple anhydrous chemical components. The products should contain most of the free energy accumulated by the algae. A microbiologist would recognize that these requirements fit fermentation processes very well. Commercial products, such as alcohol, acetone, butanol, acetic acid, are already obtained in this manner.

However, a high protein feedstock induces organisms to cease fermentation and enables them to spend their energies upon reproduction. One obtains the transfer of cell substance from one species of microorganism to another with some attendant loss. This means that a special type of fermentation must be sought which will continue under conditions which inhibit growth in the presence of plentiful nutrients. There is one quite well-known fermentation which will fill these specifications—thermophilic methane. One other possibility, recently discovered and still imperfectly explored, is thermophilic hydrogen production. Figure 41 shows a possible biological

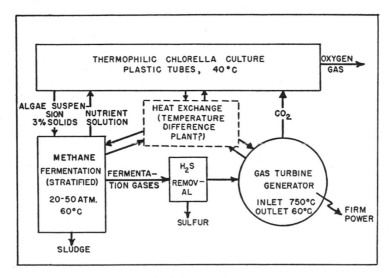

Figure 41.—A biological cycle for power production.

cycle which includes such a fermentation, and several auxiliaries, the the feasibility of which has been considered.

The first point to be established is whether the cycle as outlined is technically feasible. Much information is at hand concerning the unit processes represented by the engine generator and the culture of algae. The use of algae for methane fermentation has apparently not yet been investigated in the technical or scientific literature. No scientific work has been published on the use of protein substrates for methane fermentation. Fortunately there has been broad experience in composting and in sewage works operations. Technologists find that the only organic materials not converted to methane, carbon dioxide, and water-soluble salts are rubbers, waxes, resins, and lignin. Algae contain none of these; therefore, the technologists are confident that algae would be smoothly fermented. Calculations suggest that 65–90 per cent of the free energy is conserved in the transformation.

Whenever one deals with large-scale biological processes, the problems of poisoning and infestation must be faced. The problems for algae culture are discussed elsewhere (*3*). Infestation is no problem for methane fermentation if one operates near 60° C. Apparently a mixture of bacterial species is necessary for a speedy fermentation, so there is no need to maintain pure cultures. The problem of poisons is difficult to assess because the full biochemical mechanism for methane formation is not known (a knowledge of enzymes required and the intermediates would suggest what agents present in the medium would inhibit the formation of methane). A reasonable biochemical path was worked out using some of the current findings about dithiols by Calvin and co-workers, but this has yet to be tested experimentally. Some Dutch workers (Bannink, *et al.*; *1, 2*) investigated this area empirically and found that sulfite ion was an unusually potent poison for methane fermentation. In somewhat higher concentrations SO_2 is also an inhibitor of photosynthesis. The gases from methane fermentation are expected to contain 1–3 per cent H_2S which, when combusted in the power generation step, yields SO_2. This may diminish photosynthesis somewhat, but would almost certainly affect methane fermentation. Therefore, if it were not removed, the cycle would start strong but would steadily decline in efficiency as the sulfite ion concentration built up. There now exist standard commercial plants for extracting H_2S from principally hydrocarbon gases and oxidizing it to powdered sulfur. One interposes this new unit process between methane fermentation and power generation. No other potential defects in the over-all process were discovered or suggested.

The question of how much power can be obtained requires much more elaborate analysis before any estimate can be made. The procedure used was to determine from published experiences of investigators what inputs for each unit process, as they might be operated on a large scale, would most affect energy efficiency and cost. The experience of the Plant Biology Laboratory of the Carnegie Institution of Washington, located at Stanford, California, with mass algae culture and information concerning the efficiency of methane fermentation obtained from W. A. Barker and his co-workers was invaluable at this point. It indicated that this cycle would yield roughly ten times the dependable energy that could be obtained from the same sunlight using the best forestry techniques. Nevertheless, a very large share of the potentially useful energy was slipping away in the form of low-grade heat.

An improvement in performance of the cycle could possibly be obtained by operating a Claude process temperature difference plant as a cooling system for thermophilic algae culture, thermophilic methane fermentation, and the low-temperature side of the engine turbine. Calculations and data of Howe and co-workers indicated that one might obtain some power beyond pumping needs, if the temperature difference was greater than 15°–20° C, depending upon scale of operations.

The final product of such an operation need not be only electric power. The gases obtained from methane fermentation, Table 14, are a suitable

TABLE 14

Probable Composition of Gas
Obtained from the Thermophilic Fermentation of Algae

Methane	50%–70%
Carbon Dioxide	20%–30%
Hydrogen	2%–10%
Hydrogen Sulfide	1%– 3%
Carbon Monoxide	trace
Ammonia	trace

substitute for natural gas. The CO_2 present could be extracted and re-cycled back to photosynthesis, with the remainder being obtained from the air. Drawing upon air as a major source of CO_2 increases pumping costs, but these are important only at the time of day the Claude process plant would be producing a surplus. In other words, peak demand coincides with peak supply, while other anticipated power uses are not so nicely timed.

It is also possible to obtain liquid fuels. The CH_4-CO_2 ratio in the output gas from methane fermentation can theoretically be reacted to yield liquid hydrocarbons in the gasoline and kerosene range in a variation of the Fischer-Tropsch synthesis. Wartime research in Japan demonstrated that at least two types of catalysts bring about smooth conversion to Fischer-Tropsch synthesis gas at relatively low temperatures. The over-all yields that can be calculated while making reasonable assumptions are quite satisfactory. A yield of 35 tons of algae per acre per year in tropical conditions reduces to 6–9 tons of liquid hydrocarbons after providing for pumping and fuel requirements. Some surplus electric power may also be produced, but this output would be extremely weather sensitive.

Costs of production, based upon the present state of knowledge but assuming optimum size facilities, would still be very high according to present-day standards. Much depends upon the availability of large volumes of low-temperature cooling water, such as can be obtained from the ocean 1,500 feet or less below the surface. Power would cost from

2½–5 cents per kwhr and liquid fuels $60–$150 per ton in the better locations. Therefore there is little chance that the present state of knowledge will find application except perhaps as a part of a large food-producing facility which might have trouble disposing of bad batches of algae. If the algae were delivered free of charge, then the fuels generated from them would be economic in most locales. Such power generation or fuel production is hardly likely to exceed the needs of the food-producing facility itself.

If solar energy via biological cycles is to be made more economical, the principal cost reductions will have to be found in the photosynthesis stage. In algae culture the principal costs remaining are in the amortization of equipment and interest upon investment. Therefore further improvement implies either (*a*) more photosynthesis per unit of equipment, (*b*) reduced cost of equipment for cultivating algae, or (*c*) developing a line of valuable by-products. These possibilities will be taken up in order.

Recent work suggests that a regular exposure to light of individual cells followed by shading will, under thermophilic conditions, give an increase in efficiency of utilization of light and a net gain in yield of cell substance in algae culture. The amount of the increment that is economically practical has yet to be worked out. This is an important frontier, and one of the best hopes for getting more photosynthesis per unit area.

In the way of equipment, one finds a multiplicity of possible improvements. Plastic films that are impervious to sunlight are needed. Pumps that, by one means or another, solubilize more CO_2 from air would help greatly. Cheaper harvesting equipment is important.

By-products have hardly been looked into as yet, but the possibilities are good. For example, Fogg in England has shown that certain blue-green algae will fix all their cell nitrogen directly from the air. Current work by Arnon and Allen in Berkeley on optimal culture media for Fogg's strain suggests that dense cultures can be obtained, and that the fixing of the needed nitrogen per acre could be produced annually as a by-product. It would be delivered from the methane fermentation unit in aqueous solution mixed with other fertilizer salts. A species that grows well in sea water or strong brackish water would also be advantageous. Such a species would, of course, also need to be a thermophile. This is not a very restrictive condition because blue-green algae have been identified in hot springs and geysers where they are living in warmer environments than have ever been achieved in the laboratory with Chlorella. The organism would also have to retain its disperse nonfilamentous character. Biologists are quite encouraging at present about the chances of finding or developing such an ideal strain.

Economic Aspects of Algae as a Potential Fuel

A. W. Fisher, Jr.

The possibility of using algae as fuel has been mentioned several times in connection with discussions of their production as food. The purpose of this summary is to present briefly the status of algal culture, including its economic possibilities, so that its potential as a source of fuel may be evaluated. Since the production of organic matter by photosynthesis involves the use of sunlight, algal culture is essentially a method for converting solar energy to useful purposes. It is necessary to look at two factors in this connection. The first is the net production of energy from the sun in the form of available heat of combustion; the second is the over-all cost of producing algae ready to be burned as a fuel.

The Pilot-Plant Experiments.—Early in 1951 the Carnegie Institution of Washington retained Arthur D. Little, Inc., to demonstrate the production of algae on a scale comparable with commercial operation. Previous work had demonstrated that this operation should be technically feasible. A long series of studies in the laboratory, many of them arising from research on photosynthesis, had given a general background of the operating conditions most suited to algae cultures. Some small experimental units, using glass tubes 4 inches in diameter and 6 feet long and flat trays of as much as 30 square feet, had provided additional data.

Using all available information, the Arthur D. Little, Inc., pilot plant was built with a total area of 600 square feet. Polyethylene film 4 mils thick was used for the transparent container in the form of a flat tube 4 feet wide and 140 feet long. This was laid out in two parallel straight runs connected by semicircular end pieces (Figure 42). The 1,200 gallons of culture, which gave a depth of about $2\frac{1}{2}$ inches, was continuously circulated by a centrifugal pump and cooled in a heat exchanger. Air containing 5 per cent CO_2 was fed continuously through the tube. Algal cells were harvested by centrifuging daily to maintain a constant concentration of algae. The unit operated with the initial culture for a period of just over three months from early July to mid-October. The total production of dry algae was 75–80 pounds. Some data were obtained on the rate of growth and on other pertinent factors under the conditions of operation. The pilot-plant studies are described in detail in the recent monograph edited by J. S. Burlew, *Algal Culture from Laboratory to Pilot Plant* (*3*). This book also contains a complete bibliography on all aspects of algal culture.

We concluded that the large-scale culture of algae is entirely feasible from the technical point of view. We do not believe that the method used in the pilot-plant experiment is necessarily the best one, but it should be workable in a commercial operation. A large amount of additional research and development will be required before the optimum type of plant can be selected for a given set of conditions. However, the data obtained were adequate for a preliminary estimate of production costs.

Cost of Growing Algae.—On the basis of the pilot-plant information and additional pertinent data which were available, it was possible to project a commercial installation which we were fairly sure would operate. This was a conservative approach, since in many cases we believe that major improvements are possible which might reduce both investment and operating costs. Our analysis of costs has not previously been published. A detailed discussion will be given in a paper now in preparation.

We assumed for calculation purposes, a plant covering 100 acres of total area with 62½ acres of exposed culture. A single central plant for final harvesting, drying, and packaging of the product was included. A schematic drawing of this unit is shown in Figure 43. The layout is essentially an enlargement of the Cambridge pilot plant with polyethylene tubes laid out in straight runs, the length of which is controlled by the temperature rise of the culture between cooling installations. Continuous flow of the culture is also necessary to maintain the algae in suspension and to expose the cells uniformly to direct sunlight. A yield of 35 tons per acre per year was assumed here, since we felt that the best pilot plant yield of about 20 tons per acre per year could be appreciably increased through the use of the information obtained during our studies.

TABLE 15

Investment in 100-Acre Algal-Culture Installation

(Assumed average production—12,500 pounds per day)

Area preparation and growth tubes	$ 220,000
Circulation equipment, installed	440,000
Cooling facilities, installed	1,180,000
Preharvest equipment, installed	240,000
Central harvesting equipment, installed	234,000
Gas preparation and distribution system, installed	161,000
General facilities, equipment and buildings	211,000
Engineering and contingencies	534,000
Total	**$3,220,000**

Figure 42.—Algal-culture pilot plant at Arthur D. Little, Inc.

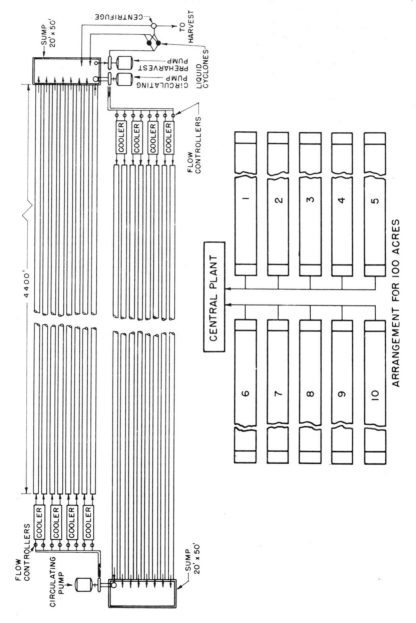

Figure 43.—Schematic plan for a 100-acre algal-culture installation, with sketch of one possible type of 10-acre unit.

Table 15 summarizes our estimate of the investment cost required for the 100–acre plant and shows the relative costs of the various portions of the plant. The investment of over $30,000 per acre is extremely high in comparison with any conventional agricultural practice. Even though the assumed yield is several times more than the best agricultural crop produced at present, the investment per unit of product will still be relatively high.

Table 16 presents an estimated cost of 25 cents per pound for producing algae in the projected plant. This does not include any allowance for general

TABLE 16

Operating Cost for 100-Acre Algal-Culture Installation

(Assumed average production—12,500 pounds per day)

	Cost per day
Labor, supervision, and plant overhead	$ 950
Utilities and supplies	360
Replacement of growth tubes	410
Insurance and taxes	460
Depreciation	920
Total	$3,100
Approximate cost per pound	$ 0.25

overhead, sales cost, or profit. The price of competitive nutritive materials today is in the range of 10 cents per pound or less. Thus, the estimated cost figure of 25 cents puts algae out of consideration for the present, at least in the United States. In underdeveloped areas of the world where protein food is either not available or must be imported, the competitive disadvantage of algae is less marked. All costs used in these tables are based on U.S. labor figures, so in underdeveloped countries the lower rates should permit lower figures for both investment and operation.

In the analysis of these figures, it should be kept in mind that there are many possibilities of reducing these costs through future research and development. We have projected some of these possibilities, such as increased yields and simplified cooling systems, and have estimated that about the best one can hope for in light of any present knowledge is a production cost in the range of 5–10 cents per pound of dry algae. Several of the assumptions used to reach these figures are still open to question from a technical point of view. We cannot visualize at present how costs lower than these could be hoped for under artificial growth conditions.

The Efficiency of Conversion of Sunlight.—The theoretical maximum for conversion of sunlight by photosynthesis to heat of combustion of organic products is approximately 12.5 per cent. This is based on the general consensus that not more than 25 per cent of the visible radiation, which is about half of the total, can be converted by photosynthesis to chemical energy in the ultimate products. The balance of the energy absorbed is converted to heat in the culture. The theoretical utilization of sunlight has never been achieved except in extremely dilute algal suspensions which would be impractical in large-scale culture. It is theoretically possible to approach this maximum through the proper use of the so-called intermittent light effect by which cells are briefly exposed to intense light and then kept in the dark until their photosynthetic processes have been completed. Mechanically, however, it does not appear likely that a practical process for achieving more than a portion of this potential can be developed. Our best estimates now are on the order of 30–40 tons per acre per year as compared with a theoretical maximum of 100–110 tons. With a heating value of approximately 10,000 Btu per pound, the daily product from 100 acres would be equivalent to about 5 tons of coal, which in modern power-plant equipment would correspond to a capacity of perhaps 600 kw. Most utility installations are at least 25,000 kw, so that tremendous acreage would be required even for a small power plant.

Discussion of Algae as a Source of Fuel.—In the operation which we have projected for the production of food, the power requirement of the system would actually exceed the fuel value of the algae produced. While we would expect that this power requirement for operation could be appreciably reduced by improved design and increased knowledge, some power will be needed. Thus, we must burn a substantial fraction of the algae as fuel. Even if we assume that only 25 per cent of the production must be converted for electrical power for the plant operation, we would expect to have to pay at least 10 cents per pound for the fuel which would create energy for outside use. The equivalent amount of coal would be about 0.8 pound, which at present prices would cost about ½ to ¾ cents. If Mr. P. C. Putnam is correct in his analysis that no fuel will be important in the future unless its cost for energy is not greater than 2 or 3 times present costs (Section I), it is our opinion that algal culture is not a potential future source of fuel.

With present knowledge of utilization of chemical energy, it should be no problem to develop systems to obtain maximum efficiency from dry algae. Dr. R. L. Meier has outlined several possible systems in his interesting discussion on algal fuel (Section VIII). As we have seen from the previous discussion, however, the major factor will be the economics of production. Even if the solar energy which goes to heat in the culture could be recovered as work at low temperature differences, the culturing of algae for fuel does not appear to be warranted economically. Such a low-temperature–difference system could be developed for solar energy or industrial waste heat without the concurrent growth of algae and in a more efficient and less expensive system.

A more optimistic viewpoint with regard to algae is its potential use as "human fuel." As produced, the algae form an excellent nutritional product, being equivalent to yeast. Normally grown Chlorella contains approximately 50 per cent protein, 20 per cent fats and other lipides, 25 per cent carbohydrates, and 5 per cent ash. It can be produced using inorganic chemicals as nutrients along with carbon dioxide, much of which could be obtained from waste gases. Otherwise useless land can be used. The use of solar energy to obtain a high-grade food in this manner seems to have real promise for the future.

Photochemical Utilization of Solar Energy

Photochemistry provides a very important long-range hope for the storage and utilization of solar energy. It is more promising than the conversion of heat into work because it is not limited, as heat is, by the requirement of a large temperature difference. In principle, it should be easy to break up a colored compound by sunlight in a chemical reaction which absorbs heat, and then allow the reaction to reverse itself and give out the heat. In practice, most reactions of this type reverse themselves too quickly for efficient storage. Search for suitable reactions should be carried out along different lines in many laboratories. The existence of photosynthesis should lend encouragement to this effort. The fundamental principles involved in the photochemical utilization of light energy are clearly discussed.

The photolysis of water in the presence of cerous and ceric ions is a significant step in the right direction. Accordingly, it is described here with technical details, more fully than most of the other subjects discussed in this book.

Another possibility in photochemical reactions involves the removal of electrons from the photo-product as fast as formed and their conduction through a wire to give a photochemical electrical cell. Further possibility lies in producing some reduced compound which can be oxidized with oxygen. The oxygen of the air is just as free as the sunlight. Photosynthesis acts thus, combining carbon dioxide and water into a carbohydrate which can be oxidized in air with the evolution of heat.

Section IX. Introduction, continued

The storage of solar energy in crystals is a long-range possibility. If one can bring about molecular dissociations or dislocations of crystal units by sunlight and preserve these energy-absorbing changes, it may be possible in some systems, yet to be found, to release the stored energy later by raising the temperature. Fundamental research may contribute eventually to some way of holding solar energy in crystals. Some crystal systems are able to trap the high energy products of photochemistry and radioactivity and thus prevent immediate recombination.

Photochemical Utilization of Light Energy

Eugene Rabinowitch

Photochemical storage of solar energy has been going on in nature on an immense scale for millions of years: all human sustenance and industry depend on it. The average efficiency of the plant blanket covering the land and of the algae swarming in the upper layers of the oceans, in storing the solar energy impinging upon them, is probably less than 1 per cent. It is a most sobering example of the limitation of today's science and technology that we cannot remotely imitate this figure. Not only do we not know how to combine carbon dioxide and water, by means of visible light, to form sugars or starch (thus achieving with one stroke a feat of power engineering and a marvel of chemical synthesis), but we do not know how to use visible light to bring about *any* chemical reaction, however trivial, in which a significant amount of absorbed light energy would be stored in reaction products in a form suitable for practical purposes—producing mechanical or electrical work. The following discussion reviews the search for energy-storing photochemical reactions outside the living cell systems (including special systems derived from living plants).

PHOTOCHEMICAL PROCESSES

The most promising types of photochemical reactions from the point of view of energy storage are *oxidation-reductions* (of which photosynthesis is an example). Stripped of various secondary processes (of which association with, or liberation of, hydrogen ions is most important), oxidation-reduction is a transfer of electrons from one molecule (or atom) to another. (For simplicity, we will talk from now on of molecules only, including atoms or atomic ions in this term.) The molecule which has lost its electron is referred to as being oxidized, and the molecule which has gained it is referred to as being reduced. The strength (or more precisely, the "free energy") with which a molecular species clings to its electrons is called its "reduction potential." Without the help of light, electrons can be transferred, in chemical reactions, only from molecular species with the higher to those with the lower reduction potential. In photosynthesis, however, electrons are raised by the action of light from molecules with a reduction potential of −0.8 volt to molecules with a potential of +0.4 volt.*

In imitating photosynthesis outside the cell (at least in its energy-storing aspect, disregarding its food-synthesizing function), we have to study various oxidation-reduction reactions which could be reversed by bombardment with light particles (photons). It turns out that the problem is not so much to raise the electrons to a higher potential as to keep them there. We begin our review with systems directly derived from plant cells.

The Hill and the Krasnovsky Reactions.—If we crush green plants or algae, separate by centrifugation whole or broken parts of the chlorophyll-carrying bodies (chloroplasts) in which photosynthesis takes place, and suspend them again in water, we find that they have lost some but not all of their capacity for conversion of light into chemical energy. As found by the British biochemist Robin Hill fifteen years ago, such illuminated chloroplasts will still accept electrons from water but are not able to raise them to as high a level as they were able to do in the living organism. However, if they cannot reduce carbon dioxide, they can, for example, reduce certain ferric salts (such as ferric oxalate) to ferrous salts, which means raising electrons about half as high up on the potential scale as they are raised in photosynthesis. However, the reduced product does not stay unchanged, but is slowly reoxidized, until the original state is restored; it is only because the oxidation of ferrous salts by oxygen is slow that Hill was at all able to detect what has since become known as the "Hill Reaction." Recently, more refined methods of experimentation have shown that electrons *can* be transferred in the Hill reaction to practically as high a level as in photosynthesis, but that they quickly return to their former state. This indicates that, in the extraction of chloroplasts, the enzymes which "trap" the unstable products in the living cells have been somehow destroyed or eliminated.

If we go one step further and extract the green pigment, chlorophyll, from the chloroplasts into solution, we find that the preparation has now lost its capacity of removing electrons from water and therefore does not liberate oxygen in light. However, a Russian physical chemist, Krasnovsky, discovered five years ago that by illuminating chlorophyll solutions it is possible to remove electrons from compounds which hold onto them less strongly than water (for example, ascorbic acid, also called Vitamin C) and transfer them to molecules with a markedly higher reduction potential.

*This is the scale of *reduction* potentials generally used in American physicochemical literature. In biochemistry, *oxidation* potentials are more commonly used, which indicate the oxidative power of the oxidized molecular form rather than the reductive power of the reduced form. The two potentials differ from each other only by the sign.

But here again the reaction goes back and the original state of the system is restored in a matter of minutes.

The Iron-Thionine System.—A particularly striking example of an oxidation-reduction system, in which light is converted to a marked proportion into chemical energy, but the latter rapidly dissipated, was studied by us at the Massachusetts Institute of Technology before the war, under the auspices of the Cabot Fund. This system is compounded of a purple dye, thionine, and the salt, ferrous sulfate, or ferrous chloride. When exposed to light, which is absorbed by thionine, electrons are removed from ferrous ions (oxidizing them to ferric ions) and transferred to the dye, which is thus converted into a colorless, reduced form, called "leucothionine." As soon as the light is switched off, the reaction goes back and the colorless solution becomes dark purple again within a few seconds. In light of moderate intensity, a "photostationary state" is established, in which one part of the dye remains continuously in the oxidized, colored form and the other in the reduced, colorless form. In fact, one can measure the intensity of illumination (at least, within a certain range) by watching the color of the thionine–ferrous sulfate mixture. We will discuss this system later as an example of how back reactions in photochemically changed chemical systems can be used to produce electric current and thus to convert, indirectly, light energy into electrical energy. First, however, we should discuss other photochemical systems, in which the oxidation products and the reduction products of the light reaction can be stablized or separated—at least to some extent—without the help of enzymes.

Photooxidation or Photoreduction of Water.—One way in which the unstable products of the light reaction can be separated is by making at least one of them precipitate out of the solution, or escape as a gas. No good example of the first kind (in which light energy is stored by means of a chemical reaction forming a precipitate) comes to mind. Better known (and more promising) are photochemical reactions which lead to the liberation of gases. In the case of photosynthesis (and the Hill reaction), one aspect of the stabilization mechanism is that the removal of electrons from water leaves behind an unstable product, which, rapidly regrouped with the help of an enzyme as yet unknown, becomes oxygen gas. The latter escapes from the solution and reacts back only slowly, if at all, with the reduction products that had remained in the cell (or in the chloroplast suspension). Similar photochemical liberation of oxygen or hydrogen (or both) from water can be obtained also in simpler inorganic systems. For example, illuminated solutions of ferric salts oxidize water and liberate oxygen, while illuminated solutions of ferrous ions reduce water and liberate hydrogen. In both cases, the system moves in light from the more stable to a less stable, energy-rich state. Theoretically at least, this energy derived indirectly from light could be utilized later—for example, by letting oxygen, produced photochemically from a ferric ion solution, reoxidize the ferrous ions remaining in solution. However, both the amount of energy stored in the reaction products and the yield of these products are extremely small. The photon raises an electron only 0.2 or 0.3 volt above its original potential; and out of a large number of photons absorbed in solution, only a very small percentage—perhaps one in a thousand or less—succeeds in producing the desired final effect, liberation of a molecule of oxygen. A particularly interesting system of this type is being investigated by Heidt at the Massachusetts Institute of Technology and is discussed in the following paper. It involves the oxidation of water by ceric ions, with the liberation of oxygen, and the reduction of water by cerous ions, with the liberation of hydrogen. Similarly with the other above-mentioned cases of photochemical oxidation or reduction of water by inorganic ions, the yields attained so far are exceedingly low. Furthermore, the reaction occurs only in ultraviolet light, or at the utmost, in the short-wave end of the visible spectrum, while the bulk of solar energy reaches us in the form of long-wave radiations—orange, red, or infrared. This difficulty leads us to the problem of sensitization.

Sensitization.—The problem of utilization of long-wave radiation for photochemical processes is familiar from photography, where ordinary photographic plates, containing only silver bromide emulsion, are sensitive only to blue, violet, or ultraviolet light, and do not differentiate between an orange, red, or black surface. The answer to this difficulty was found in the addition to the plates of certain dyestuffs which absorb green, yellow, orange, red, or even infrared light, and by some transfer mechanism, which is not yet fully understood, transmit the absorbed energy to silver bromide. In this way the latter becomes "sensitized" to light which otherwise would not affect it. This is the principle of orthochromatic, panchromatic, or infrared-sensitive photographic plates and films.

A solution of the problem of energy storage by photochemical methods could be sought in the same direction: sensitizing the storage system for all visible and, if possible, also for near infrared light, by appropriate dyes.

In the cerium salt and water system, the former acts, in the end result, as a sensitizer or "photocatalyst" (i.e., catalyst which acts only in light). The difference between it and the dye-sensitized photographic plate is merely that with cerium salts we see the mechanism of sensitization: the "photocatalyst" itself first oxidizes and then reduces water, and is first reduced and then reoxidized itself; while in the photographic plate, we can only make hypotheses about the way in which the dye accomplishes its sensitizing function.

Photochemical Peroxide Production.—Water is a very stable compound and can be decomposed directly only by the extreme ultraviolet light, far below the limit of visibility. The ceric-cerous system shows that it is possible to extend the active spectral region up to the limit of the visible spectrum by making the reaction proceed in two separate steps, and thus utilizing two photons; the "raising" of the electron to its final, unstable position is accomplished not directly but stepwise. (In photosynthesis, at least 4, and probably 6 or 8, photons operate in a similar way in achieving the final result.) While it may be possible to find the solution of the energy conversion problem in a similar co-operation of several photons or chemical reactions which requires as much energy as the decomposition of water, one should also look for chemical systems in which the energy of one photon suffices, so that the problem of sensitization reduces itself to how to convey this photon to a system which does not itself take it up, as silver bromide does not absorb green or red light.

In this connection, one may consider, for example, that water, in addition to being decomposed into oxygen and hydrogen, also can be oxidized by taking up more oxygen and forming hydrogen peroxide. The reaction between oxygen and water, which leads to hydrogen peroxide, is an oxidation-reduction reaction (oxidation of water and reduction of oxygen) with hydrogen peroxide as the only product (since it is the oxidation product of water, as well as the reduction product of oxygen). The potential difference which electrons have to overcome in moving from water to oxygen is considerable, about 1.0 volt; and if one finds a way to carry out this reaction with a good yield, in visible light, it would be a very satisfactory way of storing light energy.

Water and oxygen absorb light only in the extreme short-wave ultraviolet (and some hydrogen peroxide is formed as a result). It has been found that if water is mixed with certain oxides, such as zinc oxide, which absorb light in the near ultraviolet just below the limit of the visible spectrum, the reaction becomes sensitized to this light. In other words, water containing a suspension of such oxide will produce hydrogen peroxide if exposed to radiations in the near ultraviolet. Such rays are present in sunlight but form only a very small fraction of it. Therefore, in order to make the reaction of practical interest, one would have to find colored sensitizers, perhaps dyestuffs, which either by themselves or added to an oxide suspension would permit the oxidation of water to hydrogen peroxide to proceed with a good yield, in visible light.

Ozonization.—There is no lack of reactions which proceed with good photochemical yield in the far ultraviolet and lead to the conversion of much of the absorbed radiation energy into chemical energy. One of the best known is the conversion of oxygen into ozone, which occurs on a large scale in the upper atmosphere and is responsible for the practical absence of such radiations on the surface of the earth—a protection without which life on earth would be rapidly destroyed. When an ultraviolet photon transforms three molecules of oxygen into two molecules of ozone, quite a sizeable proportion of the energy of this photon is stored as the chemical energy of this unstable modification of oxygen; one could perhaps devise some means for utilizing this stored energy. However, it doesn't seem likely that this reaction could be sensitized so as to proceed in visible light; and studies directed at sensitized decomposition of water into hydrogen and oxygen, or sensitized oxidation of water by oxygen to hydrogen peroxide, are likely to offer more promise as approaches to the problem of utilization of solar energy.

Heterogeneous Systems.—The low yields of both direct and sensitized photochemical reactions in solutions, caused by the opportunity which the unstable primary products have to react back before they are stabilized (or removed from the mixture as gases of precipitates), may stay in the way of an efficient energy conversion until some new and ingenious method is invented to facilitate this stabilization or separation—a mechanism which will perform the task performed by enzymes in the photosynthesis of living cells. One could think in this connection of actually including in the aqueous system enzymatic components prepared from biological materials (as Vishniac, Ochoa, Tolimach, and Arnon have done recently with chloroplast-containing photochemical systems). Perhaps, however, the same role could be performed by inorganic reaction components. After all, catalysis is known to occur in simple inorganic chemical systems, and not only in enzymatic processes developed by living organisms. The most important type of catalytic action in inorganic chemistry is "heterogeneous" catalysis, which occurs on surfaces of metal powders, oxides, or other "contact catalysts." It may prove possible to devise heterogeneous systems in which the primary photochemical reaction products will be adsorbed on surfaces or dissolved in droplets of an emulsion, and in this way removed from destruction by the back reaction. In this general direction lies perhaps the most promising path along which one could search for an efficient mechanism of light-energy conversion in nonenzymatic systems. Only this general direction of studies can be suggested at the present time; it is an uncharted field.

Miscellaneous Gas Decomposition Reactions.—We have talked so far of reactions in which light transfers electrons from one molecule to another, and the problem is to separate and stabilize the resulting oxidation and reduction products. There are other photochemical reactions of interest, in which a single molecule is either split in two or its atoms are regrouped. We have seen the example of the first kind in the photolysis of water into oxygen and hydrogen, and one of the second kind in the conversion of ordinary oxygen, O_2, into ozone, O_3. Several other simple reactions, particularly of the first type (photolysis) are known which may be worth closer study from the point of view of light utilization. We can only briefly mention them.

In ultraviolet light, saturated gaseous hydrocarbons can be split into unsaturated ones and hydrogen: for example, ethane into ethylene, $C_2H_6 \rightarrow C_2H_4 + H_2$, with the storage of a considerable proportion of the absorbed light energy; or hydrogen can be split off unsaturated hydrocarbons leaving behind a still more unsaturated one, e.g., $C_2H_4 \rightarrow C_2H_2 + H_2$. Similarly, halogenated hydrocarbons can be split into hydrocarbons and halogen (for example, methyl iodide into ethane and iodine) and in some cases with storage of light energy. Some of these reactions occur in the near ultraviolet, almost at the limit of the visible spectrum

Perhaps more tempting are similar photochemical decompositions of gaseous oxides or oxyhalogenides of nitrogen such as $2NO_2 \rightarrow 2NO + O_2$, or NOCl (nitrosyl chloride) $\rightarrow NO + 1/2Cl_2$, since these vapors are colored and will therefore react in visible light—the second one even in green or yellow light.

The problems with this type of gas reactions are again the old ones: how to separate the products before they have chance to react back, which they will do immediately if left together in the reaction mixture; and how to do so without losing too much of the invested energy.

PHOTOGALVANIC PROCESSES

Finding a photochemical reaction by which light can be stored as potential chemical energy with a good conversion yield is only half the problem. The other half is how to utilize this energy, i.e., how to get it out of the system when it is needed. In mixtures containing free hydrogen, catalytically induced rehydrogenation may provide the answer; or two gaseous reaction products (e.g., O_2 and H_2) can be made to recombine explosively. In many other cases, the answer is less obvious. Let us assume, for example, that we have used light energy to decompose silver bromide in an emulsion, forming grains of silver metal. It is not unlikely that in this "photographic reaction" a good percentage of light energy is actually stored as chemical energy; and we know that this reaction can be sensitized to proceed even in the far red and infrared light. Let us assume we have exposed a sensitized silver bromide "light storage cell" until it has become saturated with photochemical products and set it aside. How are we going to go about utilizing the stored energy?

In some photochemically produced unstable systems, the back reaction could be conducted so as to produce not heat (as in an oxygen-hydrogen explosion), but (at least in part) electric energy. In other words, we can make our "light-storage battery" a *photogalvanic battery*, charged by light as a lead storage battery is charged by electric current. In both cases, "charging" means creating an unstable chemical system from which current can be taken out in the "discharge" process, which ends with the restoration of chemical equilibrium. A battery which does not discharge itself at all upon standing with open circuit would be ideal. This means that the back reaction should be infinitely slow, except if it is allowed to proceed electrochemically. This is not the case even in the best lead storage cells, which gradually lose their electromotive force upon standing. We would be doing well, however, if we could devise a light-storage battery as stable as the lead accumulator.

At the present time, the only light-storage batteries known lose their electromotive force, acquired in light, within a few seconds or minutes after the light has been switched off. (Bell's "solar battery," which can be considered as a special type of photoelectric battery, does it practically instantaneously.) In other words, the photochemical products, produced by light in these cells, react back with considerable velocity, even if they are not provided with the external circuit connection through which the reaction can be channeled. So-called photovoltaic and photogalvanic cells are of this type.

Photovoltaic and Photogalvanic Cells.—The difference between photovoltaic and photogalvanic cells is in the locus of the photochemical change. In photovoltaic cells (also called Becquerel cells) the photochemical change takes place in the surface layer on the electrode. They consist of an inert electrolyte, into which two identical electrodes dip. One is kept in the dark; the other is illuminated. The photochemical change takes place in the surface layer of the illuminated electrode—for example, in a thin layer of copper oxide covering a copper electrode. Because of the thinness of this layer, the precise nature of the chemical change is difficult to establish.

In photogalvanic cells, the photochemical change occurs in the electrolyte. It is therefore more easily identifiable, and the storage capacity of the cell can be larger. On the other hand, the problem of preventing the back reaction from also taking place in the body of the solution, and of forcing it to proceed through the external electric circuit, is more difficult to solve. To understand the mechanism of these cells, let us recall that the photochemical changes caused by light usually are oxidation-reductions, i.e., transfers of electrons from one molecule to another. If this transfer has occurred "uphill," light energy has been stored. The problem is how to reverse the process, without wasting the accumulated energy. If the back reaction is not instantaneous—in other words, if the electrons do not again assume their original positions as soon as the oxidation and reduction products encounter each other in solution—a chance is given to conduct the back reaction as a galvanic process. It may then be possible to bring the oxidation and reduction products in contact with two electrodes and let the electrons run from the reduction product into one of the electrodes, from there via the external circuit into another electrode, and thence into the oxidation product in solution. In other words, we offer the electrons a smoother channel to get back into their position of stable equilibrium, but on this path we extract electrical work from them.

The Thionine-Iron Cell.—As an example, we consider the thionine-ferrous-iron system, to which reference has been made earlier in this paper. In this system, light transfers electrons from ferrous ions to thionine molecules. A nonphotochemical back reaction takes place in the illuminated solution, transferring the electrons from the "leuco dye" back to ferric ions, and thus restoring the original system. This is why the solution which had been decolorized in light becomes purple again, in a matter of seconds, in darkness. However, this back reaction is, though fast, not instantaneous; otherwise we could not have observed the effect in the first place. In other words, the oxidation and reduction products are to some extent "stabilized," and the latter do not lose their electrons to the former upon their first encounter. If we now dip into a solution, containing ferrous ions and thionine, two inert electrodes and illuminate the solution around one of them, leaving the other in the dark, we find that the electrode surrounded by the illuminated solution becomes negative—by up to 0.5 volt—relative to the electrode surrounded by the dark solution. If the two electrodes are now connected through an external circuit, electric work will be produced in the latter as long as the illumination is sustained. The electrons acquired by the dyestuff molecules are now returned to the ferric ions not only by direct exchange in solution but also via the external circuit. We can think of the two electrodes and the metallic connection between them as a catalyst which accelerates the back reaction. While the main part of the back reaction, which takes place in the solution, wastes the stored light energy, the small electrode-catalysed part permits us to intercept the electrons on their downward course and make them do work for us—e.g., turning a tiny motor.

How high is the percentage of displaced electrons which can be made to run through the external circuit? This is a matter for experimental study. In our first estimates of this yield, in not specially designed cells, we found that up to 1 per cent of the absorbed light energy could be converted into electric energy. There is no reason to see in this accidental value anything in the nature of a limit. By systematic study of different oxidation-reduction systems which are affected by light, and by geometrical arrangements favoring the reactions at the electrode surface relative to the reactions in the volume of the solution, a considerable increase in the yield could probably be obtained. This study was interrupted by the war and not resumed since.

Conclusions.—In summing up, I would like to state my belief that the conversion of light into chemical energy is likely to prove, in the long run, as important in human technology as it is in living nature. The two general approaches which seem to me to be the most promising are:

1. Construction of artificial oxidation-reduction systems, in which light would cause a shift away from equilibrium, and in which the unstable products will be—in some ingenious way—separated from each other, slightly stabilized, and stored until they are made to release their energy by ignition or by the introduction of a catalytic agent.

2. Construction of photogalvanic systems in which the products of the light reaction will be permitted to react back immediately after they have been formed, but with the back reaction conducted mainly via an external electric circuit. The electric energy produced in this way could either be used at once or stored in ordinary storage batteries.

Photochemistry of Cerium Perchlorates in Dilute Aqueous Perchloric Acid

Lawrence J. Heidt

Introduction.—The photochemistry of cerium perchlorates in dilute aqueous perchloric acid is of interest in connection with the problem of the utilization of solar energy because it has led to the discovery of a way to decompose water photochemically into hydrogen and oxygen, thereby converting light into chemical energy available in storage (*19*). The purpose of this article is to record the steps which led to the discovery of this process and to present the over-all reactions, the nature of the photochemical and thermal reduction of ceric to cerous ions in these solutions whereby water is oxidized to oxygen gas, and the nature of the photochemical oxidation of cerous to ceric ions whereby water is reduced to hydrogen gas.

The raw materials for carrying out the process are, strangely enough, three colorless substances, namely, water, white ceric oxide, and colorless perchloric acid. These substances, however, when mixed together eventually produce an amber solution of water, cerous and ceric perchlorates, and perchloric acid.

It is important to recognize that the over-all efficiency of the process in any of the systems thus far devised is so small at present that the process cannot be utilized economically for the storage of sunlight. The amounts of the gases that have been produced, especially as regards the hydrogen, have been of the order of micromoles. Most of the work has been carried out by employing ultraviolet light of 2,537 Å, which is beyond the ultraviolet limit of the spectrum of sunlight as it reaches the earth's crust because this light is completely absorbed by the ozone layer in the outer atmosphere (*38*). A few experiments, however, have been carried out in sunlight (*19*), and these have shown that this light is capable of bringing about the process, although only microquantities of the gases have been produced by several weeks of sunshine falling on the small reaction vessels thus far employed.

The discovery of the process was the result of a program of work based on quantum-yield measurements employing monochromatic light and the simplest possible solutions of known composition under controlled and reproducible conditions (*17*). It was not the result of casual or accidental observations based on experiments carried out in the full light of an intense source of polychromatic light of unknown intensity falling on a system of uncertain composition designed to learn in a rough way what would happen without due regard to the identity of the species absorbing the light or to the fraction of the light absorbed by these species. The essential piece of equipment was the irradiation ensemble (*15, 18*) which is outlined in Figure 44. This ensemble permitted the irradiation of small

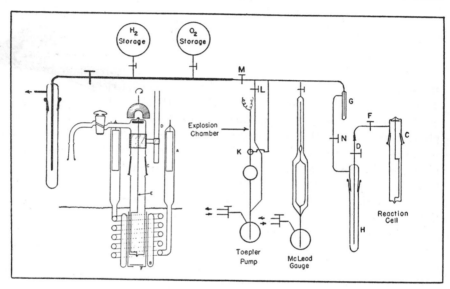

Figure 44.—Apparatus for irradiation of solutions and analysis of evolved gases.

samples of solutions at constant temperature with monochromatic light of very large flux per unit of time, and this made it possible to bring about in several hours reactions to an extent which would have required several weeks of irradiation if we had employed monochromatic light obtained with apparatus of conventional design. Moreover, the most sensitive analytical methods were employed and these were often designed especially for the purpose at hand, such as the method employed to determine the composition of the evolved gases which made use of apparatus (*16, 19*) sketched in Figure 44.

Cerium is the most abundant of the rare-earth elements. It exists in water only in the +3 and +4 states of oxidation (*37*). It occurs together with several other rare-earth elements and the radioactive element thorium in the mineral monazite, which is found in several places in alluvial sands of high specific gravity. Large quantities of the element are known to exist in Brazil, India, and the United States (*37*). One of the commonest commercial compounds of the element is the oxide, CeO_2, which is employed in gas mantles to increase the intensity of the white light they produce. The element itself is a metal; one of its commonest uses is as an alloy with iron to produce the spark of most cigarette lighters. The oxide is white but often has a pinkish cast because of the presence of small amounts of other oxides of cerium and oxides of the other rare-earths and iron (*34*). Even the purest commercial preparations may contain a few tenths of a per cent of thorium.

Cerium can be freed of the other rare-earth elements by oxidizing it to the $+4$ ceric state and precipitating the ceric hydroxide at a pH below which the other rare earths in the $+3$ state remain in solution, or by crystallizing out ceric ammonium nitrate from dilute nitric acid (*1*). Some ferric hydroxide may precipitate together with the ceric hydroxide, but the iron can be removed by taking advantage of the facts that the ceric state is reduced to the cerous state by oxalate in acid and that cerous oxalate is insoluble in solutions near the neutral point under conditions where ferric ions form water-soluble ferric oxalate complexes.

The color of solutions of ceric perchlorate in water ranges from colorless to a deep amber as the concentration of the ceric perchlorate is increased. Cerous perchlorate solutions, on the other hand, are colorless although they do absorb some of the extreme ultraviolet part of sunlight. The fraction of sunlight absorbed by cerous ions, however, is greatly decreased in the presence of ferric ions when the pH equals 1 or more. In particular, ferric ions absorb 40 per cent of 3,100 Å light at pH 2 and 25° when the ratio of ferric to cerous ions is 0.01, and an even larger fraction of this light at higher values of the pH, at higher temperatures, and at longer wave lengths.

Water solutions of either or both ceric and cerous perchlorates are acid; the pH is usually below 2 to prevent precipitation or colloidal formation of hydrated ceric oxide (*28*). Neither light nor heat reduces ceric ions in water when excess sulfate or fluoride is present. Chlorides, however, reduce ceric to cerous ions and the chloride is oxidized to chlorine (*2*, *8*); so that sulfate, chlorides, and other halides must be absent if oxygen is to be evolved by ceric ions acting on water.

The absorption spectra of cerous solutions (*35*) or ceric (*36*) solutions exhibit no sharp bands in the visible spectrum as do solutions of many of the other rare-earth elements (*37*, Chap. 3). Part of the absorption spectrum of cerous perchlorate in water is exhibited in Figure 45; its origin

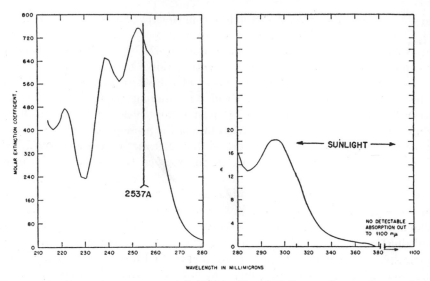

Figure 45.—Absorption spectrum of Ce(ClO₄)₃, 25 ± 0.2° C, according to Stewart (*35*).
213–280 *m*μ: 0.00147M Ce(ClO₄)₃, in 0.94M HClO₄ against 0.94M HClO₄
280–1,100 *m*μ: 0.147M Ce(ClO₄)₃, in 0.90M HClO₄ against 0.88M HClO₄

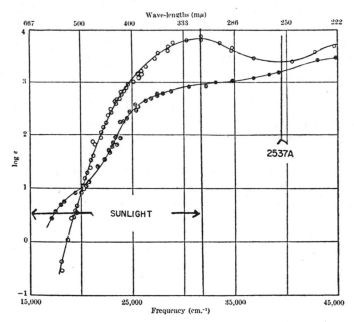

Figure 46.—Molecular extinction coefficients of ceric perchlorate (θ) and ceric sulphate (0) according to Weiss and Porret (*36*).

has been investigated (*4*). The spectra of ceric perchlorate solutions differ with the concentration of ceric ions in the solutions (*11, 21*) but over the entire visible and near ultraviolet part of the spectrum the values of the extinction coefficients of ceric are greater than those of cerous ions per gram atom of cerium. The absorption spectrum of a solution of ceric perchlorate is exhibited in Figure 46; the spectrum extends well into the visible part of the spectrum as is also evident from the amber color of ceric perchlorate solutions of moderate concentration.

The Path of Discovery and the Over-All Reactions.—The photochemistry of aqueous solutions of ceric perchlorate was studied in this laboratory to learn something about the way in which water is photochemically oxidized to oxygen, since this oxidation appears to be a fundamental part of the natural photosynthetic process in living organisms (*29*). Earlier studies on the photochemical oxidation of water to oxygen by light absorbed by persulfate anions (*12, 14*) had revealed no evidence for the intermediate formation of peroxide, although several tests had been made for peroxide because it is well known that hydrogen peroxide is made by the thermal oxidation of water by persulfate. The over-all equation for the photochemical oxidation of water by persulfate appears to be (*12, 14*)

$$S_2O_8^- + H_2O + h\nu = 2SO_4^- + 2H^+ + 1/2\ O_2$$

whereby the net effect is the transfer of two electrons from the water to the photon-activated persulfate. An intermediate species may well be the radical ion SO_4^-. The maximum quantum efficiency of the reaction is about 0.6 mole of $S_2O_8^-$ reduced to sulfate per einstein of light of 2,537 Å absorbed by the persulfate anion (*12, 14*), but the efficiency decreases rapidly as the hydrogen ions accumulate, dropping to less than 0.01 when the concentration of hydrated protons exceeds the concentration of persulfate, although conductivity measurements reveal no association of protons with persulfates under the prevailing conditions (*12, 14*).

The photochemistry of aqueous solutions of ceric perchlorate was reported in 1908 (*3*) to involve the oxidation of water to oxygen by light absorbed by the ceric ions. The over-all equation for the reaction appeared to be

$$Ce^{+4} + 1/2\ H_2O + h\nu = Ce^{+3} + H^+ + 1/4\ O_2$$

whereby the net effect is the transfer of one electron from the water to the photon-activated ceric ion. The quantum efficiency of this reaction was reported in 1937 (*36*) to be about one-tenth mole of ceric reduced to cerous ions per einstein of light absorbed by the system and the efficiency was observed to decrease rapidly as one of the products, namely, cerous ions, accumulated (*36*).

In the ceric photochemical reactions the light merely replaces the activation energy required for corresponding thermal reactions which should and do take place at a small but measurable rate; hence, none of the absorbed light is converted into chemical energy available in storage. In both the ceric and persulfate systems the light initiates an electron transfer reaction and in both cases the quantum efficiency of the reaction is markedly decreased by one of the products. An obvious difference between these reactions is that the light-absorbing unit in the persulfate system is an anion which is capable of accepting two electrons from the water, but in the cerium system the light-absorbing unit appears to be a cation which is capable of accepting only one electron. It was this difference which led me to undertake a quantitative study of the photochemistry of the ceric perchlorate system in order to determine, if possible, the nature of the cerium reactions and their bearing upon the manner in which the water is oxidized.

The results of our study of the ceric perchlorate system (*13*) eventually revealed that the quantum efficiency of the reaction was independent of the light intensity as is the case in the persulfate reaction, but that unlike the latter the efficiency in well stirred solutions depended upon the concentration of the light-absorbing species, in this case the ceric ions, even after correction for the inner filter effect of the cerous species, i.e., after correcting for the fraction of the light absorbed by the cerous species. This dependence is shown in Figure 47, where it will be seen that the quantum efficiency, ϕ, of the reaction with respect to the light absorbed by all the ceric species increases to a maximum as the formal concentration of the ceric perchlorate is increased when the ratio of the formal concentrations of ceric to cerous perchlorates and other variables is kept constant. This unusual aspect of the reaction led me to the startling conclusion that it could be explained if the photosensitive ceric species were ceric ions which had been polymerized, e.g., dimerized, in these solutions, although the solutions were one molar in perchloric acid and hydrolyzed ceric monomers such as $CeOH^{+3}$ would be expected to strongly repel each other. Fortunately it had been shown previously in this laboratory (*32*) that ceric ions are largely hydrolyzed even in one molar perchloric acid, although it had not been suspected that polymerization also took place.

The dimerization reaction between the partially hydrolyzed ceric species is believed to result from the splitting out of a molecule of water from hydroxyl groups attached to two different ceric ions, i.e., the reaction is believed to be a case of amphoterism involving ions. The problem of calculating the equilibrium constants of reactions of this kind from the quantum-yield measurements has been solved (*13*) and the concentration constants for the reactions: $2CeOH^{+3} = Ce\text{---}O\text{---}Ce^{+6} + H_2O$, $2Ce(OH)_2^{+2} = HOCe\text{---}O\text{---}CeOH^{+4} + H_2O$ and $CeOH^{+3} + Ce(OH)_2^{+2} = HO\text{---}Ce\text{---}O\text{---}Ce^{+5} + H_2O$ have been evaluated. The average value of the constants for these reactions is about 50 at 25° and an ionic strength of about unity. The formulas have been simplified by leaving out the water of hydration.

My attention was turned next to the possible evaluation of these con-

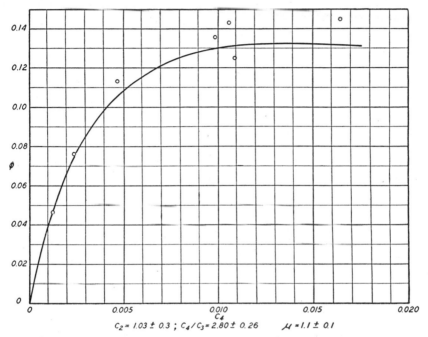

$C_2 = 1.03 \pm 0.3$; $C_4/C_3 = 2.80 \pm 0.26$ $\mu = 1.1 \pm 0.1$

Figure 47.—Dependence of the quantum yield of the photochemical reduction of ceric ions upon the concentration of ceric ions, at constant ratio of concentrations of ceric to cerous ions.

stants from the previously unexplained dependence of the emf of cells containing ceric and cerous perchlorates upon the formal concentrations of these ions. This problem too was solved (*13*), and it was gratifying to find that the average value calculated for the constants from the emf data was essentially the same as the value calculated from the quantum yield measurements and that the emf data also permitted the evaluation of the individual constants for these reactions, namely, 50, 50, and 100 respectively. Similar calculations have been made since then by Connick, Kraus, and others to evaluate the dimerization constants of similar reactions (*5, 6, 25*).

The fractions of ceric ions in the form of dimers at some values of the formal concentration of ceric perchlorate in one molar perchloric acid at 25° are tabulated below (*13*).

Formal Concentration of Ceric Ions in Moles per Liter × 10⁴	Fraction Dimerized
1	0.010
10	0.085
100	0.385
150	0.450

The dependence of the quantum yield of the photochemical reduction of ceric ions upon the reciprocal of the cerous ion concentration was found

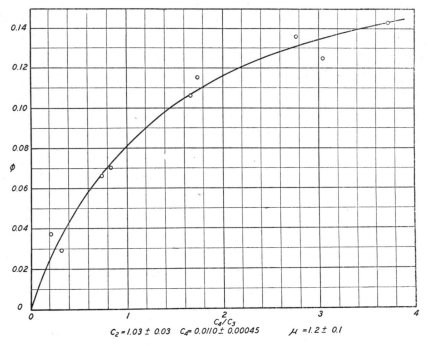

$$C_2 = 1.03 \pm 0.03 \quad C_4 = 0.0110 \pm 0.00045 \quad \mu = 1.2 \pm 0.1$$

Figure 48.—Dependence of the quantum yield of the photochemical reduction of ceric ions upon the ratio of concentration of ceric to cerous ions at constant ceric ion concentration.

to be as shown in Figure 48 after correcting for the inner filter effect of the cerous ions (*13*). The quantum yields are based on the observed decrease in the formal concentration of ceric ions. The falling off in this quantum yield as one increased the concentration of cerous ions, i.e., decreased the value of C_4/C_3 at constant C_4, suggested that the effect might be caused partly by the photochemical oxidation of the cerous to ceric ions by light absorbed by the cerous ions as well as by electron transfer from the cerous to photoactivated ceric ions without the intervening oxidation of the divalent oxygen which was originally part of the water (*13*). In order to test the hypothesis, solutions containing initially cerous but no ceric perchlorate were irradiated with light of 2,537 Å and it was found, much to our delight, that ceric ions were indeed produced (*13*). This was made evident by the formation of the orange color of ceric sulfate in the irradiated but not in the unirradiated solutions when concentrated sulfuric acid was added to them and by the oxidizing power of the irradiated but not the unirradiated solutions when treated with a solution of ferrous sulfate. Moreover, the intensity of the orange color was found to be directly proportional to the amount of ferrous ion required to bleach it (*13*).

The quantum efficiency of the photooxidation of cerous to ceric ions, however, was found to be of the order of only a few one-hundredths of 1 per cent (*13*). Calculations based on this efficiency and the extinction coefficients of the ceric and cerous species at 2,537 Å (the values of these extinction coefficients in common logarithmic units for the optical density are about 750 and 1,700 respectively per gram atom of cerium) revealed, however, that the photochemical conversion of cerous to ceric ions could account for less that 1 per cent of the observed decrease in the conversion of ceric to cerous ions with increase in the concentration of cerous ions, so the remainder of the decrease was apparently due to deactivation of the photon-activated ceric ions by cerous ions resulting either in an electron transfer from cerous to photoactivated ceric ions without the intervening decomposition of water or in the degradation of the energy of the photon-activated ceric ions as heat without electron transfer.

It was recognized at this time (*13*), nevertheless, that the photooxidation of the cerous ions might be accompanied by the production of molecular hydrogen and, if so, the photolysis of a solution of cerous and ceric perchlorates would provide a way to break down water into its elements while the amount of cerium and acid in the solution would remain unchanged. The pertinent statement was (*13*), "We did not test for hydrogen produced by the photooxidation of the cerous ions, but it is worth noting that when $E_3C_3\phi^* = E_4C_4\phi$, the amount of cerous and ceric perchlorates in the solution being irradiated would remain unchanged while water was being broken down into oxygen and hydrogen." The symbols E_3, C_3, and ϕ^*, E_4, C_4, and ϕ represent the extinction coefficients, concentrations, and quantum yields for the cerous and ceric ions respectively. The quantum yields are defined for the purpose of this equation as moles ceric converted to cerous and vice versa per einstein (mole of light quanta) of light absorbed by all of the ceric or cerous species.

There remained the problems of determining whether or not hydrogen was produced by the photooxidation of cerous to ceric ions and whether both hydrogen and oxygen could be produced by the irradiation of a solution of cerous and ceric perchlorates. Even if it was established that hydrogen could be produced by the irradiation of solutions containing initially all of the cerium in the cerous state and that oxygen could be produced by the irradiation of solutions containing ceric ions, it did not follow that both gases could be produced simultaneously from the same solution because the light absorbed by the cerous ions in the presence of ceric ions might produce only an electron transfer from the cerous to the ceric ions without the intermediate production of hydrogen, and under these conditions a similar reaction might be brought about by the light absorbed by ceric ions. There is in fact a growing literature on electron transfer reactions of this kind brought about by the agency of heat (*31*).

It soon became evident from our work that only micro amounts of hydrogen, if any, could be produced in a reasonable time by the irradiation of our cerous perchlorate solutions even at the high values of the light flux at our disposal and that if we were to collect this gas and identify it we would have to work in a gas-tight system and at very low pressures.

The construction and perfection of such a system required considerable time, but this was finally accomplished (*17*) by Dr. G. G. Palmer and we were able to irradiate our solutions under their own vapor pressure after they had been thoroughly pumped free of all gases in a system that maintained a pressure of at least 10^{-4} mm Hg overnight when cut off from the solution and the pumps. The reaction vessel was constructed of clear transparent fused quartz to let in the ultraviolet light and the solution was stirred by means of a "magnetic stirrer" operated by rotating a magnet outside the reaction vessel which drove a stirrer completely sealed within the vessel, as sketched in Figure 44.

Our first tests for the production of hydrogen by light absorbed by cerous perchlorate consisted of irradiating under its own vapor pressure a gas- and iron-free solution of cerous perchlorate at 0.01M in 1M perchloric acid with light of 2,537 Å until the solution had absorbed about one-tenth mole of light quanta. The volume of the irradiated solution was about forty ml. The vapor above the solution was then passed slowly through a cold trap immersed in liquid nitrogen in order to remove water and any other condensable gas. When the dry gas was passed over hot black cupric oxide, the main mass of oxide appeared to remain unchanged; but along the top of the tube, which was also hot and contained initially some black cupric oxide dust, there had formed a bright copper-colored mirror clearly visible from certain angles. The sealed tube with this mirror we still have. The experiment was repeated several times to insure that it was reproducible. A typical one of these experiments has been described in detail elsewhere (*17*).

There remained the task of determining whether both hydrogen and oxygen could be produced simultaneously by the irradiation of a solution containing initially both cerous and ceric perchlorates. This proved to be a more difficult task than had been encountered in obtaining evidence for the production of the hydrogen alone because any mixture of hydrogen and oxygen in approximately equivalent amounts burns to form water. Eventually, however, Dr. A. F. McMillan succeeded in constructing a gas-tight explosion chamber on the collection end of a Toepler pump which was built to handle micro quantities of gases. The explosion chamber, Toepler pump, auxiliary apparatus, and the operation of this equipment has been described in detail (*19*); part of this apparatus is sketched in Figure 44. The spark plug consisted of a pair of platinum wires separated in the chamber by a gap of about 1 mm. One of the wires was grounded; the other hung free and when an activated gas-leak–tester was touched to it a spark was produced in the chamber. Two gas reservoirs were attached to the system: one contained pure hydrogen, the other pure oxygen. Provision was made for bleeding predetermined amounts of either or both of these gases into the explosion chamber. This provided a means of determining the effect of sparking for selected intervals of time upon hydrogen, oxygen, or air, or mixtures thereof confined in the explosion chamber at selected pressures; it also provided a means of mixing any or all of these gases with gas already in the chamber. When the gas in the chamber was pure hydrogen or oxygen or dry air, a spark of short duration had no measurable effect upon the volume of gas in the chamber at constant pressure and temperature; but if the gas contained a mixture of hydrogen and oxygen under a pressure or between 20 and 50 mm Hg, a spark caused a measurable decrease in the volume which corresponded to the complete formation of water by the limiting reagent. When sufficient water was produced, part of it condensed as liquid while the rest remained in the gaseous state at the vapor pressure of water. The limiting amount of hydrogen or oxygen initially in the chamber was calculated from the decrease in the volume produced by the explosion at the known temperature and pressure.

The apparatus was constructed so that the irradiation of the solutions could be carried out independent of it. This permitted the simultaneous irradiation of several solutions under a variety of conditions while one carried out the gas measurements and analysis on those solutions which had been irradiated.

The results of these experiments gave evidence that both hydrogen and oxygen are indeed produced simultaneously by light absorbed by solutions containing both cerous and ceric perchlorates under certain conditions, provided significant fractions of this light are absorbed by both the cerous ions and ceric dimers (*19*). The efficiency of the process, however, was found to be very low under the prevailing conditions; less than one thousandth of a mole of water was found to be decomposed into its elements per mole of light quanta absorbed by the system. Hence the light absorbed by the cerous and ceric ions was mainly dissipated as heat and in bringing about the undesirable electron transfer reactions mentioned above instead of the photochemical decomposition of water. Nevertheless, ways may be found to increase the efficiency of the process, either in this or a similar system, to the point where this process will be of economic importance in the commercial production of power from sunlight.

The over-all reactions of the process are:

(1) $Ce^{+4} + 1/2 \; H_2O + Light \; (or \; Heat) = Ce^{+3} + 1/4 \; O_2 + H^+$

(2) $Ce^{+3} + H_2O + Light = Ce^{+4} + 1/2 \; H_2 + OH^-$

(3) $H^+ + OH^- = H_2O$

Twice the sum of these reactions is:

(4) $2_1Ce^{+4} + 2_2Ce^{+3} + H_2O + Light = 2_1Ce^{+3} + 2_2Ce^{+4} + H_2 + 1/2 \; O_2$

which is competing with

(5) $_1Ce^{+4} + {}_2Ce^{+3} + Light = {}_1Ce^{+3} + {}_2Ce^{+4} + Heat$

and other quenching reactions.

The reaction $Ce^{+3} + H^+ = Ce^{+4} + 1/2 \; H_2$ is endothermic (*10*) to the extent of 37.9 kcal in 0.5M $HClO_4$ at 25°. The reaction $H_2O = H_2 + 1/2 \; O_2$ is endothermic to the extent of 68.3 kcal; hence the reaction $Ce^{+4} + 1/2 \; H_2O = Ce^{+3} + H^+ + 1/4 \; O_2$ is exothermic to the extent of 3.8 kcal all at 25°.

The maximum experimental values of the quantum efficiencies of reactions 1 and 2 under conditions studied thus far are 0.15 (*13*) and 0.0013 (*16*) respectively at 25° in terms of moles ceric and cerous ions converted to the other state presumably by way of photochemical decomposition of water per mole of light quanta of 2,537 Å absorbed by the respective ions. The quantum efficiencies of the reactions at other wave lengths have not been measured, although we have found (*19*) that the reactions are brought about by sunlight presumably only by the ultraviolet part of sunlight beyond 3,500 Å (see Figure 45) in the case of the photochemical reduction of the water by the cerous ions.

The kinetics of the thermal reduction of ceric perchlorate had been studied (*22*) in the meantime and had been found to be in accord with the hypothesis that only the dimeric ceric particles, previously postulated by us to explain the photochemical results, are responsible for the oxidation of the water to oxygen. The rate of the thermal reaction was observed to be first order with respect to the concentration of these dimers and to be inversely proportional to the concentration of cerous perchlorate. Calculations based on these data reveal that about two days at 95° are required to reduce, thermally, half the ceric perchlorate in a solution containing initially about 0.3M ceric and 0.3M cerous perchlorate in 3M perchloric acid.

Since water can be oxidized to oxygen by ceric perchlorate at a convenient rate even in the dark, while its reduction to hydrogen by cerous perchlorate occurs only in light of wave lengths shorter than 3,500 Å, it is possible to construct a system whereby an aqueous solution containing both cerous and ceric perchlorates can be made to produce pure oxygen in darkness by sunlight converted into heat or in the part of sunlight of wavelengths longer than 3,500 Å, and alternatively almost pure hydrogen in the full light of the sun when the solution contains all but a negligible amount of the cerium in the fully hydrated unhydrolyzed and uncomplexed cerous state. The solution could be circulated by means of the temperature gradient established between its parts. Such a system would largely prevent ceric perchlorate from competing effectively with cerous ions for the part of sunlight absorbed by both and would enable one to collect the hydrogen and oxygen largely free from one another thereby avoiding the handling of highly explosive mixtures of these gases.

Nature of the Oxidation of Water by Ceric Perchlorate.—The following set of reactions was originally given (*13*) to account quantitatively for the photochemical oxidation of water by ceric perchlorate.

$$K_p \quad 2c_m = c_p$$

$$k_I \quad c_p + h\nu = c_p^*$$

$$k_1 \quad c_p^* + H_2O = 2c_3 + 2H^+ + 1/2\,O_2$$

$$k_2 \quad c_p^* + c_3 = c_p + c_3 + \text{heat}$$

$$k_3 \quad c_p^* + S = c_p + S + \text{heat}$$

c_m represents all ceric monomers such as $CeOH^{+3}$, $Ce(OH)_2^{+2}$, etc.

c_p represents all ceric dimers such as $Ce—O—Ce^{+6}$, $Ce—O—CeOH^{+5}$, etc.,
   which are in equilibrium with the monomers.

c_3 represents Ce^{+3}.

S represents any substance except c_3.

K_p is an equilibrium constant; the k's are rate constants. In order to
   simplify the equations the water of hydration and the charges have been
   left out of the formulas.

This set of reactions was found to give the following mathematical
relationship between the quantum yield ϕ (for the conversion of ceric to
cerous ions by light absorbed by ceric ions in all forms) and the components
of the systems:

$\phi = 2yk_1/[k_1 + k_3(S) + k_2(c_3)]$

or $\phi = y/[a + b(c_3)]$ at constant temperature and ionic strength

y = fraction of the ceric cerium in the form of dimers

If the quenching reactions were negligible, the maximum value of ϕ
would be 2 based on the third reaction in the set, but this reaction lacks a
plausible mechanism. The mechanism may be

$$*Ce—O—Ce^{+6} = Ce—O\cdot^{+3} + Ce^{+3}$$

$$Ce—O\cdot^{+3} + Ce—O—Ce^{+6} = 3Ce^{+3} + O_2$$

If this is the mechanism, the maximum possible value for ϕ would be 4
instead of 2. A forthcoming publication will deal with this problem based
on some new data obtained by us over a wider range of the independent
variables than was covered by the earlier work. No definitive evidence,
however, has been obtained for the existence of the radical ion $Ce—O\cdot^{+3}$
but it may well be the key intermediate instead of the hydroxyl radical
in a number of thermal reactions involving ceric ions. Some authors (9),
however, believe so firmly in the production of hydroxyl radicals in reactions of this kind that they discard all results which do not agree with
such an hypothesis and attribute to impurities the observation that the
quantum yield for the conversion of ceric to cerous perchlorate falls off
when the concentration of ceric perchlorate is decreased. We have re-
peatedly checked our observations concerning this matter with water
purified in a variety of ways and have found the results to be independent
of the method of purification and to be essentially the same as those we
have previously published (13).

Mention also needs to be made of a publication written in Russian by
Dain and Kachan but summarized in English in *Chemical Abstracts* (7).

They followed the photochemical oxidation of water by ceric perchlorate over the range 6° to 60° C by measuring the amount of oxygen produced by light of 313 mμ. They came to the conclusion that the production of oxygen is the result of a heterogeneous reaction which takes place on the surface of the quartz reaction vessel and that there is no production of oxygen by a thermal reaction unless preceded by the photochemical reaction. They make no mention of any attempt to determine if the stirring of their solutions could be made adequate to eliminate dependence of the quantum yield upon the rate of stirring—a very important aspect of photochemical work when most of the light is absorbed by a thin layer next to the wall of the reaction vessel.

Nature of the Reduction of Water by Photoactivated Cerous Perchlorate.—Studies (*16*) have been made on the influence of variations in the concentrations of perchloric acid and cerous perchlorate upon the quantum yield, ϕ^*, and on the conversion of cerous to ceric ions in solutions containing initially only these substances and water but no ceric perchlorate. These studies show that an increase in either or both of these concentrations increases the value of ϕ^* in such a way that the reciprocals of these quantities depend linearly upon each other. The results have been interpreted quantitatively in terms of the following set of reactions.

Forward Reactions:

(1) $Ce \cdot H_2O^{+3} + h\nu = \ ^*Ce \cdot H_2O^{+3}$

(2) $^*Ce \cdot H_2O^{+3} + H_3O^+ = Ce\!-\!OH\!-\!H_2^{+4} + H_2O$

(3) $Ce\!-\!OH\!-\!H_2^{+4} + Ce \cdot H_2O^{+3} = 2CeOH^{+3} + H_2 + H^+$

The sum of reactions 1, 2, and 3 is $2Ce \cdot H_2O^{+3} + h\nu = 2CeOH^{+3} + H_2$.

Quenching Reactions:

(1′) $^*Ce \cdot H_2O^{+3} = Ce \cdot H_2O^{+3} + heat$

(2′) $^*Ce \cdot H_2O^{+3} + H_3O^+ = Ce \cdot H_2O^{+3} + H_3O^+ + heat$

(3′) $Ce\!-\!OH\!-\!H_2^{+4} + H_2O = Ce \cdot H_2O^{+3} + H_3O^+ + heat$

Other quenching reactions can be neglected. The principal quenching reaction is 2′ which appears to take place about fourteen hundred times more often than its analogue reaction 2. The value of ϕ^* would be 2 if quenching reactions were negligible.

The meaning of the symbols in these equations is as follows: $Ce \cdot H_2O^{+3}$ or Ce^{+3} represents hydrated cerous ions, namely $(H_2O)_5Ce^{+3} \cdot H_2O$; $Ce\!-\!OH\!-\!H_2^{+4}$ represents $(H_2O)_5Ce^{+4}\!-\!OH^{-1}\!-\!H_2^+$; $^*Ce \cdot H_2O^{+3}$ represents photon activated $Ce \cdot H_2O^{+3}$; $CeOH^{+3}$ represents $(H_2O)_5CeOH^{+3}$; H^+ or H_3O^+ represents the hydrated proton. A detailed discussion of the mechanisms of these reactions is presented in reference (*16*). The same article also makes the following observations:

The set of reactions given above for the photochemical reduction of water by light absorbed by cerous ions is not necessarily a unique solution to the problem nor does it eliminate the possibility that ceric and other ions whose concentrations were negligible in our solutions may be outstandingly effective as deactivators of the transient species, or that hydrated hydrogen molecule ions may be produced by reaction 2 and subsequently reduced to hydrogen gas largely by oxidizing cerous to ceric ions and to a much lesser extent by oxidizing water to oxygen. The latter possibility exists because of the small amount of oxygen which we have always observed in the hydrogen produced by the reaction, although this oxygen may very well have been produced by the oxidation of water by light absorbed by ceric ions.

We have also examined the possibility that the reaction is initiated by light absorbed by a photosensitive cluster consisting of a hydrated ion pair of cerous and hydrogen ions. This hypothesis leads to the conclusion that the ion pair has an association constant of 14 which is incredibly large for a reaction of this kind. The set of reactions given above avoids the formation of this ion pair but replaces it essentially by a similar pair involving a photon-activated cerous ion instead of a normal cerous ion; this has the advantage of requiring only the temporary removal of a very small amount of H^+ from H_3O^+ and attributes no unusual properties to acidic solutions of cerous perchlorate in thermal equilibrium with their surroundings.

Summary.—Evidence has been presented that ultraviolet light, in particular light of 2,537 Å and the extreme ultraviolet part of sunlight of wave lengths shorter than 3,500 Å, photochemically decomposes water into hydrogen and oxygen when enough of this light is absorbed by cerous and ceric perchlorate in dilute aqueous perchloric acid. The efficiencies of these reactions in any of the systems thus far studied, however, are so low that the process is of no economic importance at present. The production of oxygen, however, can also be made to take place solely by the agency of heat acting on a solution of ceric perchlorate and a way has been given to employ this reaction in the design of a system in which sunlight can be employed to decompose water into the hydrogen and oxygen largely free from each other, thereby eliminating the hazard of handling highly explosive mixtures of these gases.

There are a host of problems still to be solved in connection with this process; some of these are the following:

1. Determine the maximum experimentally obtainable quantum efficiencies of these reactions over the temperature range 5° to 95° in simple systems and discover ways to modify the systems to increase these efficiencies.

2. Determine the dependence of net quantum yields upon the wave length of the absorbed light.
3. Determine the ratio of hydrogen and oxygen produced to cerous converted to ceric and vice versa, respectively.
4. Identify and evaluate any objectionable side reactions and determine ways to eliminate these reactions as well as species acting as inner filters and quenching agents.
5. Determine in greater detail the kinetics of the thermal reactions.
6. Learn how to alter the system in such a way that the cerous perchlorate will absorb a larger fraction of sunlight without quenching desired reactions.
7. Discover and study in a similar fashion other systems in which the process or one or the other half of it takes place.

Some persons may wish to speculate concerning the possibility that this process or a similar one may sometime be able to supply enough hydrogen (and oxygen) to furnish most of the power to run our industries, heat our homes, and do most of our work. I cannot even hazard a guess about this. The best I can say now is that we have no good reason for believing that such a process cannot become of economic importance. At present, we are very much in the research stage of the problem and are having a great deal of fun in unraveling the details of the reactions as well as in trying to find other ways to store sunlight in the form of high-grade chemical energy which can be converted efficiently into power.

High-Energy Intermediates in
Some Photochemical Processes

Henry Linschitz

The great majority of photochemical reactions which take place in the laboratory are exergonic. That is, they are thermodynamically feasible even in the dark, and the light energy absorbed by the reactants serves merely as activation energy. This energy appears ultimately as heat in the products, in addition to the over-all heat of reaction. Nevertheless, during the course of such a reaction, states are initially reached in which a great deal of the incident light energy is stored more or less briefly as potential energy of the first products of excitation. These may be, aside from the initially electronically excited molecules, free radicals, ionized fragments, rearranged forms, or reduced or oxidized intermediates.

From the standpoint of energy storage, the problem is to trap these energetic intermediates in such a way as to avoid either direct back reactions or exergonic, dissipative side reactions. Moreover, the temporary stabilization of the intermediates must be such as to permit efficient recovery of useful work when the back reactions are ultimately allowed to proceed in a controlled manner. From the standpoint of the general problems encountered in photochemistry, this is an ambitious program inasmuch as the identity of the initial energetic products are themselves usually not directly established. In some cases, the character of the absorption spectrum or detailed kinetic study of the over-all reaction yields evidence regarding the nature of the photochemical "primary-process," but for most such reactions, in particular those involving complex molecules in condensed phase, the nature of the intermediates is highly uncertain. Such knowledge is, of course, essential to any development of photochemical mechanisms for storage of light energy. In this paper we present a very brief summary of some simple photochemical experiments in rigid solvents in which it appears to be possible to stabilize some high-energy fragments long enough to permit their identification.

Various polar organic liquids of low molecular weight like ethanol or triethylamine, mixed with suitable light hydrocarbons or ether, set to clear hard glasses when cooled in liquid air. In such rigid solvents, bimolecular processes involving *solute* molecules are essentially stopped. Moreover, it is possible to trap fragments formed photochemically from solute molecules if these fragments move even small distances apart when they appear. For example, one of the elementary effects which may be conveniently studied with the rigid-solvent technique is that of direct photo-ionization (photo-oxidation, to the chemist) of complex organic molecules.

Lewis and Lipkin (*27*) found that the illumination of certain easily oxidizable substances (amines, phenols, various dyes, etc.) in rigid solvents led to the appearance of new absorption bands. The new substances were identified as ionized free radicals or semiquinones, on the basis of several cases in which the spectra corresponded with those of known semiquinones prepared by conventional chemical procedures. The photo-process thus postulated is a direct ejection of an electron from an excited molecule,

$$RH_2 \xrightarrow{h\nu} RH_2 \cdot^+ + e,$$

the electron being trapped in the glass. When the glass is softened by warming, the original spectrum is restored. We have recently been able to establish the presence of the trapped electron in the illuminated glass by working with solvents containing amines of low molecular weight. In such solvents one finds not only the spectrum of the organic free radical but also a characteristic broad band in the near infrared. This band is similar to one found in solutions of alkali metals in the same solvent and is therefore ascribed to solvated electrons.

Light energy may thus be stored in these glasses in a manner analogous to the formation of "f-centers" in ionic crystals, and this energy is released as heat when the radicals and electrons are allowed to recombine by softening the solvent. The energy required for such photooxidation processes is surprisingly low and in special cases—like the negatively charged, easily oxidized triphenylmethide ion—even visible light suffices for electron ejection. It is noteworthy that in this particular case little energy is lost by initial recombination, since there are no Coulomb forces acting between the pair of fragments.

Another application of this simple stabilization technique is in the study of photosensitization mechanisms. Plant photosynthesis may be regarded as a series of dye-sensitized hydrogen transfers from water to CO_2 yielding oxygen and carbohydrate. It is possible to set up formally analogous reactions in vitro, in which a dye-sensitized hydrogen or electron transport occurs between substances more reactive than CO_2 or water, as follows:

$$RH_2 + A \underset{\text{Dye}}{\xrightarrow{h\nu}} R + AH_2 \tag{1}$$

The donor and acceptor may be typical organic or inorganic reductants and oxidants, such as amines, ascorbic acid, iodide ion, or quinones, azo compounds, oxygen, etc., and the dye may be any of a large number, such as eosin or chlorophyll itself. One can write numerous mechanisms, of course, for the photocatalysis, but the simplest would be of the type (DH_2^* = excited dye):

$$DH_2^* + A \rightarrow DH \cdot + AH \cdot$$

$$DH \cdot + RH_2 \rightarrow DH_2 + RH \cdot$$

$$AH \cdot + RH \cdot \rightarrow R + AH_2 \tag{2}$$

Another equivalent mechanism would involve the reaction of DH_2^* first with the donor instead of the acceptor. Thus:

$$DH_2^* + RH_2 \rightarrow DH_3 \cdot + RH \cdot$$

$$DH_3 \cdot + A \rightarrow DH_2 + AH \cdot, \text{ etc.} \tag{3}$$

Studies have been made in our laboratory on rigid (alcohol, ether, isopentane) solutions of chlorophyll and quinone, containing no added reductant. Initially these glasses are clear green. Illumination with red light changes the color to yellow. The new spectrum is stable at low temperature, but when the glass is softened by warming, the original green color is restored. It may be that the new substances appearing in the illuminated glass are $DH\cdot$ and $AH\cdot$, the forward reaction taking place within a dye-substrate complex (for which there is evidence) and the back reaction being prevented by the glass.

If a basic solvent (pyridine) is used, rather than alcohol, then excited chlorophyll appears to react by reduction rather than oxidation. Reversible photo-bleaching at room temperature has been observed by Krasnovsky and co-workers (*23, 24*) when pyridine solutions of chlorophyll and various reductants (ascorbic acid, phenylhydrazine) are illuminated. In these cases, the original green color changes to pink in the light, and then gradually returns when the excitation is cut off. Possibly we are dealing here with compounds of the type $DH_3\cdot$ and $RH\cdot$.

Krasnovsky (*24*) has gone further than this and has shown that reaction can actually be made to go "uphill" even in vitro. A reversible reduction of safranine or riboflavin by ascorbic or pyruvic acid was shown to occur, when solutions of these reagents containing chlorophyll or magnesium phthalocyanine as sensitizer were illuminated. The increase in free energy for the sensitized ascorbic acid–safranine reaction is about 15 kg-cal, and since the products can conceivably be separated after the photochemical reaction, this offers a method for transformation of light energy into useful chemical energy in vitro. These studies clearly are of great interest and are now being confirmed and extended in other laboratories.

This conference has been devoted almost entirely to the scientific and engineering problems of solar-energy utilization. By and large, the picture is encouraging. The fact that straightforward engineering methods already bring the cost of solar power to within roughly a factor of ten of that of fossil fuels indicates that our race need fear no ultimate, inevitable power shortage. The real problem lies elsewhere. Even with present techniques, a small fraction of our annual armament expenditure (about $50 billion) would suffice to install a fullfledged solar power industry, and it is a good bet that the cost of a single aircraft carrier would support all the fundamental research necessary to find better methods than are now available. It is regrettably trite, but still relevant, to point out that the real difficulties to be overcome are human, not technical.

A British Viewpoint

A British report on the utilization of solar energy (*Research*, 5, 522 [1952]) was published just before the symposium by a group of eminent British scientists, under the chairmanship of Dr. E. C. Bullard. This report was pessimistic in its view of the possibilities of utilizing solar energy. An unsuccessful effort was made to bring to the symposium one who would represent the British view.

Some time later an excellent and comprehensive series of articles was written by Professor H. Heywood on the utilization of solar energy. Professor Heywood kindly gave permission to reprint some of his material in this book.

Solar Energy Applications

Harold Heywood

Taken with permission from Engineering, 176, 377, 409 (1953). *First presented to the British Association for the Advancement of Science in September, 1953.*

Research at the Imperial College.—At Imperial College, London, experimental studies commenced in 1947, and have been continued by students on various aspects of the utilization of solar energy. The first series of experiments was made on a flat-plate absorber, one foot square, covered on the front surface by plates of glass, and protected by heat insulation on the back surface. The heat collected was absorbed by means of water channels soldered on the back surface of the copper plate, through which water was circulated under constant head and the temperature rise measured. In this way the rate of heat absorption was determined for various numbers of glass plates and for various temperatures of collection.

Radiometers were constructed to record continuously the solar intensity, and the design was based on the standard Moll thermopile, though larger in size. These radiometers were calibrated by comparison with standard instruments at Kew Observatory, and the thermoelectric output could be shown on an indicator or recorded on a clock-driven drum. Concurrently with these researches on the fundamental principles of heat collection, a water heater with an area of 10 sq ft was installed at the writer's residence at Sidcup, 10 miles southeast of London. The installation was intended to be of temporary nature, but has been in operation for four years. The absorber was constructed from two sheets of corrugated galvanized iron placed in "mirror image" position so that eight water channels were formed along the length of the absorber. The edges were riveted and soldered, and square-section headers fitted at the top and bottom edges. The metal absorber with blackened front surface was enclosed in a wooden casing with heat insulation at the back and with two layers of glass over the front. A hot-water storage tank was placed at a level slightly higher than the top of the absorber, with flow and return pipes, so that the whole formed a thermosiphon circulating system. The water capacity of the absorber was 5 gallons and the storage tank was also of 5 gallons capacity, so that the total water capacity was 10 lb per square foot of absorber surface. The general arrangement is shown in Figure 49; the cost of this section of the research was covered by a grant from the Central Research Fund of the University of London.

Output tests were made during the summer of 1948, the water flow and rate of heating being related to the incident radiant energy. A three-point recorder enabled simultaneous readings to be taken of the maximum and minimum water temperatures in the system and the output from the thermopile radiometer. There are various ways of operating such an

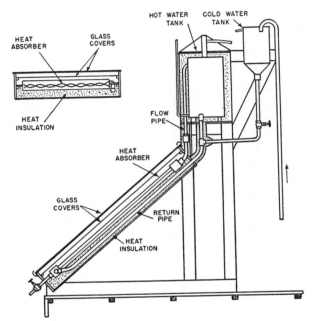

Figure 49.—An experimental solar water heater.

absorber system. One method is to allow the water to circulate naturally for the whole day without the withdrawal of any water, the total heat input being determined. This is not, however, the most effective way of collecting heat; for although during the morning increasing radiation intensity corresponds with rising water temperature, after noon the radiation decreases while the water temperature is still increasing. Hence the water reaches a maximum temperature at about 15 hours, though the radiation intensity may still be appreciable. A more effective method of operating the absorber is to withdraw the water as soon as it is hot enough for the purpose required, and replace it by cold water. In this way the mean temperature of the system can be reduced in the afternoon and an effective heat recovery obtained. In practice, the withdrawal of hot water could be controlled automatically by means of a thermostat.

Daily records of the heat collected were kept during the spring and early summer of 1949. On most days the system was left undisturbed, and the total gain in heat measured over the period 8 to 16 hours local time. The results of these tests, which apply to a water capacity of 10 lb per square foot, were averaged for each month and are shown in Table 17.

TABLE 17

Heat Collection Data

(All figures apply to period 8 to 16 hours and show averages for all days, effective days, and maximum values.)

Month in 1949	No. of days	Btu per sq ft	Max. temperature °F	Effc'y of Collection	Air temperature °F	Bright sun hours
			All Days			
March	31	294	85	47	45	2.8
April	30	575	123	48	56	5.0
May	31	577	124	52	58	4.7
June	30	611	131	54	66	4.5
		Effective Days (bright sun period exceeded 4 hours)				
March	12	477	105	43	47	5.8
April	22	704	135	48	58	6.2
May	23	678	132	56	59	5.4
June	20	774	145	56	68	6.0
			Maximum			
March	1	784	133	55	52	8.0
April	1	908	145	57	66	7.2
May	1	918	152	50	54	8.0
June	1	1,005	170	50	68	8.0

Note: Radiation during April, 1949, was exceptionally high.

The averages for all days are somewhat low, but if effective days are selected then the yield is quite satisfactory. A day is considered "effective" if the bright sunshine period exceeds approximately four hours, and this method of selection gives an indication of the yield that could be expected continuously in more favorable climates. With a reduced water capacity of 5 lb per square foot, the temperature rise is increased, though the heat collected is no greater and may even be slightly less. With this reduced capacity the water may be brought to the boiling point, and on several days the maximum temperature was held at 212° F for a period of two hours. When the absorber was emptied by draining, the maximum temperature attained was 300° F.

Another series of experiments was concerned with concentration by means of plane mirrors placed at the side of the absorbing surface. The arrangement is somewhat similar to the Tacony absorber of Shuman, but with the mirrors placed at all four sides of the square absorber plate (*1*). The shape thus resembled somewhat a square funnel and it was found later that the solar cooker designed by Adams in 1876 was of the same type, but with an octagonal base and eight mirrors forming the sides. The geometry of this system is interesting, and it can be shown that the maximum practical concentration is obtained when the length of the mirrors is three times the side of the square absorber plate. The equilibrium temperature with this arrangement was considerably above the normal boiling point of water, but the mistake was made of using back-silvered mirrors, resulting in considerable absorption by the glass. With surface-silvered mirrors it was estimated that an efficiency of 50 per cent would be attained at 170° F. This arrangement has the advantage that it is less sensitive to the accuracy of alignment than parabolic reflectors, and an error in direction of 10° makes very little difference to the heat collected.

Other experiments were made with spherical mirrors, using searchlight mirrors 36 inches in diameter (*2*). These experiments were of an exploratory character, but showed that an efficiency of 50 per cent could be obtained at a temperature of 300° F. There would thus be no difficulty in generating steam at a useful pressure by such means. Research work is being continued on various aspects of solar-energy utilization, and data are being collected which will be of great value in the subsequent design of larger operating units.

Future Possibilities of Solar-Energy Applications.—The various forms of equipment for the direct utilization of solar energy that have been described in a preceding section were more or less successful technically, but failed economically. This failure may be ascribed to the following causes: the relatively high cost of the equipment; the low yield obtained; and the low cost and ready availability of more convenient fuels such as coal and oil. The present tendency, as is well enough known, is for fuels to become more expensive, a tendency which is most unlikely to change for the better.

At the same time, methods of fabrication are improving, new materials are becoming available both for construction of equipment and for use as working fluids or heat-transfer media, and there is an increasing knowledge of thermodynamic processes. Hence it would seem that the economic balance will change favorably towards the direct utilization of solar energy, though only in suitable locations can any substantial progress be anticipated.

Though it is hazardous to prophesy, an attempt will be made to forecast the future prospects of solar-energy utilization in the various fields. In general, one can say that there is little prospect of using solar energy on a large scale in cities or towns where the population density is high and alternative sources of energy are "on tap," even though they may be expensive. The problem of intermittency and of the night period is sufficient in itself to make effective use of solar energy impossible in such circumstances. The field of application is essentially limited to rural or sparsely populated districts, where land space is cheap and where other energy sources are lacking. Such areas, however, total in the aggregate a large proportion of the habitable surface of the earth and comprise a considerable, though often unconsidered, proportion of the world's inhabitants. There are many fields of application of solar energy where improvements in the amenities of life could be effected by the use of solar energy. The primary problem is not so much one of developing new processes, but is one of design to produce simple equipment at minimum capital expense.

Utilization as Low-Grade Heat.—This field is the one that may be considered solved at the moment, for there are many designs of absorber which are simple and reasonably efficient. The heat may be used as domestic hot water, for space heating or for cooking. In semitropical countries the heat stored in the day may be used at night for house warming. Seasonal storage of heat, i.e., from the summer to the winter period, presents considerable constructional problems. It would be difficult to store the heat collected during the summer at a temperature sufficiently high for direct use in the winter, but it would be more feasible to store the heat in a large water reservoir at a few degrees above atmospheric temperature and to use this as an energy source for a heat-pump system. Such a scheme would collect the radiant energy at a high efficiency with relatively small thermal losses and would enable the advantage or performance efficiency ratio of the heat pump to be increased considerably.

The production of potable water by distillation is another application with definite possibilities in tropical countries. The simplest equipment consisting of glass-covered tanks would yield only about 0.5 lb of water per square foot per day, but improvements in design would increase this to 1 lb or even 2 lb per square foot per day, which is the maximum for direct evaporation. It has been suggested, however, that on some of the islands near Aden a combination of wind-driven thermal pump with heat collector would give a very much larger yield. There may also be scope for increasing the yield of salt by concentration in open salterns or pans, and this is under investigation in Ceylon by a former research student at the Imperial College (*3*).

Power Generation.—This is a problem that is more difficult to solve, though small power units of 5 kw to 10 kw would fulfill a great need in

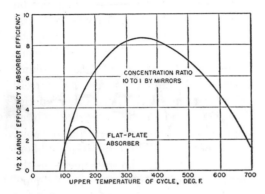

Figure 50.—Efficiencies of solar energy utilization for power for flat-plate and concentrating systems.

many localities, particularly for pumping water for irrigation. Low-temperature absorbers are simple, but the thermodynamic efficiency of conversion of heat to mechanical energy is low. The conversion efficiency increases with higher temperatures, but the absorbers become more complex and expensive. This dilemma is linked with the choice of working fluid and type of prime mover, i.e., reciprocating engine or turbine.

If it is assumed that an engine can attain half of the Carnot efficiency for the cycle, i.e., $\dfrac{(T_1 - T_2)}{T_1}$ where T_1 is the upper temperature and T_2 the lower temperature, then the probable over-all efficiencies based on incident radiation may be calculated for various absorber temperatures. The effect is shown by the curves in Figure 50, which have been calculated for a flat-plate absorber (concentration unity), and for an absorber with mirror concentration of 10 to 1. The probable over-all efficiency, which is one-half of the product of the Carnot efficiency and the absorber efficiency, is zero when either the Carnot efficiency or the absorber efficiency becomes zero, i.e., when the temperature rise is very small, or at the equilibrium temperature, respectively. At a certain intermediate temperature the product of the efficiencies is a maximum, and this defines the optimum temperature of operation for a particular degree of concentration. The Carnot efficiency is quite independent of the working fluid used, but in practical applications the characteristics of the working fluid are very important and influence the choice for a particular range of working temperatures. While steam has many advantages as a working fluid, full advantage of the low-temperature end of the cycle cannot be obtained by the reciprocating engine. The turbine is capable of utilizing effectively steam at low pressure, but against this is the fact that small turbines are inefficient. A working fluid that is more volatile than water would mean that a small but efficient reciprocating engine could be used for power generation, but the working fluid would need to be heated indirectly by water passed through the absorber.

The curves in Figure 50 show that higher efficiencies are obtainable with mirror concentration of the radiation on the absorber, but solar-energy utilization differs from normal heat-engine operation in that the energy costs nothing, and in that it is the construction of the equipment and the value of land space which represent the cost of utilization. Thus, it might be that a very simple form of fixed flat-plate absorber, though occupying greater space than a mirror absorber, would be the more economical to construct. In any case, as much use as possible should be made of fixed absorbing surfaces for the preliminary heating and evaporation of the working fluid, with perhaps a small area of mirrors for superheating the vapor. One possible design which could use the refrigerating fluid Freon-12 is shown diagrammatically in Figure 51. The flat-plate absorber which supplies the major portion of the heat is filled with water

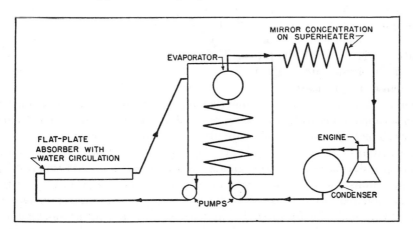

Figure 51.—Schematic representation of a solar power system using Freon–12 as a working fluid.

and the heat subsequently transferred to evaporate liquid Freon. The Freon vapor is superheated in a mirror concentration absorber and then passed to a small high-speed reciprocating engine. After condensation, the vapor is returned to the Freon boiler.

An alternative working fluid having many advantages is air, and a constant-pressure gas-turbine cycle though workable would only be efficient in large powers. A new form of hot-air engine has been developed by Dr. T. Finkelstein in conjunction with the writer (4), and this is specially intended to operate at relatively low temperatures. Thus, there are many ways in which power units could be operated directly by means of solar radiation. Which will prove to be economic, and how distant in the future, depend upon further research and development in design.

Refrigeration and Air Conditioning.—A cooling effect is the ideal load in tropical countries, for the requirement would be a maximum when solar radiation was greatest. The load could take the form of low-temperature freezing for food preservation or more moderate temperatures for air cooling. The ammonia-absorption cycle would probably be the most suitable for refrigeration, the pressure range being modified to suit the heating temperature most convenient. The problem of operation in the day period only could be overcome by increasing the heat-absorbing area either to give a storage of heat which would continue to operate the refrigerator during the night, or a storage of "cold" sufficient to maintain a low temperature in the cooling chamber.

Air cooling could be effected by the lithium-bromide–water-vapor absorption system, in which the diluted lithium-bromide solution would be reconcentrated in the solar heater. As an alternative, the air could be cooled directly by expansion, and turbine machines would be most effective if these were efficient in small sizes. An arrangement is shown diagrammatically in Figure 52. A compressor is driven by two turbines, a power unit, and an expansion unit. A fraction of the air from the compressor passes through the solar heater and then to the power-unit turbine; the remainder of the air, after cooling to atmospheric temperature, passes to the expansion-unit turbine, doing work and being rejected at a temperature below atmospheric. The higher the temperature attained in the solar heater, the smaller the fraction of the compressed air which passes through this part of the circuit, and consequently the greater the coefficient of performance for the system as a whole. The special hot-air engine mentioned in the preceding section has been designed to be reversible, and a similar system to the above could be operated by an engine unit driving a cooling unit. From a study of the literature, little research appears to have been conducted on this aspect of the utilization of solar energy, yet the field is a most promising one.

Conclusions.—The possibilities of using solar energy must be examined impartially against the background of future developments in the fuel-supply situation, and the present economics must not be stressed too greatly. Overoptimism is as great a danger as undue pessimism, for it is clear that applications in the near future are limited, though the potential applications are significant. It is evident that solar-energy utilization has no prospect of success in large communities, but in isolated areas with semitropical climates there are many fields of application ready for development. As fuels become more scarce and costly, so will the economic balance become more favorable, and experience gained now may prove of the

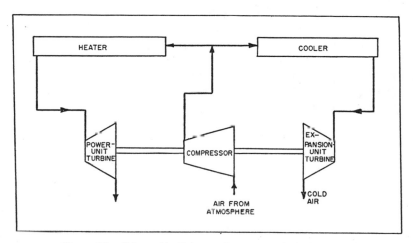

Figure 52.—Schematic diagram of an expansion air-cooler.

greatest value in the future. Many of the possibilities which have been described in this paper involve no new principles, but success is dependent upon careful design and the introduction of new materials of construction as these become available.

Research on solar-energy utilization ranges over many fields of science: solar physics, meteorology, the physics of heat transfer, thermodynamics, thermoelectricity, plant growth, and chemical synthesis. Once an interest in the subject has been roused, few will relinquish the hope of achieving an objective that could benefit many peoples in countries at present only partly developed, and would enable "two ears of corn, or two blades of grass, to grow upon a spot of ground where only one grew before."

Section XI

Miscellaneous Applications of Solar Energy and Suggestions for Further Research

Several miscellaneous applications of solar-energy utilization and related subjects such as the storage of intermittent power are grouped together in this section.

Conversion of Agricultural Products to Power

Farrington Daniels

The older method of converting agricultural products into useful mechanical power was through the feeding of horses and other animals. Many of the early steam engines used wood to heat the boilers. Fossil fuels, although essentially irreplacable, are so cheap and so convenient that they have displaced the annually recurring agricultural fuels except in isolated areas or under special conditions. Sawdust, produced as a by-product in saw mills, has been used to heat the boilers of steam engines which operate the mill. The straw-burning steam engines for threshing machines in wheat harvesting have given way to engines operated by petroleum products. When gasoline was very difficult to obtain during the War, charcoal was used in some countries to provide producer gas or water gas, which was stored in large bags on the roofs of busses and automobiles. These gases contain carbon monoxide, or carbon monoxide and hydrogen, which operate an internal combustion engine. Under normal economic conditions in industrialized countries the cost of collecting wood or other agricultural crops is too high. Ideas for utilizing the mass culture of algae are discussed in Section VIII.

Is new research likely to make the use of agricultural crops more attractive in competition with coal, oil, and gas? Two approaches are possible: one, the Fisher-Tropsch method for preparing liquid fuels, is here, but it is too expensive; the other, the fuel cell, has possibilities which should be explored through more intensive research.

By heating organic material with steam at high temperatures, it is possible to obtain a mixture of carbon monoxide and hydrogen known as synthesis gas. The organic material may come from trees, or grass, or from stalks and leaves obtained as a by-product in agricultural crops. These gases can be combined under pressure in the presence of special catalysts, containing iron and cobalt, to give liquid alcohols and hydrocarbons. These liquid fuels produced by the Fisher-Tropsch process are valuable for operating internal-combustion engines, but they are now too expensive.

Synthesis gas, consisting of carbon monoxide and hydrogen, or producer gas, consisting of carbon monoxide, can be used not only for producing liquid fuels, but they can be used directly in gas engines or converted into electricity through the use of the so-called "fuel cell." Thermodynamics shows that the burning of carbon or hydrogen in air can give about as many calories of work as calories of heat. Only the heat has been used thus far in any practical way, and when it is used to operate an engine only one-third or one-quarter or less is converted into useful work.

Instead of burning hydrogen and oxygen in a heat engine, the hydrogen may be bubbled over one platinum electrode, and oxygen over another electrode, while both are immersed in an acid or alkaline solution. A difference in potential is set up which can be used in an electrochemical battery to produce a current and operate a motor. The operation of hydrogen and oxygen electrodes has been known for nearly half a century.

Theoretically, a similar battery can be made with oxygen bubbling over one electrode and carbon monoxide, methane, or any oxidizable organic material bubbling over the second electrode. It is difficult to find conditions which will produce a suitable electrically conducting ion in equilibrium with carbon or carbon monoxide, and there are serious practical difficulties. Recently, however, there has been considerable activity in the development of fuel cells.

J. A. N. Keletaar of Amsterdam exhibited a fuel cell in 1953, at a meeting of the Netherlands Chemical Society, which operates in a fused bath of sodium phosphate at 600° C. Air is passed through small holes in one electrode and an oxidizable gas such as carbon monoxide or methane is passed through a second electrode. One volt is generated and the current is about 10 amperes per square decimeter. Under these conditions, laboratory experiments showed a 70 per cent conversion of the maximum chemical energy directly into electricity and a 30 per cent conversion into heat. This 70 per cent conversion into useful electricity is more than twice as high as can be expected in a modern heat engine. The 30 per cent of the energy which is generated as heat maintains the high temperature of the fused salt bath. Experiments at the University of Cambridge with nickel electrodes in concentrated potassium hydroxide solution gave nearly 1 volt with a current of 100 amperes per square foot. Hydrogen and oxygen were introduced at the electrodes under a pressure of 30 atmospheres (9, 10).

Dr. Everett Gorin of the Pittsburgh Consolidation Coal Company has carried out experiments on the fuel cell (7, 8) in which the fuel gasification and the operation of the fuel cell are integrated with each other giving a 70 to 75 per cent conversion of the maximum chemical energy into electricity.

Storage of Intermittent Power

Farrington Daniels

Implicit in all the symposium discussion of solar engines was the realization that solar energy is intermittent and that ways must be devised for carrying over the sun's daytime radiation for use at night or for a period of cloudy weather.

In principle, the energy can be stored by pumping water to a higher level and letting it flow back through a water turbine which operates an electrical dynamo. Such a process was carried out in New Mexico, where for many years a small mine was lighted day and night by electric lights fed by a solar engine and dynamo. J. A. Harrington built a parabolic mirror which focused the sun's radiation onto a boiler. It operated an engine and pumped water 20 feet up into a tank of 5,000 gallons capacity.

In practice, very large water reservoirs would be required to meet extensive demands for nighttime electricity. In some locations it would be possible to combine solar engines or generators with hydroelectric plants operated from reservoirs and dams. When the sun is shining, electricity could be generated directly from solar energy and the amount of water allowed to flow through the water turbine could be reduced accordingly. At night or on cloudy days the hydroelectric plant would take over, with the help of the extra water saved by the operation of the solar engines. Again, solar engines can be integrated with a power grid and used to save coal when the sun is shining.

In the long-range future, if solar energy becomes important, it is conceivable that those cities which are adjacent to large, high plateaus suitable for constructing water reservoirs may be favored. Perhaps those cities which have nearby abandoned mines or other large underground space suitable for water reservoirs could store the energy by pumping water to the surface and allowing it to flow back through a turbine situated at the lower level.

Another obvious way of storing solar energy is through the use of storage batteries. Although the lead storage battery is very efficient, it is expensive and of limited life. It has been highly developed as a portable unit for use in automobiles. Radical reduction in the cost and weight of such portable storage batteries could bring back the electrically propelled automobiles. For the storage of electricity produced by solar generators, however, portability of the storage batteries is not necessary and easy change from charging to discharging is not important. It is conceivable that some electrochemical process could be used for the large-scale storage of energy, as, for example, in the electrochemical production of aluminum. The electrodeposition of aluminum from fused salts is highly efficient, and in principle the aluminum plates produced could be set into large installations of primary electrical batteries. After these batteries were run down, the aluminum could be recovered from the spent electrolytes and the operations continued indefinitely in such a way as to be essentially equivalent to a storage battery.

Research on new types of storage batteries is important to support the possible development of solar energy. The batteries for large solar power plants of the future would not have to be light in weight and transportable, they would not have to store the electricity for long periods of time, they would not have to be completely automatic, and the charging reaction would not have to be the identical reverse of the chemical reaction which takes place in the discharging process. With the removal of these limitations, new ideas may be forthcoming.

Seasoning of Timber with Solar Energy

M. L. Ghai

Seasoning of timber requires heat at low potential which might be obtained from solar energy. Results of a theoretical investigation conducted by the author to determine means of applying solar heat to the present methods of seasoning timber are briefly given below to indicate possible research in the future.

The simplest method of seasoning wood is the "air drying method." It is generally not considered as a very desirable method because of the long time required and because of uneven seasoning with surface cracking caused by dry air. It is, however, still in use because of the low initial investment required. Some of the defects of this method might be removed by expediting seasoning with solar energy. The wood to be seasoned may be stacked in a tank covered by glass sheets to trap solar heat, and having side reflectors for diverting additional solar energy. The tank is partly filled with water which maintains the desired humidity. The tank is so arranged that most of the solar energy transmitted by the glass sheets is not received by the timber directly.

For the continuously operated seasoning kiln with controlled temperature and humidity, a number of different systems employing solar energy were studied. A description of the system which appeared to be most satisfactory follows. Air delivered to the kiln is passed through a solar-heat collector, that is, a hot box with a water tank to give the necessary moisture. Part of the air discharged from the kiln is exhausted to the atmosphere, whereas the rest is mixed with fresh air and is conditioned by passage through solar-heat collectors before delivery to the kiln. Inside the kiln, dehumidifying coils are installed to remove part of the moisture given up by the wood. The dehumidifying coils are cooled by circulating water.

Storage of Solar Energy in the Ground

F. A. Brooks

Present commercial agricultural practices for raising the mean temperature of the soil are mainly as follows:

1. Covering seed beds by: (a) Muslin or lightweight canvas, but opening to sunshine from 9 A.M. to 4 P.M. Such a cover conserves solar energy by shielding from wind and decreasing nocturnal cooling. (b) Dark paper, to minimize soil evaporation while still absorbing sunshine. This increases soil temperature 5° to 7° F if the cold frame is covered by muslin from 4 P.M. to 9 A.M. (c) Glass for off-season production. These are described by Minges and Associates (5).

2. Covering seedlings in the field by paper caps. Tests by F. W. Zink (6) show that these raise soil temperature under the caps about 5° F in the winter at latitude 34° N.

3. Forming east-west seed beds with surface sloped downward to the south, to improve the angle of incidence of direct sunshine. A 40 per cent slope increases total irradiation about 39 per cent in January.

4. Adding east-west shields of paper to south-sloping east-west seed beds. Figure 53 shows this system with peppers. Frost damage occurred only at the ends. This system conserves solar energy by: (a) decreasing surface wind, thus increasing soil intake of insolation; (b) decreasing nocturnal radiation loss; (c) adding diffuse reflection of direct sunshine to seed bed. Separate unpublished tests by S. A. Hart (Assistant Agricultural Engineer, University of California, Davis) and F. W. Zink show no significant differences between brown paper and paper with aluminum foil on either or both sides. Heat-transfer calculations on this system by Brooks (1) show 27 per cent gain in total irradiation on beds sloped 40 per cent. This is less radiation gain than in item 3 because of shading until nearly 9 A.M., but the total effect is much better than without paper. Many vegetable growers in the Coachella Valley are spending nearly $90 per acre annually on such systems.

5. Removing cover crop in deciduous orchards before spring frosts and compacting the soil moderately to improve intake of insolation and also to decrease the soil-surface temperature drop at night, when nearly

80 per cent of the nocturnal radiation loss per acre is ultimately drawn from the ground. This practice in large orchards has decreased frost hazard 1° to 2° F, which is often sufficient to avoid artificial frost protection (*2, 3*). It is to be noted that frost protection is primarily an economic problem and no system is acceptable to California citrus growers now unless the installation cost is less than $400 per acre and the average operating cost less than $3.50 per acre hour.

6. Spreading of coal dust or cinders. A report (*4*) from Kazakstan, Russia, claims an advance in cotton ripening by a month or more by increasing the solar-energy intake of the soil by blackening it, using about 100 pounds of coal dust per acre.

There are other important uses for dark surfaces, such as to reduce glare. Furthermore, the possibilities of increasing the intake of solar energy by using plants with minimum foliage as small windbreaks have not yet been thoroughly investigated.

Figure 53.—Photograph of peppers in the Coachella Valley, California, grown on sloped beds with paper shields running east and west. The plants at the ends are recovering from frost damage. Photo courtesy Department of Vegetable Crops, University of California, Davis.

Some Ideas on Solar Energy Utilization

L. M. K. Boelter

The purpose of the following comments will be to present additional ideas relative to the conversion of solar energy to work or to store this energy for use at greater rates and flux densities. However, some overlap with the formal and informal discussion at the Wisconsin symposium may occur.

1. The phenomenon of radiation pressure is described and supported theoretically. The Crookes Radiometer utilizes this principle to accomplish direct conversion. It is to be noted that early explanations of its performance were incorrect.

2. Dolazalck proposed utilizing the $T\Delta S$ (the difference between the free energy and the enthalpy) absorbed from the surroundings by electrolytic cells as a source of electrical power, for instance cells with the proper $\left(\frac{dE}{dT}\right)_p$ would be placed in a hot room and used to charge cells in a cold room. The difference in energy would be available for useful work. Present cells possess characteristics which keep the efficiency of this process down. However, continuous exploration for new cell materials and their relative geometrical arrangements appears to be desirable. Cells for the storage of energy should also be studied.

3. Expansion and contraction of substances and materials is a source now used in certain instruments and controls and equipment for which small amounts of power are required.

4. Is it possible to conceive of an excellent absorber with high thermal conductivity which will be arranged to transmit thermal energy with little loss of entropy to a working fluid? An arrangement such as the Ljungstrom heat exchanger may be worthy of consideration.

5. The irradiation of the earth per unit area is increased as a cloud edge passes over the sun. Although farfetched, it is proposed that an artificial cloud be maintained in a position to increase the energy received on the surface of the earth per unit area at a given place.

6. The air under certain atmospheric conditions stores heat close to the earth. This air can be moved to places on the earth's surface where

needed, as was presented by Professor F. A. Brooks. In a similar manner the earth's surface can be treated by cultivation, cover, etc., to accept or reject more radiant energy. Environmental treatment of the landscape, orientation and construction of the buildings, and other means can be used to control the heat absorbed and make it available when and where needed.

7. The windmill was omitted from consideration by the Wisconsin symposium. Here it seems proper to mention that great improvements were effected before the war by Th. von Karman and through the efforts of Palmer Putnam. Wind forces are a secondary effect, only partially generated through thermal forces. Windpower is discussed by Putnam in Section VI.

8. Wave motors are not directly related to solar utilization, but it will be noted that by recourse to the resonance effect in vertical stand pipes reasonable power outputs are a possibility.

9. A thorough thermodynamic analysis of the heat-power component of the Abbot reflector-engine system appears to be a worthy task.

10. Finally, there is need for an economic study which is designed to present results in a general form so that the parameters for a given locality and time may be inserted to discover the economic feasibility of a given proposed system.

This proposal is the converse of making an economic study of a given solar utilization system and then attempting to discover whether it can be operated economically anywhere in the world.

Conclusions

Farrington Daniels

No effort was made to record or summarize the proceedings of the symposium. The discussions were entirely informal, and emphasis was placed on new ideas and on the areas of research which should be encouraged in order to bring about a greater utilization of solar energy.

It seemed to be the general impression that solar heating is already here, that the solar distillation of fresh water from sea water may not be far away, that efficient solar engines will be very expensive for a considerable time to come, and that the long-range hope of utilizing solar energy lies in photochemistry and in the direct conversion of sunlight into electricity.

House heating, with its modest demands for temperatures only slightly above those of the surroundings, is one of the simplest applications of solar energy. Here good progress has been made. Two different types of heat storage are promising, one in which salt hydrates or other systems undergo a chemical transformation and one in which the heat is stored by raising the temperature of a pebble bed of stones. The first is more efficient; the second is cheaper to build. More research is needed on heat-storage systems and on the collecting surfaces. Fundamental research is needed on the reflection of daylight solar radiation and on the nighttime radiation from the surface. Wind cooling and other meteorological factors need further detailed study. The fact remains, however, that houses have been built and heated entirely with radiation from the sun. A rapid development is expected particularly in areas where the winters are not too severe. Emphasis is likely to be placed on solar heating which can be supplemented with fuel heating on abnormally cold days or in continuing cloudy weather. The cost of the double system will have to be low and the saving in fuel adequate to permit competition with the conventional houses which are heated by fuel. The combination of solar house heating with the electrical heat pump appears promising. The cooling of houses by solar energy is possible but much more difficult than the heating of houses. The demand for cooling is large, however. The solar evaporation of a low-boiling liquid can be used for cooling in a manner similar to that used in certain types of refrigerators. Perhaps cooling systems which give only partial relief from excessively hot weather will come first.

The great handicap in the utilization of solar energy is the very large collecting area required. An acre of concrete or an acre of glass, each, may cost in the neighborhood of $10,000. A capital investment as great as this requires a large return in heat, electricity, fresh water, or other product. New possibilities have been introduced with the large-scale production of thin sheets of inexpensive plastics and thin metal foils such as aluminum. An acre of land can be covered with thin plastic material for a few hundred dollars. More information is needed on cost, light transmission, reflection, and weathering of these plastics. Long-range, outdoor tests are also needed, not only on mechanical strength but also on dust collection, cleanability, water wetting, and other properties. Investigation of thin plastics would be helpful with reference to the distillation of sea water and the storage of heat and even for inexpensive solar engines.

Although it is generally recognized that solar engines cannot compete in industrial areas of the United States with internal combustion engines operated with gasoline or other cheap fuel, the technical possibilities always arouse interest. Solar-engine designs are of two general types. In one, high thermodynamic efficiency is achieved by the use of higher temperatures produced by focusing the sun's radiation with parabolic mirrors arranged mechanically to follow the sun. In the other type only a moderately high temperature, somewhat above 100° C, is achieved with layers of glass plates to minimize reradiation. There are no moving parts and no requirement for an unclouded sun for focusing. The flat-plate collectors are considerably cheaper, but they give a considerably lower temperature and are less efficient in converting heat into work.

Even though solar engines are not now competitive with electricity and with internal combustion engines, their use would tend to reduce the drains on our irreplacable supply of fossil fuels and they might find acceptance in isolated areas, far removed from available electricity and fuel supplies. An inefficient solar engine of only 1 to 5 per cent efficiency might be welcome in such places. Where land and sunshine are cheap, a low efficiency can be tolerated if only the capital cost of the equipment and repairs can be kept sufficiently low. Special efforts should be made to develop inexpensive solar engines even if they are inefficient, emphasizing new designs and new materials quite different from those used in modern fuel-operated engines with efficiencies of over 25 per cent.

Heat engines are limited in their efficiency by the difference between the highest and the lowest temperatures of the engines. Any utilization of slight differences in temperatures for doing useful work would be welcome. Such a utilization would also open up possibilities of utilizing differences in earth temperatures and waste heat from fuel engines. Here again if the problem of using small temperature differences can be solved it may be wise in some areas to sacrifice efficiency of operation for low capital investment. For low-cost engines operating on small temperature differences, studies should be made on vapor engines with low-boiling liquids and on gas-expansion engines which have transparent containing walls of large area which are exposed alternately to periods of sunlight and shade.

The difficulty with solar-energy utilization is the low temperatures ordinarily produced by sunlight. It is an anomoly, therefore, to find that the best furnaces for experimental work at very high temperatures are heated by the sun. Large and perfect parabolic mirrors focusing the sunlight on a small area can give temperatures of 3,000° C and more. These solar furnaces are finding uses in the study of physical properties and chemical reactions of solids at these very high temperatures.

Photochemical reactions, in constrast, do not depend on the conversion of heat into work and they are not limited in efficiency by temperature differences. Chemical reactions of the proper kind would store nearly all the solar energy and give back the full heat when the reaction is reversed in the dark. Suitable practical reactions of this type are difficult to find. The photodecomposition of water by ultraviolet light in the presence of ceric and cerous perchlorate appears to be an important step in the right direction. The fact that photosynthesis of carbohydrates from carbon dioxide and water actually does take place in nature gives encouragement to those who seek new photochemical reactions for storing the sun's energy. Such photochemical reactions need not be limited to water solutions; the search should be carried also to organic systems and crystals.

One of the difficulties of storing solar energy photochemically, or converting it into electricity, is the fact that the photoproducts are apt to recombine or react instantaneously with the other materials which are present. Advantage can be taken of this fact in the case of photochemical reductions which liberate electrons. In certain photoreduction processes the sunlight produces organic products with the liberation of electrons. If these electrons are removed instantly, the reaction cannot reverse itself and the liberated electrons passing through a wire produce a current of electricity which can be utilized directly. Electrodes placed in a suitable, electrically-conducting solution constitute photoreduction and photo-oxidation electrochemical cells which give promise of further progress which might lead to results of practical value. Rabinowitch described this type of cell in Section IX.

The theory of photovoltaic cells has been reviewed earlier in this book. The direct conversion of light into electricity through solid semiconductors appears to be one of the best ways of converting sunlight directly into electricity. A few months after the symposium, an important announcement was made by the Bell Telephone Company. With the use of a boron-treated silicon transistor, electrical energy of 50 watts can be produced continuously by sunlight falling on a square yard of surface. This is an invention of real promise for the direct utilization of solar energy. These silicon transistors can be very thin, but they require material of extraordinary purity and are very expensive. It is to be hoped that they can be produced in large quantity at a price which will make them generally available.

The symposium profited greatly by bringing together scientists from many different fields. Meteorologists contributed much in reviewing the available data on solar radiation and the additional type of data which would be valuable. They pointed out many possibilities, not only in the design of solar-heated houses, but in the retardation of frost, the early melting of snows, the use of windmills, and geophysical processes.

It is hoped that the material discussed at the symposium and the ideas presented here may serve to encourage further research so that our abundant supply of solar energy may be still better utilized.

Appendix

A Survey of United States Patents Pertaining to Utilization of Solar Energy

John A. Duffie

The aid of Mrs. Patricia Orcutt in preparing this patent survey is acknowledged with thanks.

Listed below are some 240 United States patents, dating from Ulysses Pratt's 1852 patent on an "Improvement in Processes of Bleaching Ivory," to the present, and relating to the utilization of solar energy. This list undoubtedly will overlook some pertinent patents; however, it represents an extensive and interesting collection of ideas and developments, some practical and some otherwise, a few of which are outlined below.

Many of these patents could well have been included in the bibliographies of the proceeding sections; and, in fact, some were, where authors have made specific reference to them. The general subject of the patents is indicated by the title and by the classification notes described below. A complete subject file of these patents would include such headings as radiation measurements; hot-water and hot-air collectors; energy storage; concentrating mirrors, lenses and their positioning devices; furnaces; house-heating systems; solar stills; engines using NH_3, SO_2, steam, air, or other working fluids; photoelectric and thermoelectric generating devices; air-conditioning systems; devices for industrial use; water heaters and water-heating systems; devices for therapeutic purposes; solar dryers; bleaching apparatus; and others.

The earliest patents in this listing relate to the use of solar radiation in bleaching processes. In addition to Pratt's 1852 patent, Welling (1855), Miller (1883), and others have described apparatus for bleaching of ivory; Welling's device consisted of a pyramidal glass case in which plates of ivory were set on edge and placed on a north-south line "so that in the morning the sun will shine on one side of the ivory plates while the other receives the reflected light and heat from the pyramidal glass case and the

255

next plate of ivory, and in the afternoon the opposite action takes place." Miller, on the other hand, placed the ivory in "hermetically-closed glass covered vessels" and exposed it to the sun while keeping it at low temperature by immersion in water. Solar bleaching of Irish moss is described in two recent patents (Siehrs, 1950).

Solar dryers were also the subject of a number of early solar-energy patents. They consisted usually of glass covers, provision for ventilation, trays upon which the fruit or other material to be dried could be placed, and in some cases a stove or other source of auxiliary heat. Rice (1867) noted such a device, which had "a glass door to admit rays of heat and intercept their return." Keeler (1877) described a fruit dryer in which the drying space was an inclined chest or chamber, with an inverted V-shaped top to permit passage of solar radiation. The transparent plates were so arranged that condensate which formed on them would run down into a collecting trough, in a manner similar to that of the stationary type solar stills described in Section V of this book. Other solar dryers were described for treating fruit, raisins, fish, and brick. In 1928, Shipman patented a solar-heat dryer in which peat and similar materials to be dried are placed on a conveyor and moved through a housing with a transparent top and air-circulating means. Dunkak, in a more recent patent (1949), describes a solar-activated dehumidifier, a device for application to breather tubes in which a desicant is regenerated by solar energy.

Some of the principles upon which recent developments in solar-energy utilization are based were recognized by early patentees and noted in their patents. Hittell and Dietzler (1877), in a broad patent, described an assembly of a collecting device, a mass of iron or other material, insulated for heat storage, and a flue in which the heated mass was to be placed and in which a draft of heated air for "industrial or other purposes" was to be produced. Weston (1888) claimed a "combination of a thermopile, a means arranged to concentrate or converge solar rays thereon, and a secondary or storage cell in circuit with said thermopile." Early note of the idea of using water tubes "spaced apart, and sheets of copper between the respective tubes," similar to those in use in some modern collectors, was made by Bailey (1910). Emmet (1911) proposed the use of small high-pressure boilers to raise the temperature and thus the thermal efficiency of a solar engine, and Severy (1896), in one of a series of patents, claimed "a solar boiler or heat receiver consisting of a thin box-like chamber of small cubical contents relative to the area of the cross-section of the solar beam it interrupts, one or more thicknesses of glass or similar material transparent to the sun's rays but opaque to dark heat rays, placed over the front surface of the heat receiver and separated therefrom and from each other by an air space." Rice (1867) also noted the use of glass to admit the sun's radiations and "intercept their return," and Willsie (1915) noted that "sheets of other transparent substances, as insoluble gelatin, celluloid, paper, etc., may be used in the place of glass."

A great variety of concentrating devices, positioning devices, and heliostats have been described in the patent literature. Some of the better-known devices are those patented by Eneas (1901), Shuman and Boys (1917), and Abbot (1932, *et seq.*). Numerous types of flat-plate collectors and water heaters have also been designed and patented; water heaters have been the most popular subject of inventions.

Space-heating and air-conditioning patents have also been issued. Morse (1881) proposed mounting a vertical collector on the outside of a wall, with air openings and louvers at the bottom and top of the collector to both the inside room space and the outside atmosphere. Thus he claimed that by opening combinations of the louvers he could heat outside air and send it to the room, heat room air and recycle it to the room, or draw air from the room, all by natural draft. Very recently Miller (1954) patented a "Solar Heat Trap" which is the same as the collectors described by Löf in Section III of this volume. Newton (1944 and 1946) described heating and cooling systems using a common daytime collector and night-time radiator, with high and low temperature chemical heat storage, with control systems. Wilson (1951) patented a combined solar-energy–heat-pump heating system which included a collector built of a blackened copper plate with multiple channels attached and connected to a water reservoir which had in it the evaporator coils of the heat pump. The condenser of the heat pump was in a secondary reservoir from which heating water was drawn to provide heat for the house. Solar distillation has also been the subject of a number of patents, particularly those dealing with plastic stills for life-raft use developed during World War II. Single-effect stills are described by Ushakoff, Delano, Barnes, and others; and Ginnings (1948) described a multiple-effect plastic still. Abbot (1938) patented a solar distiller which used a cylindrical parabolic mirror to focus radiation on a boiling tube.

During the course of perusal of these several hundreds of patents, a number of unusual applications of solar energy were noted. Rieke (1898) patented a "Stump-Burner and Insect Exterminator," which consisted of a large converging lens mounted on a wagon in a fashion so that solar radiation could be focused on a plate which was to be positioned immediately over the stump. Parker (1917) proposed a "Solder Heating Tool" which had a lens and solder pot mounted on a handle.

Lee (1945) proposed the use of an "apparatus for forming artificial thermals for sail-plane use, . . . a black body positioned to permit solar rays to impinge thereon to heat said body and in turn to heat the adjacent atmosphere thereby causing it to ascend." Kim (1949) patented a "Cocoon Sun Sweat Suit," described as a transparent plastic "health suit." Several other uses of solar energy for therapeutic purposes have been described.

Patents on subjects not directly pertinent to use of solar radiation have not been included in this listing. For example, there are a large number of patents on thermoelectric generators, but only those that specifically mention solar energy (e.g., Weston) are included. There are also interesting patents on heat pumps, heating and air-conditioning systems which use as heat sources the ground or other sources in which heat is solar in origin. However, these have not been included, except for Wilson, because of space and time limitations and because those located do not specifically involve combined solar-energy–heat-pump systems.

Listing of Patents.—The list of patents is arranged chronologically, with patentee, number, date and title, and the general subject matter is indicated under one or more of the following headings:

1. Collectors: Includes flat-plate type air or liquid heaters and boilers. Most of this group are water heaters.
2. Concentrating Devices: Includes mirrors, lenses, positioners, and accessories. Most of these are by nature liquid heaters or boilers, although many of the patents do not specify use for the energy.
3. Storage: Includes specific-heat type and chemical type energy storage.
4. Engines and Pumps: Includes engines or pumps using steam, air, SO_2, NH_3, or other working fluids.
5. Distillers.
6. Cookers.
7. Heating Systems: Includes heating and air-conditioning systems, hot-water systems, etc.
8. Miscellaneous: Includes dryers, bleaching devices, solar thermoelectric generators, therapeutic devices, etc.

The combination of one or more of these numbered classes, plus the title of the invention, will serve to indicate in a convenient manner the subject matter of the patents.

Patentee	Patent	Date	Type	Description
U. Pratt	8,639	6 Jan. 1852	8	Improvement in processes of bleaching ivory
W. M. Welling	13,928	11 Dec. 1855	8	Improvement in devices for bleaching ivory

Patentee	Patent	Date	Type	Description
J. Phyfe	15,983	28 Oct. 1856	8	Ivory bleaching apparatus
B. Robinson	48,723	11 July 1865	8	Apparatus for curing & drying fish
D. Rice	68,459	3 Sept. 1867	8	Machine for drying fruit
D. K. Tuttle	85,875	12 Jan. 1869	8	Bleaching ivory, bone, etc.
E. Sperry	117,476	25 July 1871	7	Improvement in cooking apparatus
G. A. Dietz	172,398	18 Jan. 1876	8	Fruit driers
W. Crookes	182,172	12 Sept. 1876	8	Apparatus for indicating the intensity of radiation
J. S. Hittell & G. W. Deitzler	188,517	20 Mar. 1877	2, 3, 7	Apparatus for collecting, storing & utilizing solar heat
J. M. Keeler	189,472	10 Apr. 1877	8	Fruit-driers
E. Moreau	201,439	19 Mar. 1878	1	Apparatus for the production of hot air
A. Viol & C. P. Duflot	202,078	2 Apr. 1878	8	Process for bleaching feathers
J. R. Mauzey	227,028	27 Apr. 1880	2	Solar heater
E. F. Ely	229,109	22 June 1880	8	Drying apparatus
E. J. Molera & J. C. Cebrian	230,323	20 July 1880	1	Boilers & condensers for vapor engines
E. S. Morse	246,626	6 Sept. 1881	1, 7	Warming & ventilating apartments by sun's rays
G. W. Deitzler	257,560	9 May 1882	2	Apparatus for utilizing solar heat
W. Calver	260,657	4 July 1882	1, 4	Method of & means for utilizing rays of the sun
N. S. Willet	280,271	26 June 1883	8	Brick drying apparatus
W. P. Kirkland	281,084	10 July 1883	2, 8	Solar fruit dryer
J. Miller	281,780	24 July, 1883	8	Method of & apparatus for bleaching ivory
W. Calver	290,851	25 Dec. 1883	2, 3, 4	Apparatus for storing & distributing solar heat
W. Calver	290,852	25 Dec. 1883	1, 8	Water lens for solar heaters
W. Calver	291,146	1 Jan. 1884	2, 8	Solar reflector
W. Calver	291,147	1 Jan. 1884	2, 8	Controlling the temperature of solar heaters
W. Calver	291,491	8 Jan. 1884	2	Utilizing the rays of the sun
W. Calver	294,117	26 Feb. 1884	1, 2	Condensing solar rays
W. A. Meeker	300,995	24 June 1884	8	Fruit-drier
H. A. W. Braune	326,711	22 Sept. 1885	2	Self-acting solar reflector
E. Weston	389,124	4 Sept. 1888	2, 3	Apparatus for utilizing solar radiant energy
E. Weston	389,125	4 Sept. 1888	2, 3	Utilizing solar radiant energy
A. L. Reynolds	408,929	13 Aug. 1889	2, 4	Solar water-lifting apparatus

Patentee	Patent	Date	Type	Description
W. Calver	412,724	15 Oct. 1889	2	Solar reflecting apparatus
W. Calver	412,725	15 Oct. 1889	1, 2	Solar stove
J. Dennis	415,407	19 Nov. 1889	8	Rack for drying brick
C. Tellier	433,055	29 July 1890	1, 4	Apparatus for utilizing atmospheric or solar heat for raising water
C. M. Kemp	451,384	28 Apr. 1891	1	Apparatus for utilizing the sun's rays for heating water
M. L. Severy	495,163	11 Apr. 1893	1, 2, 3	Apparatus for obtaining continuous power from the sun
M. L. Severy	496,959	9 May 1893	2	Apparatus for utilizing solar heat
M. L. Severy	497,079	9 May 1893	2, 4	Apparatus for the utilization of solar heat
M. L. Severy	503,004	8 Aug. 1893	2	Reflector for radiant energy
E. C. Ohmart	504,890	12 Sept. 1893	2	Device for reflecting & refracting radiant energy
H. E. Paine	509,390	28 Nov. 1893	1, 2	Solar heater
H. E. Paine	509,391	28 Nov. 1893	2	Solar heater
H. E. Paine	509,392	28 Nov. 1893	2	Solar heater
H. E. Paine	509,393	28 Nov. 1893	2	Solar heater
L. W. Allingham	514,669	13 Feb. 1894	2	Heliomotor
F. H. Monks & M. L. Severy	528,255	30 Oct. 1894	2, 4	Apparatus for utilizing solar energy
C. G. O. Barr	561,755	9 June 1896	1, 2, 4	Apparatus for producing motive power by means of heat of the sun
H. C. Reagan, Jr.	588,177	17 Aug. 1897	8	Application of solar heat to thermo batteries
M. L. Severy	567,618	15 Sept. 1896	1	Apparatus for utilization of solar heat
W. Calver	603,317	3 May 1898	1, 2	Solar apparatus
H. F. Cottle	608,755	9 Aug. 1898	2, 3, 8	Apparatus for storing & using solar heat
V. Rieke	612,675	18 Oct. 1898	2, 8	Stump-burner & insect exterminator
C. A. Davis	629,122	18 July 1899	1	Solar water-heater
H. Tudor	658,195	18 Sept. 1900	1, 3	Solar heater
E. H. McHenry	659,450	9 Oct. 1900	1	Apparatus for obtaining power from solar heat
A. G. Eneas	670,916	26 Mar. 1901	2, 4	Solar generator
A. G. Eneas	670,917	26 Mar. 1901	2	Solar generator
M. M. Baker	679,451	30 July 1901	1	Solar water heater & steam generator
M. M. Baker	681,095	20 Aug. 1901	6	Solar oven & cooker
J. M. Wishart	682,658	17 Sept. 1901	1	Solar heater

Patentee	Patent	Date	Type	Description
K. C. Wideen	683,088	24 Sept. 1901	1, 2	System for collecting & utilizing solar heat
M. M. Baker	695,136	11 Mar. 1902	1	Solar water heater
M. de la Garza	696,326	25 Mar. 1902	2	Solar heating apparatus
P. G. Hubert	705,350	22 July 1902	1	Solar heater
J. M. Browning	748,696	5 Jan. 1904	1	Solar heater
E. Moss	761,596	31 May 1904	2	Solar heater
A. Beurrier	776,106	29 Nov. 1904	4	Apparatus for raising fluids by solar heat
E. C. Ketchum	784,005	28 Feb. 1905	2, 3, 4	Apparatus for utilizing solar heat
E. P. Brown	787,145	11 Apr. 1905	1, 2	Solar motor
W. M. Fulton	795,761	25 July 1905	4	Atmospheric pressure & temperature motor
M. A. G. Himalaya	797,891	22 Aug. 1905	2	Solar apparatus for producing high temperatures
W. S. Sides & J. P. Klensch	807,642	19 Dec. 1905	1	Solar heater
A. Carter	811,274	30 Jan. 1906	1, 2	Solar furnace
M. T. Cunniff	819,342	1 May 1906	1	Solar water heater
C. H. Pope	820,127	8 May 1906	2	Apparatus for the utilization of solar heat
C. L. Haskell	842,658	29 Jan. 1907	1	Solar heater
F. M. Huntoon	842,788	29 Jan. 1907	1	Solar heater
F. M. Huntoon	895,761	11 Aug. 1908	1	Solar water heater
G. N. Saegmuller	917,799	13 Apr. 1909	8	Solar attachment
P. T. Glass	921,976	18 May 1909	1	Solar water heater
M. L. Severy	937,013	12 Oct. 1909	1, 2	Means for utilizing solar heat
M. L. Little	965,391	26 July 1910	2	Solar heating plant
W. J. Bailey	966,070	2 Aug. 1910	1	Solar heater
W. L. R. Emmet	980,505	3 Jan. 1911	1, 2	Apparatus for utilizing solar heat
A. M. Brosius	983,434	7 Feb. 1911	5	Solar still
E. H. McHenry	984,585	21 Feb. 1911	1, 4	Solar heat motor
E. H. McHenry	991,161	2 May 1911	1, 4	Solar heat motor
C. S. Bradley	995,219	13 June 1911	1, 3, 5	Utilizing natural heat
F. Shuman	1,002,768	5 Sept. 1911	1, 4	Utilizing heat for the development of power
L. L. Rountree	1,003,514	19 Sept. 1911	1	Solar heater
R. S. McIntyre	1,004,888	3 Oct. 1911	1	Solar water heater
T. F. Nichols	1,014,972	16 Jan. 1912	2	Solar heater
J. M. Kennedy & J. O'Hara	1,034,465	6 Aug. 1912	1	Solar water heater
A. H. Evans	1,042,418	29 Oct. 1912	1	Device for utilizing solar heat
T. F. Nichols	1,047,554	17 Dec. 1912	1, 2	Solar steam-generator
T. W. Walker	1,056,861	25 Mar. 1913	1	Solar heater

Patentee	Patent	Date	Type	Description
D. A. Harrison	1,068,650	29 July 1913	1	Solar water heater
C. Barnard	1,073,729	23 Sept. 1913	8	Drier
F. A. Skiff	1,074,219	30 Sept. 1913	2	Solar heater
M. de la Garza	1,081,098	9 Dec. 1913	2	Solar heating apparatus
A. C. Thring	1,093,498	14 Apr. 1914	1, 2	Sun-power water heater
H. L. Foresman	1,093,925	21 Apr. 1914	1	Solar heater
H. E. Willsie	1,101,000	23 June 1914	1, 4	Apparatus for utilizing solar heat
H. E. Willsie	1,101,001	23 June 1914	2, 4	Method for utilizing solar energy
H. D. Smelser	1,111,239	22 Sept. 1914	2	Device for concentrating rays of the sun
C. E. Burnap	1,119,063	1 Dec. 1914	1	Boiler
H. E. Willsie	1,130,870	9 Mar. 1915	1, 3	Apparatus for utilizing solar heat
H. E. Willsie	1,130,871	9 Mar. 1915	1, 2, 3	Solar apparatus
H. A. Cherrier	1,158,175	26 Oct. 1915	6	Solar cooker
T. F. Nichols	1,162,505	30 Nov. 1915	2	Solar boiler
R. B. Ryder	1,213,957	30 Jan. 1917	8	Drying-house
R. A. Fessenden	1,217,165	27 Feb. 1917	1, 3	Power plant
B. C. Goff	1,220,091	20 Mar. 1917	2	Solar device
J. O. Parker	1,224,011	24 Apr. 1917	8	Solder heating tool
M. Burlew	1,233,974	17 July 1917	8	Raisin-curing apparatus
F. Shuman & C. V. Boys	1,240,890	25 Sept. 1917	2	Sun-boiler
W. T. Bailey	1,242,511	9 Oct. 1917	1	Solar heater
G. Wilcox	1,250,260	18 Dec. 1917	1	Solar heater
D. A. Harrison	1,258,405	5 Mar. 1918	1	Solar heater
E. Stevens	1,300,670	15 Apr. 1919	8	Evaporator
F. A. Graham	1,302,363	29 Apr. 1919	5	Distilling apparatus
G. J. Trosper	1,325,596	23 Dec. 1919	2	Solar heater
E. D. Arthur	1,338,644	27 Apr. 1920	1	Solar heater
P. Okey	1,343,577	15 June 1920	1, 4	Heat engine
A. V. Folson	1,345,758	6 July 1920	2	Solar steam generator
C. Barnard & H. H. Gates	1,362,216	14 Dec. 1920	8	Sun fruit-drier
W. J. Harvey	1,386,781	9 Aug. 1921	2, 4	Solar motor
M. E. Moreau	1,424,932	8 Aug. 1922	2, 4	Solar heating device
W. G. Cartter & E. D. Arthur	1,425,174	8 Aug. 1922	1, 3	Solar heat collecting apparatus
C. J. Nutt	1,442,696	16 Jan. 1923	2	Heating device
F. E. Danner	1,473,018	6 Nov. 1923	1	Solar heater
M. E. Moreau	1,479,923	8 Jan. 1924	2	Solar furnace
F. Merz	1,493,368	6 May 1924	4	Production of motive force
W. A. Anderson	1,575,309	2 Mar. 1926	2	Solar heating element
A. Marcuse	1,599,481	14 Sept. 1926	2	Solar heater
H. Metzech & F. C. Werner	1,658,455	7 Feb. 1928	2	Solar heater

Patentee	Patent	Date	Type	Description
W. Christiansen	1,672,750	5 June 1928	2	Solar heater
P. L. Vinson	1,673,429	12 June 1928	2	Sun-ray heater
L. H. Shipman	1,678,711	31 July 1928	8	Solar-heat drier
L. H. Shipman	1,683,266	4 Sept. 1928	2	Solar heating apparatus
R. H. Goddard	1,700,675	29 Jan. 1929	1, 2	Vaporizer for use with solar energy
E. B. Maxwell	1,705,988	19 Mar. 1929	2, 3	Solar heater
J. A. Gould	1,747,826	18 Feb. 1930	1	Solar water heater
H. A. Wheeler	1,753,227	8 Apr. 1930	1, 7	Solar water heating system
C. H. Drane, Jr.	1,765,136	17 June 1930	1, 4	Apparatus for utilizing solar heat
E. Kempton	1,772,219	5 Aug. 1930	8	Solar bath
A. P. Ousdal	1,784,382	9 Dec. 1930	8	Apparatus for utilizing solar radiations for therapeutic purposes
T. Romagnoli	1,785,651	16 Dec. 1930	1, 4	Sun heat motor
R. W. Eaton	1,802,635	28 Apr. 1931	1, 7	Solar water heater
G. W. Dooley	1,812,516	30 June 1931	5	Means for purifying water
E. J. D. Coxe	1,814,897	14 July 1931	2	Apparatus for utilizing solar heat
W. J. Harvey	1,822,029	8 Sept. 1931	2, 8	Sunlight control & concentrating device
C. F. Kunz	1,837,449	22 Dec. 1931	1	Solar heater
H. A. Wheeler & F. J. Bentz	1,853,480	12 Apr. 1932	1, 7	Solar water heater
C. G. Abbot	1,855,815	26 Apr. 1932	2	Apparatus for utilizing solar heat
H. A. Wheeler	1,873,854	23 Aug. 1932	1, 7	Solar water heating system
W. L. R. Emmet	1,880,938	4 Oct. 1932	2	Apparatus for utilizing solar heat
W. F. Clark	1,888,620	22 Nov. 1932	1	Solar heater
W. F. Clark	1,889,238	29 Nov. 1932	1	Solar heater
C. G. Abbot	1,946,184	6 Feb. 1934	2	Solar heater
R. H. Goddard	1,951,403	20 Mar. 1934	1	Heat absorbing apparatus for use with solar energy
R. H. Goddard	1,951,404	20 Mar. 1934	2	Focusing mirror & directing mechanism therefor
K. Sawada	1,952,945	27 Mar. 1934	8	Solar ray therapeutic apparatus
D. K. Warner	1,957,624	8 May 1934	7	Air conditioning with ground cooling & solar heat
R. H. Goddard	1,969,839	14 Aug. 1934	2	Apparatus for absorbing solar energy
H. A. Wheeler	1,971,242	21 Aug. 1934	1, 7	Solar water heater
M. Niederle	1,989,999	5 Feb. 1935	2	Solar water heater
F. A. Gill	1,993,213	5 Mar. 1935	2, 3, 4	Solar ray apparatus
E. H. Pendleton	1,997,598	16 Apr. 1935	8	Sun valve

Patentee	Patent	Date	Type	Description
H. Hodgson	2,064,345	15 Dec. 1936	1	Solar heater
H. M. Carruthers	2,065,653	29 Dec. 1936	1	Solar water heater
O. H. Mohr	2,122,821	5 July 1938	1, 3	Solar heater
C. G. Abbot	2,133,649	18 Oct. 1938	2	Solar heater
J. M. Arthuys	2,135,997	8 Nov. 1938	2	Automatic heliostat
C. G. Abbot	2,141,330	27 Dec. 1938	2, 5	Solar distilling apparatus
S. A. Courtis & W. F. Courtis	2,182,222	5 Dec. 1939	2	Solar heater
O. H. Mohr	2,202,019	28 May 1940	1, 7	Solar actuated cooler
C. G. Abbot	2,205,378	25 June 1940	2	Solar flash boiler
B. H. Cally	2,208,789	23 July 1940	1	Solar water heater
E. J. Barry	2,213,894	3 Sept. 1940	1	Solar water heater
C. M. Heck	2,234,122	4 Mar. 1941	8	Method of controlling the temperature of objects
C. G. Abbot	2,247,830	1 July 1941	2, 3	Solar heater
E. T. Turner	2,249,642	15 July 1941	1, 3, 4	Solar power apparatus
A. De Bogory	2,257,524	30 Sept. 1941	1	Solar water heater
J. D. McCain	2,259,902	21 Oct. 1941	2	Solar heater
C. A. Scott	2,311,579	16 Feb. 1943	1	Solar heater
C. A. Scott	2,316,191	13 Apr. 1943	1	Solar heater
B. H. Bohmfalk	2,332,294	19 Oct. 1943	2, 5	Distilling apparatus
T. C. Schenk	2,342,062	15 Feb. 1944	5	Device for producing potable water from sea water
S. C. Kain	2,342,201	22 Feb. 1944	5	Distillation device
A. B. Newton	2,342,211	22 Feb. 1944	1, 3, 7	Utilization of natural heating & cooling effects
C. A. Routh, R. W. Routh & O. O. Summer	2,358,476	19 Sept. 1944	1	Solar water heater
R. S. Dean	2,366,184	2 Jan. 1945	8	Production of potable water from saline solutions
F. W. Lee	2,371,629	20 Mar. 1945	8	Means for producing artificial thermals
H. A. Kezer	2,382,722	14 Aug. 1945	2	Solar heater
W. S. Barnes	2,383,234	21 Aug. 1945	5	Solar water still
R. Bloch & I. Schnerb	2,383,762	28 Aug. 1945	8	Preparation of a green dyestuff & starting material therefor
R. Bloch & I. Schnerb	2,383,763	28 Aug. 1945	8	Crystallization of salts from aqueous solutions
R. H. Taylor	2,388,940	13 Nov. 1945	1	Solar heater
A. B. Newton	2,396,338	12 Mar. 1946	1, 3, 7	Radiation heating & cooling system
W. R. P. Delano	2,398,291	9 Apr. 1946	5	Collapsible distillation apparatus
W. R. P. Delano	2,398,292	9 Apr. 1946	5	Solar distilling apparatus
W. J. Harkness	2,402,326	18 June 1946	1	Solar heater
W. R. P. Delano	2,402,737	25 June 1946	5	Process & apparatus for distilling liquids

Patentee	Patent	Date	Type	Description
W. R. P. Delano & W. E. Meissner	2,405,118	6 Aug. 1946	5	Solar distillation apparatus
W. R. P. Delano	2,405,877	13 Aug. 1946	5	Apparatus for solar distillation
J. M. Brady	2,410,421	5 Nov. 1946	2, 8	Solar operated electric switch
W. H. Miller, Jr.	2,412,466	10 Dec. 1946	5	Inflatable floating solar still with capillary feed
W. R. P. Delano	2,413,101	24 Dec. 1946	5	Solar still with nonfogging window
H. S. Bimpson & E. J. Palmer	2,424,142	15 July 1947	5	Solar salt water distilling apparatus
W. R. P. Delano	2,427,262	9 Sept. 1947	5	Inflatable solar still
D. Ginnings	2,445,350	20 July 1948	5	Multiple-effect solar still
E. E. Zideck	2,448,648	7 Sept. 1948	1	Solar water heater
E. A. Ushakoff	2,455,834	7 Dec. 1948	5	Inflatable solar still
E. A. Ushakoff	2,455,835	7 Dec. 1948	5	Inflatable solar still
C. G. Abbot	2,460,482	1 Feb. 1949	2	Solar heat collector
E. B. Dunkak	2,462,952	1 Mar. 1949	8	Solar activated dehumidifier
W. J. Freund	2,467,885	19 Apr. 1949	1, 2	Solar heater for heating liquids
E. del Cueto	2,475,544	5 July 1949	1	Radiant energy collector
C. J. Kim	2,478,765	9 Aug. 1949	8	Cocoon sun sweat suit
W. J. Freund	2,486,833	1 Nov. 1949	1, 3	Heat storage & supply means
R. E. Snyder	2,490,659	6 Dec. 1949	5	Solar heated vacuum still
S. Wilcox	2,508,700	23 May 1950	8	Sun switch
A. E. Siehrs	2,516,023	18 July 1950	8	Treatment of Irish moss
A. E. Siehrs	2,516,024	18 July 1950	8	Treatment of Irish moss
S. D. Lesesne	2,532,924	5 Dec. 1950	8	Solar evaporation of brines
L. W. Cornwall	2,553,302	15 May 1951	1, 3, 7	Solar heating assembly
L. T. Wilson	2,575,478	20 Nov. 1951	1, 3, 7	Method & system for utilizing solar energy
C. L. Stockstill	2,594,232	22 Apr. 1952	1	Solar heater & heat exchanger
M. Telkes	2,595,905	6 May 1952	1, 3	Radiant energy heat transfer device
M. H. Moseley	2,608,968	2 Sept. 1952	2	Solar heat converter
C. W. Harris	2,625,930	20 Jan. 1953	1, 3	Solar-heating structure
E. A. Agnew	2,636,129	21 Apr. 1953	4, 5	Solar engine
A. Poliansky	2,646,720	28 July 1953	2	Sunbeam receiving & reflecting device
C. R. Hooe	2,653,612	29 Sept. 1953	8	Sunray heat cabinet
C. W. Harris	2,671,441	9 Mar. 1954	1	Variable heat insulating apparatus & solar heating system comprising same
K. W. Miller	2,680,437	8 June 1954	1	Solar heat trap

Bibliography
Index

Bibliography

GENERAL REFERENCES

1 Abbot, C. G., *Smithsonian Inst. Misc. Collections, 98*, No. 5 (1939). Utilizing Heat from the Sun.

2 Ackerman, A. S. E., *Smithsonian Inst. Ann. Rept. 1915*, p. 141. Utilization of Solar Energy.

3 *Proc. Am. Acad. Arts Sci., 79*, No. 4 (1951). Conference on the Sun in the Service of Man.

4 C. and E. N. Staff Report, *Chem. Eng. News, 31*, 2057 (1953). Solar Energy.

5 Daniels, F., *Science, 109*, 51 (1949). Solar Energy.

6 Daniels, F., in *Science in Progress*, 7th Series, Yale University Press, p. 251 (1951). Atomic and Solar Power.

7 Heywood, H., *Engineering, 176*, 377, 409 (1953). Solar Energy: Past, Present and Future Applications.

8 Hottel, H. C., *Smithsonian Inst. Ann. Rept. 1941*, p. 151. Artificial Converters of Solar Energy.

9 Hottel, H. C., *et al.*, *Space Heating with Solar Energy*, the proceedings of the August, 1950, symposium at the Massachusetts Institute of Technology, ed. R. W. Hamilton (1954).

10 *Ohio J. Sci., 53*, No. 5 (1953). The Trapping of Solar Energy.

11 Pope, C. H., *Solar Heat, Its Practical Application*, Charles H. Pope, Boston (1903).

12 Thurston, R. H., *Smithsonian Inst. Ann. Rept. 1901*, p. 263. Utilizing the Sun's Energy.

13 *The Nation Looks at Its Resources*, Resources for the Future, Inc., Washington, D. C. (1954). Chapter 5, Energy Resource Problems.

14 *Utilization of Solar Energy: List of References*. A bibliography compiled by INSDOC for National Institute of Sciences of India—UNESCO Symposium on Solar Energy and Wind Power, New Delhi, October 22–25, 1954.

15 Symposium on Solar Energy and Wind Power, New Delhi, India, October 22–25, 1954. Forthcoming publication of UNESCO.

16 Pleijel, Gunnar, *The Computation of Natural Radiation in Architecture and Town Planning*, Statens Nämnd för Byggnadsforskning, Stockholm (1954).

SECTION I

1   Ayres, Eugene, and Scarlott, C. A., *Energy Sources*, McGraw-Hill Book Co., New York (1952).
2   The President's Materials Policy Commission, *Resources for Freedom*, Vol. *IV: The Promise of Technology*, U.S. Gov't. Printing Office, Washington, D.C. (June, 1952).
3   Putnam, Palmer Cossett, *Energy in the Future*, D. Van Nostrand Co., New York (1953).
4   Rabinowitch, E., *Proc. Am. Acad. Arts Sci.*, *79*, 296 (1951). The World's Energy Supplies and Their Utilization.
5   Furnas, C. C., *Ind. Eng. Chem.*, *46*, 2446 (1954). Energy Sources of the Future.

SECTION II

1   Abbot, C. G., Fowle, F. E., and Aldrich, L. B., *Smithsonian Inst. Misc. Collections*, *74*, No. 7 (1923). The Distribution of Energy in the Spectra of the Sun and Stars.
2   Abbot, C. G., and Aldrich, L. B., *Smithsonian Inst. Misc. Collections*, *92*, No. 13 (1934). The Scale of Solar Radiation.
3   Abbot, C. G., *Smithsonian Inst. Misc. Collections*, *94*, No. 10 (1935). Solar Radiation and Weather Studies.
4   Am. Soc. Heating Ventilating Engrs., *Heating, Ventilating, Air Conditioning Guide*, ed. 32, pp. 274–78 (1954).
5   Brooks, F. A., *Climatic Environment: A Thermal System*, ASCA Store, University of California, Davis, Calif. (1951).
6   Brooks, C. F., and Brooks, E. S., *J. Meteorol.*, *4*, 105 (1947). Sunshine Recorders: A Comparative Study of the Burning Glass and Thermomatic Systems.
7   Brooks, F. A., *J. Meteorol.*, *9*, No. 1, 41 (1952). Atmospheric Radiation and Its Reflection from the Ground.
8   Commission for Instruments and Methods of Observations, Rept. Progress No. 9 of United Nations World Meteorological Organization No. 19, Geneva (1953). Abridged Final Report of the First Session, Toronto (14 Aug.–4 Sept., 1953).
9   Dunkle, R. V., Am. Soc. Mech. Engrs., Paper No. 53–A–20, presented at the Annual Meeting, New York (1953). Thermal Radiation Tables and Applications.
10 Elder, T., and Strong, J., *J. Franklin Inst.*, *255*, No. 3, 189 (1953). The Infrared Transmission of Atmospheric Windows.
11 Fritz, S., *Compendium of Meteorology*, Am. Meteorol. Soc. (1951). Solar Radiant Energy and Its Modification by the Earth and Its Atmosphere.
12 Fritz, S., *Heating and Ventilating*, *46*, 69 (Jan., 1949). Solar Radiation during Cloudless Days.

13 Fritz, S., and MacDonald, T. H., *ibid.*, *46*, 61 (July, 1949). Average Solar Radiation in the United States.

14 Gebbie, H. A., *et al.*, *Proc. Roy. Soc. (London)*, Series A, *206*, 87 (March, 1951). Atmospheric Transmission in the 1 to 14 μ Region.

15 Gier, T. J., and Dunkle, R. V., *Trans. Am. Inst. Elec. Engrs.*, *70*, (1951). Total Hemispherical Radiometers.

16 Hand, I. F., *Heating and Ventilating*, *44*, 80 (Dec., 1947). Solar Energy for House Heating.

17 Hand, I. F., *ibid.*, *47*, 92 (Jan., 1950). Insolation on Clear Days at the Time of Solstices and Equinoxes for Latitude 42° N.

18 Hand, I. F., *ibid.*, *50*, 73 (July, 1953). Distribution of Solar Energy over the United States.

19 Hand, I. F., *ibid.*, *51*, 97 (Feb., 1954). Insolation on Cloudless Days—at the Time of Solstices and Equinoxes.

20 Hand, I. F., *Monthly Weather Review*, *69*, 95 (1941). A Summary of Total Solar and Sky Radiation Measurements in U. S.

21 Hand, I. F., *Pyrheliometers and Pyrheliometric Measurements*, U. S. Weather Bureau, Washington, D. C. (1946).

22 Hand, I. F., *Trans. Am. Geophys. Union 28*, 705 (1947). Preliminary Measurements of Solar Energy Received on Vertical Surfaces.

23 Hand, I. F., *U. S. Weather Bur. Tech. Rept.*, No. 11 (1949). Weekly Mean Values of Daily Total Solar and Sky Radiation.

24 Haurwitz, B., *J. Meteorol.*, *5*, No. 3, 110 (June, 1948). Insolation in Relation to Cloud Type.

25 Johnson, F. S., *J. Meteorol.*, *11*, No. 6, 431 (Dec., 1954). The Solar Constant.

26 Jordan, R. C., and Threlkeld, J. L., *Heating, Piping, Air Conditioning*, *25*, 111 (Dec., 1953). Solar Energy Availability for Heating in the United States.

27 Kelly, C. F., Bond, T. E., and Ittner, N. R., *Agric. Engr.*, *31*, No. 12, 601 (1950). Thermal Design of Livestock Shades.

28 Kennedy, R. E., *Bull. Am. Meteorol. Soc.*, *30*, No. 6, 208 (June, 1949). Computation of Daily Insolation Energy.

29 Kimball, H. H., *U. S. Monthly Weather Rev.*, *52*, No. 10, 473 (Oct., 1924). Records of Total Radiation Intensity and Their Relation to Daylight Intensity.

30 Klein, W. H., *J. Meteorol.*, *5*, No. 4, 119 (August, 1948). Calculation of Solar Radiation and the Solar Heat Load on Man.

31 Linke, F., *Handbuch der Geophysik*, Band VIII, N. 1, 2, 3, Gebruder Borntraeger, Berlin (1942).

32 List, R. J. (ed.), *Smithsonian Inst. Misc. Collections*, *114*, 416 (1951).

33 McAdams, W. H., *Heat Transmission*, 3rd ed., McGraw-Hill Book Co., New York (1954). See p. 60.

34 Moon, P., *J. Franklin Inst.*, *230*, 583 (1940). Proposed Standard Solar Radiation Curves for Engineering Use.

35 Shaw, J. H., *Ohio J. Sci.*, *53*, No. 5, 258 (1953). Solar Radiation.

SECTION III

1   Anon., *Architectural Record, 112,* 179 (July, 1952). Analysis of Tests on House Heat Pumps.

2   Anon., *Edison Elec. Inst. Bull., 20,* 168 (May, 1952). Chemical Heat Storage for Heat Pumps.

3   Anon., *ibid., 21,* 355 (Sept., 1953). Research Results Concerning Earth as a Heat Source or Sink.

4   Ayres, Eugene, and Scarlott, C. A., *Energy Sources,* McGraw-Hill Book Co., New York (1952).

5   Baumer, H., *Ohio State U. Engineering Expt. Sta. News, 19,* 38 (June, 1947). Solar Design.

6   *Edison Elect. Inst. Publication,* No. 53–4 (1953). Bibliography of the Heat Pump through 1951.

7   Borg, C., *Elec. Engr., 72,* 122 (1953); Kidder, A. H., and Weber, J. H., *ibid., 72,* 123 (1953); Harlow, J. H., and Klopper, G. E., *ibid., 72,* 124 (1953). Residential Heat Pump Experiments, I, II, and III.

8   Brooks, F. A., *Smithsonian Inst. Ann. Rept. 1939,* p. 157. Use of Solar Energy for Heating Water.

9   Dietz, A. G. H., and Czapek, E. L., *Am. Soc. Heating Ventilating Engrs. Trans., 56,* 121 (1950). Solar Heating of Houses by Vertical South Wall Storage Panels.

10 Ghai, M. L., *J. Sci. Ind. Research (New Delhi), 12A,* 117 (March, 1953). Solar Heat for Cooking.

11 Ghai, M. L., Bansal, T. D., and Kaul, B. N., *ibid., 12A,* 165 (April, 1953). Design of Reflector Type Direct Solar Cookers.

12 Goethe, S. P., Sutton, G. E., and Loeffler, W. A., Technical Paper, No. 45, Engr. and Ind. Expt. Station, Univ. of Florida (1950).

13 Goss, J. R., unpublished manuscript, Agricultural Engineering Dept., Univ. of California, Davis (1954).

14 Hawkins, H. M., *U. of Florida Engr. and Ind. Expt. Sta. Bulletin,* No. 18 (1947). Domestic Solar Heating in Florida.

15 Heywood, H., *Engineering (London), 176,* 377 and 409 (1953). Solar Energy: Past, Present and Future Applications.

16 Heywood, H., paper presented to the Institute of Fuel, Institution of Mechanical Engineers, London (March 23, 1954). Solar Energy for Water and Space Heating.

17 Hollingsworth, F. N., *Heating and Ventilating, 44,* 76 (May, 1947). Solar Heat Test Structure at MIT.

18 Hottel, H. C., and Whillier, A., Energy Storage in Cyclical Heating-Cooling Operations, published in reference 20: *Space Heating with Solar Energy.*

19 Hottel, H. C., *Proc. Am. Acad. Arts Sci., 79,* 313 (1951). The Engineering Utilization of Solar Energy.

20 Hottel, H. C., *et al., Space Heating with Solar Energy,* the proceedings of the

August, 1950, symposium at the Massachusetts Institute of Technology, ed. R. W. Hamilton (1954).

21 Hottel, H. C., and Woertz, B. B., *Trans. Am. Soc. Mech. Engrs., 64*, 91 (1942). The Performance of Flat Plate Solar Heat Collectors.

22 Hutchinson, F. W., *Heating and Ventilating, 42*, 96 (Sept., 1945). The Solar House, a Full-Scale Experimental Study.

23 Hutchinson, F. W., *ibid., 43*, 55 (March, 1946). The Solar House, a Research Progress Report.

24 Hutchinson, F. W., *Heating, Piping, Air Conditioning, 21*, 102 (Aug., 1949). Solar Irradiation of Walls and Windows.

25 Hutchinson, F. W., and Chapman, W. P., *Am. Soc. Heating Ventilating Engrs. Trans., 52*, 305 (1946). A National Basis for Solar Heating Analysis.

26 Hutchinson, F. W., *Heating and Ventilating, 44*, 55 (March, 1947). The Solar House, a Second Research Progress Report.

27 Ingersoll, L. R., Adler, F. T., Plass, H. J., and Ingersoll, A. C., *Am. Soc. Heating Ventilating Engrs. Trans., 57*, 167 (1951). Theory of Earth Heat Exchangers for the Heat Pump.

28 Jordan, R. C., and Threlkeld, J. L., *Heating, Piping, Air Conditioning, 25*, 111 (Dec., 1953). Solar Energy Availability for Heating in the United States.

29 Jordan, R. C., and Threkeld, J. L., *ibid., 26*, 122 (Feb., 1954). Design and Economics of Solar Energy Heat Pump Systems.

30 Kirpichev, M. V., and Baum, V. A., *Priroda, 43*, 45 (Jan., 1954). Application of Solar Energy (in Russian).

31 Kuraku, H., *J. Chem. Soc. Japan, 63*, 1147, 1512 (1942).

32 Löf, G. O. G., *Arch. Forum, 86*, 121 (Feb., 1947). Solar House Heater Yields Twenty Per Cent Fuel Saving in University of Colorado Experimental Installation.

33 Löf, G. O. G., and Hawley, R. W., *Ind. Eng. Chem., 40*, 1061 (1948). Unsteady State Heat Transfer Between Air and Loose Solids.

34 Löf, G. O. G., and Nevens, T., *Ohio J. Sci., 53*, 272 (1953). Heating of Air by Solar Energy.

35 Löf, G. O. G., *et al.*, Report No. PB 25375, Office of Technical Services, Department of Commerce, Washington, D. C. (1946). Solar Energy Utilization for House Heating.

36 Masson, H., *Bulletin* of Institute Francais d'Afrique Moire, Dakar, No. 14, 389 (1952). Contribution to the Study of the Heating of Water by Solar Radiation.

37 Osteotag, A., *Schweiz. Bauztg., 65*, 426 (1947). Sutter-Adank Solar Heat Accumulator.

38 Parmelee, G. V., Aubele, W. W., and Huebscher, R., *Heating, Piping, Air Conditioning, 20*, 158 (1948). Measurement of Solar Heat Transmission through Flat Glass.

39 Parmelee, G. V., and Aubele, W. W., *ibid., 20*, 116 (June, 1948). Solar and Total Heat Gain through Double Flat Glass.

40   Parmelee, G. V., and Aubele, W. W., *ibid.*, *21*, 111 (Sept., 1949). Solar Energy Transmittance of Eight Inch Hollow Glass Blocks.

41   Parmelee, G. V., and Aubele, W. W., *ibid.*, *22*, 123 (June, 1950). Heat Flow through Unshaded Glass: Design Data for Use in Load Calculations.

42   Parmelee, G. V., and Aubele, W. W., *ibid.*, *23*, 124 (Feb., 1951). Solar Energy Transmittance of Figured Rolled Glass.

43   Parmelee, G. V., and Aubele, W. W., *ibid.*, *23*, 120 (Nov., 1951). Radiant Energy Emission of Atmosphere and Ground—A Design Factor in Heat Gain and Heat Loss.

44   Parmelee, G. V., *ibid.*, *17*, 562 (Oct.-Nov., 1945). Transmission of Solar Radiation through Flat Glass under Summer Conditions.

45   The President's Materials Policy Commission, *Resources for Freedom*, Vol. *IV: The Promise of Technology*, U. S. Gov't Printing Office, Washington, D. C. (June, 1952).

46   Putnam, P. C., *Energy in the Future*, D. Van Nostrand Co., New York (1953).

47   Simon, M. J. (ed.), *Your Solar House*, Simon and Schuster, New York (1947).

48   Sporn, P., and Ambrose, E. R., *Heating and Ventilating*, *50*, 86 (Sept., 1953). Progress of the Heat Pump during the Past Decade.

49   Telkes, M., *ibid.*, *44*, 68 (May, 1947). Solar House Heating, a Problem of Heat Storage.

50   Telkes, M., *ibid.*, *46*, 68 (Sept., 1949). A Review of Solar House Heating.

51   Telkes, M., and Raymond, E., *ibid.*, *46*, 80 (Nov., 1949). Storing Solar Heat in Chemicals. A Report on the Dover House.

52   Telkes, M., *ibid.*, *47*, 72 (Aug., 1950). A Low Cost Solar Heated House.

53   Telkes, M., *Ind. Eng. Chem.*, *44*, 1308 (1952). Nucleation of Supersaturated Inorganic Salt Solutions.

54   Telkes, M., *Sci. Monthly*, *69*, 394 (Dec., 1949).

55   Telkes, M., unpublished report to the Massachusetts Institute of Technology Solar Energy Conversion Project (October, 1945).

56   Threlkeld, J. L., and Jordan, R. C., *Heating, Piping, Air Conditioning*, *26*, 193 (Jan., 1954). Utilization of Solar Energy for House Heating.

57   Whillier, A., *S. African Inst. Mech. Engrs.*, p. 261 (April, 1953). The Utilization of Solar Energy in South Africa.

58   Whillier, A., Solar Energy Collection and Its Utilization for House Heating, Sc.D. Thesis, Massachusetts Institute of Technology, 1953.

59   Mackey, C. O., and Gay, N. R., *Heating, Piping, Air Conditioning*, *26*, 123 (Aug., 1954). Cooling Loads from Sunlit Glass and Walls.

60   Parmelee, G. V., *ibid.*, *26*, 129 (Aug., 1954). Irradiation of Vertical and Horizontal Surfaces by Diffuse Solar Radiation from Cloudless Skys.

61   *Heating and Ventilating*, *51*, 96 (April, 1954). Solar Heat Collectors Used with Heat Pumps.

62   *Bibliography on Domestic and Industrial Applications of Solar Heating*, Engineering Societies Library, New York (1950).

63   Petukhov, B. V., and Krizanovskii, G. M., *Solar Water Heating Devices*, Inst. of Energetics, Academy of Sciences, Moscow (1953). (In Russian.)

SECTION IV

1 Abbot, C. G., *The Military Engr., 35*, 70 (Feb., 1943). Solar Radiation as a Power Source.
2 Abbot, C. G., *Smithsonian Inst. Ann. Rept. 1943*, p. 99. Solar Radiation as a Power Source.
3 Abbot, C. G., *Smithsonian Inst. Misc. Collections, 98*, No. 5 (1939). Utilizing Heat from the Sun.
1 Green, F., J. Meteorol., 4, 60 (1947). Note on the Theory of Nocturnal Radiation Cooling of the Earth's Surface.
5 Heywood, H., *Engineering (London), 176*, 377, 409 (1953). Solar Energy: Past, Present and Future Applications.
6 Hottel, H. C., *Proc. Am. Acad. Arts Sci., 79*, 313 (1951). The Engineering Utilization of Solar Energy.
7 Hottel, H. C., and Woertz, B. B., *Trans. Am. Soc. Mech. Engrs., 64*, 91 (1942). The Performance of Flat Plate Solar-Heat Collectors.
8 Moorehouse, C. F., *Elec. Engr. and Merchandiser (Melbourne) 28*, 75 (1951). Power from Solar Radiation.

SECTION V

1 Abbot, C. G., Publ. No. 3530, *Smithsonian Inst. Misc. Collections, 98*, No. 5 (1930).
2 Anon., *Chem. Eng. News, 31*, 2001 (May 11, 1953).
3 Armstrong, E. F., and Miall, L. M., *Raw Materials from the Sea*, Chemical Publishing Co., Brooklyn, N. Y. (1946).
4 Bloch, M. R., Farkas, L., and Spiegler, K. S., *Ind. Eng. Chem., 43*, 1544 (1951). Solar Evaporation of Salt Brines.
5 Bloch, R., and Martin, H., D. R. P. 660 490 (May 27, 1938, CL. 12a.2).
6 Bloch, R., and Schnerb, I., U. S. Patents No. 2,383,762 and 2,383,763, August 28, 1945. Preparation of a green dyestuff and starting material therefor. Crystallization of salts from aqueous solutions.
7 Bloch, R., *Proc. U. N. Sci. Conf. on the Conservation of Resources*, Lake Success, 1949, Section 7 (b). Use of Solar Energy in Evaporation of Dead Sea Brine.
8 Boutaric, A., *Chaleur & ind., 11*, 59, 147 (1930).
9 Boutaric, A., *Recherches et inventions, 8*, 205 (1927).
10 Bowen, I. S., *Phys. Rev., 27B*, 779 (1926). The Ratio of Heat Loss by Conduction and by Evaporation from Any Water Surface.
11 Cummings, N. W., *Trans. Am. Geophys. Union, 21*, 512 (1940, II). The Evaporation Energy Equations and Their Practical Applications.
12 Cummings, N. W., *ibid., 27*, 81 (1946). The Reliability and Usefulness of the Energy Equations for Evaporation.

13 Cummings, N. W., *ibid.*, *29*, 408 (1948). Discussion of "Some Recent Evaporation Investigations" by Arthur R. Young.

14 Cummings, N. W., and Richardson, B., *Phys. Rev.*, *30*, 527 (1927). Evaporation from Lakes.

15 Dornig, M., *L'Ingegnere*, *17*, 11 (1939).

16 Ginnings, D. C., U. S. Patent 2,445,350, July 20, 1948. Multiple effect solar still.

17 Harding, J., *Proc. Civil Eng. Inst.*, *73*, 248 (1883).

18 Herlihy, J. T., Physical Chemical Studies of the Solar Evaporation of Salt Water, M.S. Thesis, Univ. of Wisconsin, 1953.

19 Hollingsworth, F. M., *Heating and Ventilating*, *45*, 99 (Aug., 1948). Solar Energy to Provide Water Supply for Island.

20 Howe, E. D., *J. Am. Water Works Assoc.*, *44*, 690 (Aug., 1952). Sea Water as a Source of Fresh Water.

21 Pasteur, F., *Compt. rend.*, *30*, 187 (1928).

22 Telkes, M., *Ind. Eng. Chem.*, *45*, 1108 (1953). Fresh Water from Sea Water by Solar Distillation.

23 Telkes, M., Massachusetts Institute of Technology Report, January, 1943.

24 Telkes, M., *OSRD Report* PB 21120 (May, 1945). Solar Distiller for Life Rafts.

25 U. S. Air Force, WPAFB–(A)–0–11, *Instructions for Obtaining Drinking Water with Distillation Kit, Sea Water, Solar Type A-1* (April, 1951).

26 U. S. Dept. of the Interior, *Demineralization of Saline Waters* (October, 1952).

27 U. S. Dept. of Interior, *Second Annual Report on Saline Water Conversion* (January, 1954).

SECTION VI

1 Billig, E., and Plessner, K. W., *Phil. Mag.*, *40*, 568 (1949). The Efficiency of the Selenium Barrier-Photocell when Used as a Converter of Light into Electrical Energy.

2 Brunt, D., *Physical and Dynamical Meteorology*, Cambridge University Press, p. 285 *et seq.* (1941).

3 Chapin, D. N., Fuller, C. S., and Pearson, G. L., *J. Appl. Phys.*, *25*, 676 (1954). A New Silicon p-n Junction Photocell for Converting Solar Radiation into Electrical Power.

4 Chapman, S., *The Earth's Magnetism*, Methuen and Co., London (1951).

5 Chapman, S., and Bartels, J., *Geomagnetism*, Oxford, Clarendon Press (1940).

6 Coblentz, W. W., *Sci. Am.*, *127*, 324 (1922). Harnessing Heat from the Sun.

7 Fleming, J. A. (ed.), *Terrestrial Magnetism and Electricity*, McGraw-Hill Book Co., New York (1939).

8 Fritz, S., *J. Meteorol.*, *6*, 277 (1949). The Albedo of the Planet Earth and of Clouds.

9 Gish, O. H., and Wait, G. R., *J. Geophys. Research*, *55*, 473 (1950). Thunderstorms and the Earth's General Electrification.

10 Graybeal, J. D., A Study of Certain Thermocells as a Means of Utilizing Solar Energy, M.S. Thesis, Univ. of Wisconsin, 1953.

11 Hottel, H. C., *Smithsonian Inst. Ann. Rept. 1941*, p. 151. Artificial Converters of Solar Energy.

12 Kettering, C., *S.A.E. Journal*, *59*, 17 (Dec., 1951). Direct to the Sun for Power.

13 Kingsbury, E. F., and Ohl, R. S., *Bell System Tech. J.*, *31*, 802 (1952). Photo-electric Properties of Ionically Bombarded Silicon.

14 Putnam, P. C., *Energy in the Future*, D. Van Nostrand Co., New York (1953).

15 Putnam, P. C., *Power from the Wind*, D. Van Nostrand Co., New York (1948).

16 Rabinowitch, E., *J. Chem. Phys.*, *8*, 551 (1940). The Photogalvanic Effect: I, The Photochemical Properties of the Thionine Iron System.

17 Rabinowitch, E., *ibid.*, *8*, 560 (1940). The Photogalvanic Effect: II, The Photogalvanic Properties of the Thionine-Iron System.

18 Schonland, B. F. J., *Atmospheric Electricity*, Methuen and Co., London (1953).

19 Telkes, M., *J. Appl. Phys.*, *18*, 1116 (1947). The Efficiency of Thermo-Electric Generators.

20 Telkes, M., *J. Appl. Phys.*, *25*, 765 (1954). Solar Thermoelectric Generators.

21 Trivich, D., *Ohio J. Sci.*, *53*, No. 5, 300 (1953). Photovoltaic Cells and Their Possible Use as Power Converters for Solar Energy.

22 Vestine, E. H., *J. Geophys. Res.*, *58*, 539 (1953). Note on Geomagnetic Disturbance as an Atmospheric Phenomenon.

23 Vestine, E. H., *ibid.*, *59*, 93 (1954). Winds in the Upper Atmosphere Deduced from the Dynamo Theory of Geomagnetic Disturbance.

24 Wulf, O. R., and Davis, L., Jr., *J. Meteorol.*, *9*, 79 (1952). On the Efficiency of the Engine Driving the Atmospheric Circulation.

SECTION VII

1 Buffon, G. L. L., *Supplement a l'Histoire naturelle générale et particulière*, I. Imprimerie Royale (1774).

2 Conn, W. M., *Ceram. Soc. Bull.*, *33*, 69 (March 15, 1954). Use of the Solar Furnace for Studying the System Alumina-Silica.

3 Conn, W. M., and Braught, G., *J. Opt. Soc. Am.*, *44*, 45 (1954). Separation of Incident and Emitted Radiations in a Solar Furnace by Means of Rotating Sectors.

4 Conn, W. M., *Rev. Sci. Instr.*, *22*, 945 (1951). A Solar Furnace of 120'' Diameter for Studying Highly Refractory Substances.

5 Conn, W. M., *Z. angew. Phys.*, *6*, 284 (1954). Gesichtspunkte für den Entwurf von Sonnen-Spiegelöfen für Hochtemperaturforschung und -Entwicklung.

5a Conn, W. M., *J. Franklin Inst.*, *257*, 1 (1954). Recent Progress in Solar Furnaces for High-Temperature Research and Development Work.

6 Couchet, G., *Compt. rend.*, *236*, No. 12, 40 (1953).

7 Davis, G. E., *J. Opt. Soc. Am.*, *39*, 541 (1949). A Method of Measuring High Intensities at the Focus of a Parabolic Reflector with Large Relative Aperture.

8   Hynek, J. A., *Ohio J. Sci.*, *53*, No. 5, 314 (1953). The Use of Optical Systems in the Utilization of Solar Energy.
9   Stock, A., and Heyneman, H., *Ber. deut. chem. Ges.*, *42*, 2863 (1909).
10 Straubel, H., *Z. angew. Phys.*, *1*, 542 (1949). Der Sonnen-Schmelzspiegel.
11 Wood, R. W., *Astrophys. J.*, *29*, 164 (1909). The Mercury Paraboloid as a Reflecting Telescope.

Continued Bibliography from the Mont-Louis Solar Energy Laboratory, Supplied by F. Trombe.

12 Trombe, F., Foex, M., and La Blanchetais, Ch., *Compt. rend.*, *225*, 1073 (1947). Synthèse de l'acide nitrique par concentration du rayonnement solaire.
13 Trombe, F., Foex, M., and La Blanchetais, Ch., *Ann. Chim.* 12ème série, *2*, 385 (1947). Concentration d'énergie solaire pour la réalisation de très hautes températures.
14 Trombe, F., Foex, M., and La Blanchetais, Ch., *Journal des recherches du C.N.R.S.*, *2*, 61 (1948). Utilisation de l'énergie solaire.
15 Trombe, F., Foex, M., and La Blanchetais, Ch., *Compt. rend.*, *226*, 83 (1948). Sur la Fusion continue des substances au four solaire.
16 Trombe, F., *ibid.*, *228*, 786 (1949). Sur des Conditions de traitement des substances au four solaire.
17 Trombe, F., Foex, M., and La Blanchetais, Ch., *ibid.*, *228*, 1107 (1949). Sur la Fusion de l'alumine au four solaire.
18 Trombe, F., and Foex, M., *ibid.*, *230*, 2294 (1950). Réduction de l'oxyde de chrome Cr_2O_3 par l'hydrogène au four solaire.
19 Trombe, F., Foex, M., and La Blanchetais, Ch., *ibid.*, *231*, 44 (1950). Fours à accumulation d'énergie solaire.
20 Trombe, F., "Les Fours solaires," extrait de *Les hautes Températures et leurs utilisations en chimie*, Masson, éd., Paris (1950).
21 Trombe, F., Foex, M., and Wyart, J., *Compt. rend.*, *233*, 172 (1951). Propriétés de la zircone fondue au four solaire.
22 Trombe, F., and Foex, M., *ibid.*, *233*, 254 (1951). Sur les Céramiques à base de zircone et d'oxyde de lanthane.
23 Trombe, F., Foex, M., and La Blanchetais, Ch., *ibid.*, *233*, 311 (1951). Nouveaux Essais de synthèse de l'acide nitrique à l'aide de l'énergie solaire.
24 Trombe, F., and Foex, M., *Rev. mét.*, *48*, 353 (1951). Essais sidérurgiques au four solaire.
25 Trombe, F., and Foex, M., *ibid.*, *48*, 359 (1951). Essai de métallurgie du chrome par l'hydrogène au four solaire.
26 Trombe, F., and Foex, M., *Journal des recherches du C.N.R.S.*, *4*, 1 (1951). Les Propriétés des céramiques à base de zircone et d'oxyde de lanthane.
27 Trombe, F., *ibid.*, *4*, 189 (1952). L'Alimentation en eau des terres arides.
28 Trombe, F., Foex, M., and La Blanchetais, Ch., *Compt. rend.*, *234*, 1451 (1952). Quelque Essais récents sur la production d'acide nitrique à l'aide du rayonnement solaire.

29   Trombe, F., and Foex, M., *ibid.*, *235*, 571 (1952). Fours centrifuges à accumulation d'énergie solaire.
30   Trombe, F., *ibid.*, *235*, 704 (1952). Sur la Réalisation d'un four solaire semi-industriel au Laboratoire de Mont-Louis (Pyrénées-Orientales).
31   Trombe, F., *ibid.*, *235*, 1211 (1952). Sur quelques Détails de montage du four solaire semi-industriel de Mont-Louis.
32   Trombe, F., and Foex, M., *ibid.*, *236*, 1167 (1953). Sur quelques Propriétés du système P_2O_5—CaO et la préparation de phosphates assimilables par traitement à haute température.
33   Trombe, F., and Foex, M., *ibid.*, *236*, 1783 (1953). Etude de la conductibilité électrique du système zircone-chaux à haute température.
34   Trombe, F., *Bull. soc. chim. France* (mémoires), 5ème série, *20*, 352 (1953). Le Laboratoire de l'Énergie Solaire de Mont-Louis.
35   Trombe, F., and Foex, M., Techniques d'utilisation d'un rayonnement à haute concentration énergétique, IIIème Congrès International d'Electrothermie, Section VI, No. 610 (1953).
36   Trombe, F., and Foex, M., Sur quelques propriétés des solutions solides à base d'oxyde réfractaire utilisables pour la confection de résistances chauffantes à haute température, IIIème Congrès International d'Electrothermie, Section VI, No. 617 (1953).
37   Lebeau, P., Foex, M., Cheylan, E., and Chaigneau, M., *Compt. rend.*, *237*, 220 (1953). Fusion au four solaire d'oxyde d'uranium de forte densité.
38   Trombe, F., and Foex, M., LXXVIIIème Congrès des Sociétés Savantes (1953). Essais de préparation de ferrochromes au four solaire.
39   Chalmin, R., *Compt. rend.*, *236*, 1638 (1953). Utilisation d'un four à accumulation d'énergie solaire pour des études dilatométriques.
40   Chalmin, R., *ibid.*, *236*, 1875 (1953). Etude dilatométrique du silicate de zirconium (zircon) au four solaire.
41   Foex, M., and Chalmin, R., *ibid.*, *237*, 177 (1953). Influence d'addition de magnésie sur la vitesse pratique d'hydration de la chaux.
42   Trombe, F., *Journal des recherches du C.N.R.S.*, No. 25, 23 (Dec. 1953). Utilisation de l'énergie solaire—Etat actuel et perspectives d'avenir.
43   Trombe, F., and Foex, M., *Compt. rend.*, *238*, 1419 (1954). Purification de quelques substances réfractaires par traitement au four solaire.
44   Cabannes, F., and Le Phat Vinh, A., *J. phys. radium*, *15*, 817 (1954). Calcul de la répartition de l'énergie solaire réfléchie par un miroir parabolique.

SECTION VIII

1   Bannink, H. F., and Muller, F. M., *Leeuwenhock J. Microbiology*, *18*, 45 (1952).
2   Bannink, H. F., and Muller, F. M., *ibid.*, *17*, 151 (1951).
3   Burlew, J. S. (ed.), *Algal Culture from Laboratory to Pilot Plant*, Carnegie Institution of Washington Publication No. 600, Washington, D. C. (1953).

4   Daniels, F., *Proc. Am. Acad. Arts Sci.*, *79*, 188 (1951). Efficiency in Biological Photosynthesis.
5   Franck, J., and Loomis, W. E., *Photosynthesis in Plants*. Iowa State College Press, Ames, Iowa (1949).
6   Glesinger, E., *The Coming Age of Wood*, Simon and Schuster, New York (1949).
7   Hollaender, A., *Radiation Biology*, Vol. *III*, McGraw-Hill Book Co., New York (1955). Chapter 4, "Energy Efficiency in Photosynthesis," by F. Daniels.
8   Morimura, Y., and Tamiya, N., *Food Technol.*, *8*, 179 (1954). Preliminary Experiments in the Use of Chlorella as Human Food.
9   Myers, J., paper presented to AIBS meeting, Madison, Wis. (September, 1953).
10 Nishimura, M. S., Whittingham, C. P., and Emerson, R., "The Maximum Efficiency of Photosynthesis," Symposia of the Society for Experimental Biology, V, Carbon Dioxide Fixation and Photosynthesis, Great Britain (1951).
11 Ogura, T., and Nagai, H., *J. Soc. Chem. Ind. Japan*, *45*, 170 (1942).
12 Rabinowitch, E. I., *Photosynthesis and Related Processes*, Vol. *II*, Interscience Publishers, Inc., New York (1951).
13 Warburg, O., Burk, D., Shoken, V., and Hendricks, S. B., *Biochimica et Biophysica Acta.*, *4*, 335 (1950). The Quantum Efficiency of Photosynthesis.
14 Yuan, E. L., Evans, R. W., and Daniels, F., *ibid.* (1955). Energy Efficiency of Photosynthesis by Chlorella.
15 Franck, J., *Arch. Biochem. Biophys.*, *45*, 190 (1953).

SECTION IX

1   Ahmann, D. H., AECD–3205, declassified July 16, 1951.
2   Anderegg, J. A., and Duke, F. R., ISC–223 of USAEC July 1951.
3   Baur, E., *Z. physik. Chem.*, *63*, 683 (1908). Über ein Modill der Kohlensäure-assimilation.
4   Bose, D. M., and Mukherji, P. C., *Phil. Mag.*, *26*, 768 (1938). Origin of Color of Paramagnetic Ions in Solution.
5   Connick, R. E., and Reas, W. H., *J. Am. Chem. Soc.*, *73*, 1171 (1951). The Hydrolysis and Polymerization of Zirconium in Perchloric Acid Solution.
6   Connick, R. E., and McVey, W. H., *ibid.*, *73*, 1798 (1951). Oxidation Potentials of the Pu(III)—Pu(IV) and Fe(II)—Fe(III) Couples of Perchloric Acid Solution—Heat Content and Entropy Changes.
7   Dain, B. Ya, and Kachan, A. A., *Doklady. Akad. Nauk. S. S. S. R.*, *67*, 85 (1949). Heterogeneous Phenomena in the Reduction of Quadrivalent Cerium Ions. A summary of this article is given in English in *C. A.*, *43*, 7349 (1949).
8   Duke, F. R., and Borchers, C. E., *J. Am. Chem. Soc.*, *75*, 5186 (1953).
9   Evans, M. G. and Uri, N., *Nature*, *166*, 602 (1950). Photooxidation of Water by Ceric Ions.
10 Fontana, B. J., *National Nuclear Energy Ser.*, Div. IV, 19B, Chem. and Met. Misc. Materials, 321 (1950).

11   Hardwick, T. J., and Robertson, E., *Can. J. Chem.*, *29*, 818 (1951). Ionic Species in Ceric Perchlorate Solutions.

12   Heidt, L. J., *J. Chem. Phys.*, *10*, 297 (1942). The Photolysis of Persulfate.

13   Heidt, L. J., and Smith, M. E., *J. Am. Chem. Soc.*, *70*, 2476 (1948). Quantum Yields of the Photochemical Reduction of Ceric Ions by Water and Evidence for the Dimerization of Ceric Ions.

14   Heidt, L. J., Mann, J. B., and Schneider, H. R., *ibid.*, *70*, 3011 (1948). The Photolysis of Persulfate: II, The Quantum Yield in Water and the Effect of Sodium Chloride in Dilute Alkaline Solution.

15   Heidt, L. J., and Doyles, H. B., *ibid.*, *73*, 5728 (1951). Influence of Several Variables Encountered in Photochemical Work upon the Intensity of Light of λ, 254 mμ . . . .

16   Heidt, L. J., and McMillan, A. F., *ibid.*, *76*, 2135 (1954). Influence of Perchloric Acid and Cerous Perchlorate upon the Photochemical Oxidation of Cerous to Ceric Ions in Dilute Aqueous Perchloric Acid.

17   Heidt, L. J., *Proc. Am. Acad. Arts Sci.*, *79*, 228 (1951). Non-Biological Photosynthesis.

18   Heidt, L. J., *Science*, *90*, 473 (1939). An Arrangement of Apparatus for the Isolation of Monochromatic Light of High Intensity at λ, 254 mμ.

19   Heidt, L. J., and McMillan, A. F., *ibid.*, *117*, 75 (1953). Conversion of Sunlight into Chemical Energy Available in Storage for Man's Use.

20   Herzberg, G., *Molecular Spectra and Molecular Structure*, D. van Nostrand, New York (1950).

21   King, E. L., and Pandow, M. L., *J. Am. Chem. Soc.*, *74*, 1966 (1952). The Spectra of Cerium(IV) in Perchloric Acid. Evidence for Polymeric Species.

22   Klop, D., and Thomas, H. C., *ibid.*, *71*, 3047 (1949). Rates of Water Oxidation in Ceric Perchlorate Solutions.

23   Krasnovsky, *Compt. rend. acad. sci. USSR*, *60*, 421 (1948).

24   Krasnovsky, *ibid.*, *61*, 91 (1948).

25   Kraus, K. A., and Nelson, F., *J. Am. Chem. Soc.*, *72*, 3901 (1950).

26   Latimer, W. M., *The Oxidation States of the Elements and Their Potentials in Aqueous Solutions*, 2nd ed., Prentice Hall, New York (1952).

27   Lewis, G. N., and Lipkin, D., *J. Am. Chem. Soc.*, *64*, 2801 (1942). Reversible Photochemical Processes in Rigid Media: The Dissociation of Organic Molecules into Radicals and Ions.

28   Moeller, T., and Kremers, H. E., *Chem. Rev.*, *37*, 97 (1945). The Basicity Characteristics of Scandium, Yttrium and the Rare Earth Elements.

29   Rabinowitch, E. I., *Photosynthesis and Related Processes*, Interscience Publishers, Inc., New York (1951).

30   Rabinowitch, E., and Stockmayer, W. H., *J. Am. Chem. Soc.*, *64*, 335 (1942). Association of Ferric Ions with Chloride, Bromide and Hydroxyl Ions. . . .

31   Seiler, J. A., Rubinson, W., and Edwards, R. R., *National Nuclear Energy Ser.*, Div. IV, 9, Radiochem. Studies, The Fission Products, Book 3, 1702 (1951).

32   Sherrill, M. S., King, C. B., and Spooner, R. C., *J. Am. Chem. Soc.*, *65*, 170 (1943). The Oxidation Potential of Cerous-Ceric Perchlorates.

33   Siddall, T. H., and Vosburgh, W. C., *ibid.*, *73*, 4270 (1951). A Spectrophoto-
     metric Study of the Hydrolysis of Iron (III) Ions.
34   Spencer, J. F., *J. Chem. Soc.*, *107*, 1265 (1915). Studies on Cerium Compounds:
     Part I, Basic Ceric Sulphates and the Colour of Cerium Dioxide.
35   Stewart, D. C., AECD–2389.
36   Weiss, J., and Porret, D., *Nature*, *139*, 1019 (1937).
37   Yost, D. M., Russell, H., Jr., and Garner, C. S., *Rare-Earth Elements and Their
     Compounds*, John Wiley and Sons, Inc., New York (1947).
38   Ze, N. T., and Piaw, S., *Compt. rend.*, *196*, 916 (1933).

SECTION X

1   Banerjee, D., Univ. London Thesis, M.Sc. (Engr) (1948).
2   Banerjee, S. L., and Banerjee, S. M., Dipl. Imperial College Theses (1950).
3   Chinnappa and Selvaratnum, Ceylon Assoc. for the Advancement of Science
    (1952).
4   Finkelstein, T., University of London Thesis, Ph.D. (1953).
5   National Physical Laboratory Committee Report, *Research*, *5*, 522 (1952).
    Utilization of Solar Energy.
6   Heywood, H., *Engineering*, *176*, 377, 409 (1953). Solar Energy: Past, Present
    and Future Applications.

SECTION XI

1   Brooks, F. A., *Climatic Environment*: *A Thermal System*, ASCA Store, U. of
    California, Davis (1951).
2   Brooks, F. A., *et al.*, *Agr. Engr.*, *33*, 74, 143, and 154 (1952). Heat Transfer in
    Citrus Orchards Using Wind Machines for Frost Protection.
3   Brooks, F. A., and Rhoades, D. G., *Trans. Am. Geophys. Union*, *35*, No. 1, 145
    (Feb., 1954). Daytime Partition of Irradiation and the Evaporative Chilling
    of the Ground.
4   Editorial Items, *Science*, *80*, 2078; Supplement, p. 7 (Oct. 26, 1934).
5   Minges, Kendrick, Spurlock, and Holmburg, *Tomato Propagation*, Univ. of
    California, Agr. Extension Serv., Circ. 160, (Jan., 1950).
6   Zink, F. W., *Proc. Am. Soc. for Horticultural Sci.*, *5*, 64 (1954). Evaluation of
    Plastic Hot Caps on Muskmellons.
7   Gorin, E., U. S. Patent 2,570,543, June 17, 1950. Conversion of carbon to
    electrical energy.
8   Gorin, E., U. S. Patent 2,581,651, Aug. 31, 1951. Integrated gasification
    electro-chemical system.
9   Watson, R. G. H., *Research*, *7*, 34–40 (1954).
10 Bacon, T. T., *The Engineer*, *198*, 226–28 (1954).

Index

ABBOT, C. G.: identified, v; "Solar Power from Collecting Mirrors," 91–95; patents of, 257, 263, 264, 265; mentioned, 66, 111

Absorbers. *See* Collectors

Absorption of heat: control of, 248

Absorption refrigeration. *See* Refrigeration

Absorption spectra: of cerous and ceric solutions, 205–7

Adams: design of cooker, 66, 230

Agricultural yields with photosynthesis, 176

Air conditioning: systems for, 43–44, 64, 100–101, 234, 235; cost of, 45; possibilities of, 251; patents for, 257, 258–65 *passim. See also* Heat pumps; Refrigeration

Air drying, 243

Air heaters. *See* Collectors

Algae: mass culture of, 176, 179–84 *passim,* 185–89; as food, 180, 184, 189; as fuel, 180–84, 188–89; fermentation of, 180–83; cost of producing, 183–84; 186–87; efficiency of in conversion of sunlight, 187–88, 193

Allen: algal research of, 184

Aluminum: in electrochemical storage of energy, 242

Ambrose, E. R., 72

American Meteorological Society, 19

Ammonia: use in cooling cycles or heat engines, 64, 101, 234, 258

Anderson, Lawrence B.: identified, v; "Solar Heating Design Problems," 47–56; mentioned, 75

Angot: research with parabolic reflectors, 160

Aperture in paraboloidal reflectors: constant, 163–64; variable, 164; size in existing installations, 166

Archimedes, 157–58, 169, 170

Architectural design: as factor in solar house-heating, 33, 47–50, 60

Arnon: research in algae and photochemistry, 184, 198

Arthur D. Little, Inc., 185

Ascorbic acid, 194

Atmosphere: transmissivity of, 19–22, 99; radiation by, 24; circulation in, 129–30; as thermal engine, 129–30, 133; processes for storing solar energy in, 130–32

Atomic energy, 3, 4, 9, 10–11

Auxiliary heat, 37, 38, 48, 55, 71, 251

Averani: experiment with burning glass, 158

BAILEY, W. J., 256

Bannink, H. F., 182

Barker, W. A., 182

Barnes, W. S., 257, 264

Bartels, J., 132

Batteries, solar, 200, 241–42, 247, 254. *See also* Photogalvanic cells; Photovoltaic cells

Baum, Werner A.: identified, v; "Meteorology and the Utilization of Solar Energy," 15–17

Bell Telephone Company, 200, 254

Billig, E., 152

Bleaching, 255, 258–65 *passim*